HUNTING WARBIRDS

The Obsessive Quest for the
Lost Aircraft of World War II

Carl Hoffman

BALLANTINE BOOKS • NEW YORK

A Ballantine Book
Published by The Ballantine Publishing Group
Copyright © 2001 by Carl Hoffman

www.randomhouse.com/BB/

LIBRARY OF CONGRESS CATALOGING-IN-PUBLICATION DATA
Hoffman, Carl, 1960–
Hunting warbirds : the obsessive quest for the lost aircraft
of World War II / Carl Hoffman.
p.   cm.
ISBN 0-345-43617-2
1. Airplanes, Military—Collectors and collecting.   2. World War, 1939–1945—
Aerial operations.   3. Kee Bird (Airplane)   4. Excavations (Archaeology)
I. Title.
UG1240 .H64 2001
623.7'46'075—dc21
00-067473

Text design by Holly Johnson

Manufactured in the United States of America

First Edition: April 2001

10   9   8   7   6   5   4   3   2   1

For Lindsey
and
Lily, Max, and Charlotte

CONTENTS

——

Author's Note   ix

Introduction: Freeze-Dried Memories   1

One: Today's the Day   7

Two: The Last Flight of the *Kee Bird*   13

Three: Superfort on Ice   29

Four: Warbird Fever   37

Five: First Come, First Served   51

Six: The Laboratory Is Open   72

Seven: Living the Fantasy   84

Eight: A Bear by the Tail   97

Nine: Cry Uncle   123

Ten: Fire and Ice   135

Eleven: Smoke   160

Twelve: Precious Metal   165

Thirteen: A Peculiar Passion   178

Fourteen: *Sooner*   191

Fifteen: *Later*   214

Sixteen: The Last Good Machines   223

Epilogue: Return of the *Kee Bird*   239

Acknowledgments   242

AUTHOR'S NOTE

—

This is a true story. The three major expeditions described in it took place in Greenland and Alaska, covering a total of sixteen weeks spread out over almost seven years. Because I was present for nine of those weeks and witnessed some events firsthand and not others, I have taken the unusual step of writing in both the first person and the third person. What I did not see firsthand I reconstructed from extensive and often multiple interviews with all the participants, many of whom also shared with me their personal photographs, videotapes, letters, and journals.

Chapter two, "The Last Flight of the *Kee Bird*," was reconstructed from official U.S. Air Force accident reports, still photographs and 16-millimeter film, news reports, unpublished memoirs, and, most important, extensive personal interviews. When I got involved in the story, in 1994, six of the eleven original crewmembers were still alive, and I was fortunate enough to meet all of them. By the time I started writing this book, one more had died, but four of the remaining five spoke with me repeatedly. I also was able to interview Maynard White, the commanding officer of the 46th Reconnaissance Squadron at Ladd Field (Fairbanks, Alaska) in 1947, Bobbie Joe Cavnar, the pilot who rescued the *Kee Bird*'s crew, and a Danish radio operator stationed at Thule (Greenland) in February of 1947.

Some of the stories I heard over the years sounded pretty fantastic, and wherever possible I verified them with the institutions involved or confirmed them with a second source. Information on U.S. government trading was confirmed through records of the U.S. Air Force Museum, in Dayton, Ohio, and sources at the Smithsonian National Air and Space Museum. Information regarding salvage permits came from the Danish Polar Center and the Danish Ministry of Foreign Affairs.

INTRODUCTION

—

FREEZE-DRIED MEMORIES

In 1965, two decades after Hiroshima, the air battles of World War II came alive for me in an attic aerie in Newport, Rhode Island. Flopping onto a blue iron bed whose mattress felt as sloped and bumpy as a grassy hillside, I watched a P-38 Lightning race through a sky thick with antiaircraft flak. Above it was a formation of olive-drab B-17 Flying Fortresses, bristling with .50-caliber machine guns pointing from turrets on the nose and fuselage. Behind my head, water-stained but still vivid, big-headed caricatures of Mussolini, Hitler, and Hirohito plummeted to the ground in bumper-car-sized Messerschmitts and Zeros.

I was five and this was my father's childhood room. He had been twelve years old when the Japanese bombed Pearl Harbor in 1941 and he had papered nearly every square inch of the sloping attic walls with poster-sized centerfolds of Lightnings and Hellcats and Flying Fortresses (and, invisible until you closed the bedroom door, a wall of beckoning Vargas girls, their legs and breasts impossibly long and high). Now the room was mine for two whole weeks. Every summer my parents and my sister and I climbed into our 1962 Ford Falcon station wagon and drove from Washington, D.C., to Newport. It was a long day's drive, made longer still by the ferry between Jamestown and Newport. Washington was hot and muggy,

Newport cool and foggy, and the minute we finally arrived at the home of my grandparents, I raced up three flights of stairs and flopped down onto that bed like the proud new owner I was; that year, for the first time, I was old enough to stay in the attic of the big Victorian house all by myself. Every summer for many years thereafter I repeated the arrival ritual, dashing up to the "airplane room," listening to the foghorn wail, breathing in the musty smell of the mattress, and discovering a Corsair or Hellcat that I hadn't noticed before.

In Newport, partly because my father had grown up there during the war and his house and bedroom were virtually unchanged from those years, and partly because even in the 1960s elements of the Atlantic Fleet were still based in Newport, World War II seemed part of the town's fabric. At home, in Washington, the war was ancient history. But in Newport nearly every building and street offered a romantic World War II memory. My dad had scouted the skies for enemy airplanes from the belfry of the chapel at Saint George's School (one day rooting around in a closet I found his airplane identification book); he also helped out at the nightclub owned by his parents, the Ideal Café, a favorite Navy hangout (the showgirls bunked across the hall from my dad's airplane room), and closed the black shades every evening to keep Newport's lighted glow from reaching German U-boats lurking offshore.

Throughout my childhood, my father brought home plastic airplane models for me to build. In a gluey mess, I stuck together a P-38, a twin-boomed fighter-interceptor that the Japanese called "the fork tailed devil." "There was almost no plane faster," said my dad, whose childhood dream of being an aeronautical engineer was dashed by his inability to master basic algebra. I built a PBY Catalina, a flying boat with big observation blisters, whose wings sported retractable sponsons and a pair of torpedoes. And I loved my B-29 Superfortress, with its tail gun, rotating machine-gun turrets, and all-glass nose. In the battles on my bedroom floor, the planes wreaked havoc, the Catalina rescued downed aviators, and

2

the Superfortress earned its distinction as the highest-flying, fastest, and deadliest bomber of its time. One year I built a more modern B-52 Stratofortress, but I never loved the airplane. All sleek swept-wing jet with no bristling machine guns, no turrets, no props, and certainly no sense of heritage, it just wasn't the same.

The warbirds of the airplane room had saved the world from the crazed caricatures leering over my bed and had been romanticized in countless dramas of the fifties and sixties, from the B-17s flown by Gregory Peck in *Twelve O'Clock High* to the SBD Dauntlesses and Corsairs of *McHale's Navy*. The B-52? It didn't even have any pro-pellers! And it was sending rolling thunder over the rice paddies of Vietnam, a faraway place from which my parents wanted us out. The classic warbirds weren't just old airplanes, they were touch-stones to a glory that even a kid could recognize.

When I returned for a visit twenty years later, the models were long gone, victims of maternal housecleaning and an adolescent frenzy of fireworks experimentation (the B-52 was the first to blow). Gone also were the posters in the airplane room. "We finally fixed up that old room," my grandmother said the summer I graduated from college, and I rushed upstairs two at a time to find the blue bed painted glossy white, the 1940s museum of airplane centerfolds and Vargas girls vanished, the white walls sporting a pair of framed Am-erica's Cup posters. My grandmother beamed, but I was crushed. It was, I couldn't help feeling, the final blow to childhood.

It was time to grow up and move on.

Another decade passed and, truth be told, I pretty much forgot about the Hellcats and Superforts of my childhood. I even missed a few summers of going to Newport. Then one April I was sent to Greenland and spent three weeks at the American air base in Thule. I was a freelance writer and *Air & Space/Smithsonian* maga-zine asked me to write an article about the hunt for submarines by Navy P-3 Orion airplanes. Also marked on the navigation charts of this featureless landscape was a downed plane, a B-29 bomber called the *Kee Bird*. One day, returning from a flight, the crew suggested we take a detour and find it. April is still frigid in the high Arctic, and below us an expanse of white, frozen ocean and white, snow-covered glacier stretched in all directions. We buzzed a team of dogs pulling a wooden sledge at the frozen ocean's edge, followed the trail of sled tracks along the coast past the Inuit village of Qaanaaq, and turned east, heading inland. If we found the B-29 I imagined we'd see only the desiccated skeleton of a wing or tail poking through the snow. But when we swooped over a hill and dove into a wide snow-covered bowl at 150 knots, my heart raced. The *Kee Bird* was lying on top of the snow, a silvery B-29 Superfortress right out of the posters of my airplane room, literally frozen in time. Save a missing rudder and four bent props, the plane looked perfect, as if it had landed yesterday. I could see the yellow letters of *"Kee Bird"* written on the nose, its panes of glass still intact. Four .50-caliber machine guns pointed forward from the top turret.

We banked hard to the left, and swung around for another look in stunned silence. "You know," said the pilot finally over the intercom, as he swept eighty-five feet above the *Kee Bird*, "I heard that some guys came to the plane last summer and actually got an engine started."

"No way," I said, mesmerized by the ghost of an airplane I had worshiped for years and which, as far as I could remember, I had never seen in real life.

The pilot circled for another low pass. "Apparently they changed the spark plugs in one of the engines, connected it to a battery, and it fired right up. And they're coming back this summer to fly it out."

The *Kee Bird* touched a powerful nerve, like hearing a song or smelling a scent that instantly returned me to the wonder of childhood. I couldn't shake the image of it sitting there on the snow, a talisman from an age that seemed more exciting and romantic than my own. I wanted to see it fly, to hear its engines roar.

It turned out I wasn't alone. I discovered that the *Kee Bird* was an obsession among a growing subculture of warbird fanatics. There were warbird museums and warbird magazines, warbird restoration schools, warbird travel tours, and warbird airshows where tens of thousands of people flocked to admire them and even fly in them. You could hardly surf late-night cable television without finding historical footage of B-17s bombing Germany or Corsairs fighting Zeros on the Discovery Channel or the History Channel. Rich collectors spent tens of millions of dollars acquiring warbirds, while U.S. government museums traded them in shady deals and fought over them in court, and a few men routinely journeyed to the ends of the earth to find and recover them. And at the time I was flying over it, the *Kee Bird* was the most legendary airplane of them all, a tantalizing treasure long known of yet just out of reach. Salvors, collectors, and warbird buffs had been dreaming about it for years, scheming about how to get it, planning expeditions that never left home.

Not long after that P-3 flight I found the telephone number for something called the Institute for Aeronautical Archaeological Research, the organization whose people had gotten the engine started the previous summer. *Destination Discovery,* a magazine published by the Discovery Channel, agreed to send me on assignment with the next *Kee Bird* salvage expedition, and three months later I found myself immersed in the quest for winged treasure, a quest that eventually took me far beyond the *Kee Bird.*

Hunting Warbirds is an old-fashioned adventure story about expeditions to recover the *Kee Bird* and three other World War II airplanes. But it is also more than that. It is a story about two outsized men in more or less the same line of work, a flyer turned salvor and a salvor turned flyer, who, despite their similarities, have such profoundly different philosophies that they can't work together. It explores the unique experience of collecting objects that for millions of Americans are icons with profound and deep emotional attachments. It delves into the art and craft of vintage aircraft restoration. But most important of all, it is a search for the answer to a not-so-simple question: Why do the airplanes of World War II, highly efficient killing machines, after all, inspire such passion in so many of us?

Today, World War II aircraft are exceedingly rare. The rarer something is, of course, the more sought-after it usually becomes. But scarceness alone doesn't explain why grown men cry when they hear the sound of a certain kind of engine. Or why someone like me, a child of an entirely different generation, with neither the money nor the inclination to collect rare airplanes, should be moved by the sight and sound of one. Perhaps part of the answer lies in the oft-cited myth of the Phoenix, of a rebirth from fire. When B-29s dropped two atomic bombs on Japan in 1945 and the war ended, the world and our sense of our own place in it changed forever. In the course of the adventures I describe in this book, I began to think that it isn't winged treasure that these collectors are trying so hard to recover. It is something much more intangible—something unseen that, just as surely, went up in flames with Hiroshima and Nagasaki. The world was hardly a simple place when the propeller and piston engine reigned. But to hear a B-17's seventy-two pistons thrum, or see a P-51 Mustang roll in the wild blue yonder, you can almost believe that it was.

ONE

—

TODAY'S THE DAY

Daugaard Jensen Land, Greenland; May 1995

"Hey! Wake up! Today's the day. I'm ready." I opened my eyes and heard Darryl Greenamyer's boots crunching across the snow on his morning reveille. The tent was hot and bright. Steam rose from my sleeping bag. I crawled from the damp bag, unzipped the tent flaps and poked my head out. Last week it was blowing seventy miles an hour, the wind chill was fifty degrees below zero Fahrenheit, and I couldn't see five feet out of the tent. Today there wasn't a cloud in the sky and the cold air was still and gin-clear. The white snow and blue sky were dazzling, nearly blinding. Just the day we'd been waiting for. Even for a notorious former test pilot like Darryl Greenamyer, a frozen desert 500 miles south of the North Pole in northern Greenland was a hell of a place to take wing in a forty-five-ton, four-engine bomber that hadn't moved in forty-eight years. The weather had to be perfect.

I slid a pair of heavy fleece pants over my long johns and pulled on my coveralls. The murmur of voices from the mess tent carried across the snow and I crunched over to join them. The shiny B-29, Darryl's obsession for three years, stood nearby on its big tires, a winged aluminum cylinder lying on the Arctic plain. A winter's worth of snow rose around it, littered with a junkyard of oil drums, air compressors, tattered boxes, and batteries. There was not a tree or bush for 800 miles in any direction. To the east, above the surrounding snow-covered hills, glowed the Humboldt Glacier, 10,000 feet thick. The Inuit village of Qaanaaq lay 150 miles to the south, Thule Air Base another hundred miles beyond. To the north was nothing but ice and then the frozen Arctic Ocean stretching to the Pole.

For forty-eight years—since 1947—the *Kee Bird* had been an inanimate chunk of aluminum. Today, it would have a chance to move again. But the *Kee Bird* didn't just have to move, it had to compete with the gods and fly. The very idea seemed both glorious and impossible. Nine months ago on this barren stage, Rick Kriege had shivered helplessly in his sleeping bag and Cecelio Grande prayed on his knees in despair. A few days ago two tents had been shredded into oblivion by the raging wind. But now, through force of will and mechanical ingenuity, in one of the remotest places on earth, Darryl and his band of mechanics had installed four new engines, new propellers, new tires, new flight controls, a new rudder, and new wiring, all without the aid of governments or corporations. No one had ever done anything like that before.

This whole business of recovering airplanes from the far corners of the world was new, and it combined many of the challenges of an expedition to the North Pole or a climb to the top of Everest with the challenge of recovering something huge and fragile and mechanical. Beyond the physical and mental stamina demanded of a polar explorer or a mountain climber, this quest required mechanical savvy, a mountain of tools and heavy equipment, and razor-sharp piloting skills. And unlike climbing a mountain, there was no template for how it should be done. This was new territory, and it was more like something from the time of Shackleton or Peary or the Wright Brothers, when no one knew what they were doing. The rules were invented as they went along.

The mess tent was primitive green Army surplus canvas, floorless, and scarred with long tears from last week's near-hurricane-force winds. Inside, Darryl was sipping a cup of steaming tea. "You nervous?" I asked.

"No," he said, cupping the hot mug in grease-stained hands. A week's worth of gray stubble covered his chin and cheeks. He was small, with twinkly blue eyes, dimples, and a big smile that made him appear elfin, innocent, especially in his baggy brown Carhartt coveralls. A bulky green wool cap covered his head. "I've always thought that if something bad was going to happen I'd know it and have time to react. And anyway," he said, "when your time comes there's nothing you can do." It was a typical Darryl answer, but so far he'd been right. He was fifty-nine years old and few men had ever flown as fast or as high as Darryl Greenamyer. Still, he'd never flown a B-29. Ever. And certainly not one whose exact weight was unknown, whose engines hadn't ever run more than a few minutes, and which would be taking off from a makeshift runway of crusty snow two feet thick.

"Yeah, we'd better clean up that cockpit," said Matt Jackson. "When you blast off it'll be wild in there. Hoo, wha! Shit'll be flying all over the place." Matt was thirty-six, brash and barrel-chested with a maniacal laugh, an air racer and talented aviation mechanic who'd idolized Darryl ever since he was a kid. "And we've got to get out of here," he said, suddenly serious. "This place sucks." Any hour a maelstrom of wind and snow might howl into camp, and even a two-week delay could take us to the onset of spring when the lake—Darryl's runway—would melt. "We'll heat up engine number two, move to number one, and hopefully they'll stay warm while we work on three and four."

We trudged out to the *Kee Bird*. Darryl grabbed the bottom rung of the ladder trailing from the nose and swung himself into the cockpit. A rat's nest of wires clogged the floor. The green Bakelite yokes that controlled the plane were cracked and the glass cockpit windows were made opaque by a spiderweb of hairline fractures. Gauges were missing. Insulation hung from the ceiling. The back of the pilot's seat cushion was gone, so Darryl stuffed an old pillow behind him, sat down, and latched his wide cotton seatbelt. The only new pieces of equipment in the cockpit were the radio and GPS satellite navigation system.

Al Hanson, an old friend of Darryl's and a pilot and collector of exotic airplanes, climbed into the copilot's seat, followed by Thad Dulin, who settled into the flight engineer's seat on the *Kee Bird*'s right side, his back to the copilot. A big, round former Texas oilman with a drawl as thick as the crude he'd once hunted, Thad was a lover of World War II–era warplanes and one of the few men under seventy qualified by the Federal Aviation Administration as a B-29 flight engineer.

Facing the panel of gauges and switches and throttles in quadruplicate that controlled the bomber's four 2,200-horsepower piston engines, Thad started flicking switches to engine number two. Battery switch: on. The voltage meters flickered, the age-bleached needles rising slowly to twenty-eight volts. Auxiliary power unit: on. Mixture levers: auto rich. Throttle: cracked open half an inch. Booster pumps: on. Start circuit breakers: on. Booster coil: on.

Darryl stuck his fingers out of the small window to his left and twirled his hand. "Clear," he shouted.

Thad hit the start and prime switches simultaneously. The starter emitted a metallic, high-pitched whine. The propeller jerked and then slowly began to spin. After it completed two revolutions, Thad hit the magneto, sending a spark to the engine. A cloud of black smoke and a tongue of orange flame exploded from the exhaust like the crack of a cannon. The engine coughed, the prop stopped a moment but then twirled faster. More cannon shots and clouds of black smoke spit from the exhaust pipe. Finally engine number two exploded to life with a roar. The *Kee Bird* quivered as the prop beat in a resonant bass. Thad watched with satisfaction as the oil pressure and oil temperature rose safely into the green. It wouldn't be long, he knew. He was still scared, though. He didn't want to die.

Ten minutes later, engine number one started in a hail of noxious smoke as Darryl's head peered out the open cockpit window. An hour after that, three and four roared on, all four engines and 8,800 horsepower now thundering in a symphony of pistons. Clouds of snow billowed from behind the props, and the bomber was suddenly no longer an inanimate object but a thawed beast with open eyes and beating heart. The engines drummed and the frozen ground shook under my feet just twenty feet away, the pulse of seventy-two pistons and four sets of sixteen-foot-long propellers more intoxicating than any whining jet engine or turboprop. We scurried to clear the last hoses, fuel drums, cans of lubricant, and batteries away from the nose wheel.

"You've got the throttles now, Darryl," Thad said over the intercom.

Darryl placed his left hand across the four throttle levers. Thad, at the flight engineer's station, placed his hand over a duplicate set. Clutching the yoke with his right hand, his feet on the rudder pedals, Darryl eased the four levers forward as Thad adjusted the propellers' pitch, or angle, so they'd bite into the air like screws biting into wood. B-29s had no nose-wheel steering, and aerodynamic control from the rudder wouldn't kick in until the plane hit sixty-five miles an hour. Until then the pilot used only the engines and the brakes to turn. Darryl hoped he'd be able to steer the plane. Louder and louder the engines thundered and screamed, shaking the ground. The plane strained and shook but didn't budge, as if it were chained to the ground. Then it moved forward an inch. Darryl throttled up even further. Near maximum power, the *Kee Bird* suddenly jerked out of its icy hole, then paused an instant as Darryl eased back on the power. He turned the plane to the right and picked up speed. Inside, it felt like being in the grip of a giant paint shaker. Bouncing violently on the rough, windblown snow, Darryl struggled to control the airplane. Al's body jerked against his seatbelt. Thad could barely keep his hands on the throttle as Darryl made a wide, arcing turn to the right.

"Go, Darryl, go!" Matt screamed, leaping up and down, as the *Kee Bird* bounded past him across the snow. Four white rooster tails streaming fifty feet behind the engines, a ghost was thundering to life across the Arctic for the first time since February 1947, when 1st Lt. Vern Arnett took off from Ladd Field in Fairbanks, Alaska, on what was supposed to be just another routine mission.

TWO

—

THE LAST FLIGHT OF THE *KEE BIRD*

Fairbanks, Alaska; February 1947

You've heard the wail of the siren
As an ambulance sped down the street
And maybe you've heard the lion's deep roar
Down in Africa's grim desert heat,

Or the piercing cry of the tiger
At night, as he stalks his prey,
Or the locomotive's high shrill whistle
As it sped though the night on its way.

But these sounds sink to a whisper—
You've heard naught, I assure, till I've told
Of the bloodcurdling cry of the Kee Bird
In the Arctic's cruel frigid cold.

This bird looks just like a buzzard—
It's large, it's hideous, it's bold.
In the night as it circles the North Pole,
Crying, "Kee-Kee-Keerist but it's cold!"

—ED PRITZINGER

An hour and a half behind schedule, in weak afternoon sunlight and a temperature of twenty below zero, B-29/F-13 number 45-21768 lifted heavily into the sky from the runway at Ladd Field. It was February 20, 1947, and the *Kee Bird*'s mission was classified top se-cret. Carrying eleven men and weighing 140,000 pounds, more than 60,000 of which was enough fuel to fly twenty-six nonstop hours, she banked over the frozen Chena River, lumbered above scrubby pine trees and snow-covered hills, and climbed slowly toward Point Barrow, Alaska, her cruising altitude 12,000 feet.

Flight engineer 2d Lt. Robert "Lucky" Luedke was jazzed. A short, powerfully built twenty-four-year-old with dark, deep-set eyes, a broad face, and thin lips, he'd been chasing adventure ever since he volunteered for the Army Air Force cadet program in 1943. First he'd figured he would fly P-51 Mustang fighters and get some combat action for sure. But he was too late: when he finished flight school it was the end of 1944 and there were already tens of thousands of able fighter pilots. The sleek B-29 Superfortress was just being introduced, however, and Luedke qualified as pilot and flight engineer. In 1945, at last, he was sent to the Pacific. Then came Hiroshima, and just as Luedke made it there, his only task was to ferry Superforts home. Finally, he'd volunteered for the 46th Re-connaissance Squadron in Fairbanks. It wasn't war and no one was shooting at him, but Alaska offered the next best thing. It was cold and wild, and the top-secret 46th was flying uncharted routes over the North Pole and the edges of the Soviet Union. Up here naviga-tion was tricky and you never knew what might happen. This was only his third mission but Luedke had already survived one crash and earned his nickname.

At 12,000 feet, pilot 1st Lt. Vern Arnett leveled off, seeking maximum fuel efficiency at 150 knots, a bit less than half the B-29's top speed. The *Kee Bird* felt mushy and slightly heavy on the left side and he had trouble maintaining airspeed. Luedke checked his fuel gauges. She was drinking slightly more fuel than normal. Ar-nett edged the yoke forward and the fuel-laden *Kee Bird* descended.

In the denser air at 10,000 feet she seemed to be happier, flying more smoothly. Here in the high Arctic, near the magnetic anomalies of the Pole, magnetic compasses grew unreliable, and every thirty minutes navigator 1st Lt. Burl Cowan charted the *Kee Bird*'s position by shooting the sun with a sextant or, once it got dark, taking a three-star celestial fix.

Although top secret, the *Kee Bird*'s flight was supposed to be anything but harrowing. At the end of the war, the B-29's ability to fly long range, made longer still by adding extra fuel tanks in place of bombs, made it the perfect long-distance reconnaissance airplane. Fearing Soviet bases on the high Arctic's islands and massive ice floes, the 46th was formed and assigned Project Nanook, the first mission of the newly created Strategic Air Command. Using B-29s, Project Nanook's goal was to map and photograph the Arctic and to master the techniques of grid navigation required for flying—and fighting a war—in the high latitudes. Outfitted with cameras and radar scopes and stripped of guns to increase their range, the B-29s were dubbed F-13s.

On August 14, 1946, a B-29 identified a seventeen-mile-long, nine-mile-wide ice floe near the North Pole. Called Target X, it was the largest floe ever seen. SAC kept it a closely held secret, fearing its use by the Soviets as a forward military installation. The *Kee Bird*, which had not been completely converted and was still armed with a full complement of weapons and its four gun turrets, was to examine and photograph Target X by radar, fly to the Pole, turn around, and head for home. Just another routine mission.

At Point Barrow, three hours after takeoff, the *Kee Bird* turned forty-five degrees north, making straight for the North Pole. It was dark, but the sky was clear. From here on there would be absolute radio silence. Photographer S.Sgt. Ernie Stewart peered out of his round window. Like Luedke, he was happy to be flying. Not normally part of the *Kee Bird*'s crew, he had been a last-minute addition, assigned to take the place of a crew member grounded with a bad cold. He loved the view of the Brooks Range as the planes headed north over Alaska. As for adventure, the tall, fair-haired veteran had already had enough, having survived forty-five combat missions in the Pacific as a gunner in B-24 Liberators. Once, bombing a Japanese airfield in Formosa in late 1944, a Japanese antiaircraft shell had blown a four-inch-wide hole in the fuselage eighteen inches from his head. The attack shot out two of the B-24's four engines and Stewart had crash-landed in the Philippines. It was 1947 now, and that was all over. Unlike the B-24, the Superfort was warm and pressurized. *And thank God,* thought Stewart, gazing at the frozen sea beneath him, *up here no one is shooting at me.*

The *Kee Bird* was ninety feet long with a wingspan of 141 feet, a sleek aluminum barracuda with an oversized tail painted bright red. Her underside was as black as the night sky she was hiding in, the yellow, cockeyed letters spelling *Kee Bird* tumbling across her left nose, next to a comical, confused-looking half-duck, half-chicken pacing atop a pile of snow. Wingless and unable to fly south for the winter, according to 46th Recce Squadron lore, the *Kee Bird's* namesake would skitter back and forth all winter muttering its "bloodcurdling cry." But there was nothing funny about the plane. Four turbo supercharged Wright Cyclone 3350 engines, the biggest, most powerful assemblage of horsepower in the world in 1945, drove her through the darkness. At the end of the war no other airplane could fly higher, farther, or carry a heavier load, and no other bomber could fly faster.

Conceived and born in record time during the world's most destructive war, the Boeing B-29 Superfortress represented the pinnacle of American technology, the most complex machine ever built and manufactured by the world's most powerful nation. More engineers labored over the B-29 than had ever worked on a single project before. No other single weapon cost as much to design or produce, including the atomic bomb. When Germany attacked Poland in September 1939, its deadly Stuka dive-bombers carried 1,540 pounds of bombs, had a single machine gun, had a cruising speed of 187 miles per hour at 15,000 feet, and could fly 370 miles

without refueling. During America's first raid on the Japanese main-
land since 1942, on June 5, 1944, just thirty-eight months after
Boeing signed its first contract for a plane that had not yet been
built, much less flown, the forty-seven attacking B-29s each carried
20,000 pounds of bombs and flew at nearly 400 miles per hour over
a distance of 3,700 miles and at altitudes as high as 35,000 feet, and
they could do it in clouds, bad weather, or at night. Tens of thousands of men and women spit them out of factories in Nebraska,
Washington, Kansas, and Georgia at the peak rate of more than two
hundred a month. They were pressurized and heated and they
protected their crews behind thick armor plating. They carried ten
.50-caliber machine guns in four remotely operated turrets, plus
two .50-caliber guns in the tail. They had self-sealing, rubberized
fuel tanks, flush-headed rivets, primitive fire-control computers,
radar, and Loran (a navigation aid in which a receiver establishes a
line of position by triangulating between two low-frequency radio
signals). All this technology contributed to a machine with an as-
tonishing ability to rain destruction down on vast areas and numbers of people. On November 24, 1944, eighty-five B-29s bombed
Tokyo. Three weeks later, another eighty-four firebombed Hankow,
(then occupied by the Japanese) and on January 3, 1945, sixty-three
hit Nagoya. In low-altitude night raids on March 9, 330 B-29s in
three 400-mile-long streams incinerated fifteen square miles of Tokyo,
killing 83,793 people and destroying 267,171 buildings. By mid-
June, four wings of 180 B-29s each were making two raids a week,
hitting three or four towns on each run.

Finally, on August 6, 1945, the B-29 *Enola Gay* released the
9,790-pound "Little Boy" atomic bomb over Hiroshima, and three
days later a second B-29, named *Bock's Car*, dropped a similar bomb
over Nagasaki. No other airplane in the world had the payload or
range to carry those bombs. World War II was over and the B-29
had delivered the coup de grâce.

———

17

At eight P.M., five and a half hours after takeoff, the *Kee Bird* entered a bank of clouds. Arnett pulled the yoke back and increased the throttle and she climbed back up to 12,000 feet, above the overcast. Stewart munched on a peanut butter and jelly sandwich. In the waist of the plane, radar observer 1st Lt. Howard Adams peered through his radarscope. He, too, was a combat veteran, flying B-29s out of Guam. Once, kamikaze interceptors had rammed his Superfort and he'd limped to Iwo Jima on two engines. But those days of adventure and danger were over. With his radar tuned to its highest resolution, Adams could see items as small as the individual ties of a railroad track, even through darkness and thick cloud cover.

Near midnight, the *Kee Bird* reached Target X and overflew the Pole. At 12:17 A.M., she headed home. At 1:50, navigator Burl Cowan made a celestial fix. And then things started going wrong. At 2:30, even at 12,000 feet, the *Kee Bird* hit more clouds and increased turbulence. Ice formed on the prop tips and the wings. The magnetic compass was useless and the windows showed nothing but blackness and clouds. Cowan struggled unsuccessfully to get a fix on their location. Copilot 1st Lt. Russell Jordan, at the controls, started climbing. With fuel precious, he climbed slowly, finally punching out of the overcast at 24,000 feet at 4:20 A.M. But with the first glimmer of dawn illuminating a sky still covered with a high, wispy haze of clouds, stars were elusive. Cowan squinted into the night through his Plexiglas blister; there was a star here, a star there, but he couldn't get three good bright ones to make a fix. The *Kee Bird* droned on, slowly descending to 14,000 feet.

At five A.M., fifteen hours into the mission, Adams looked into his radarscope, tuned to its one-hundred-mile range. "Burl!" he yelled into the intercom. "You're not going to believe this, but there's land eighty miles south."

"You're kidding!" Cowan said. The *Kee Bird* wasn't supposed to hit the Alaskan coast for another hour and a half. Cowan studied the land through his scope. Nothing looked familiar. Jordan descended to 12,000 feet and in the slowly strengthening daylight, the sun still obscured by clouds, noticed mountain peaks piercing the clouds. Cowan tried to shoot the sun, but it was three degrees below the horizon and his navigation guides drew a blank. The compass was swinging violently through 360 degrees.

"Where are we?" Stewart heard over his headset.

Jordan turned left along the coastline, hoping to recognize something.

"Go back the way we just came," Cowan said, "and maybe we'll see something familiar." Jordan turned 180 degrees. Nothing.

"How much fuel left?" Arnett asked.

"Six hours," Luedke said. That was strange, too, because the *Kee Bird* should have had another eleven hours of fuel.

Under Cowan's direction, Jordan turned left, right, and left again. By then, Cowan was as lost as a kid in the woods. He didn't know which direction was east, west, north or south. The *Kee Bird* was flying blind over the Arctic in February, and fuel was running out.

Jordan fiddled with his radio compass, praying to find his favorite radio station, KFMR in Fairbanks. He hit a strong signal and followed it for thirty minutes. Then the signal died.

Deciding to break radio silence, radio operator S.Sgt. Robert Leader contacted Point Barrow in Morse code, asking for a radio fix on their position and heading, the request duly relayed to their base at Ladd Field back in Anchorage. We'll get back to you, the Ladd operators said.

"We're lost and I don't know what to do," navigator Burl Cowan said to pilot Vern Arnett. "I guess you should just follow the sun; at least that's generally east and we'll be heading away from Russia."

"Five hours of fuel left," engineer Luedke reported.

The crewmen of the *Kee Bird* were in trouble. Big trouble. It was as if they had crossed some time warp into another world. Radio waves traveled thousands of miles at night, and yet they couldn't get one signal strong enough to navigate by. If they had been nearly anywhere else they might have descended low enough to find a landmark, or follow a river, or road, or railroad track. But below was nothing but snow and frozen ocean and mountains, a black, cold world without any distinguishing feature. They were as lost as it was possible to be in the modern world. And every minute used up more fuel, shortening their time of relative safety in the air. If they flew until their fuel ran out, they'd have to crash wherever they were, be it over mountains or even open ocean.

With no way of taking a fix until darkness—if the sky was even clear enough to see the stars—and their fuel diminishing, Arnett decided he'd have to land sooner or later, and it might as well be sooner, with fuel and light enough to pick the spot. Leader radioed Ladd: "We're heading into the sun and we're going to crash-land."

Still in occasionally heavy clouds, the *Kee Bird* flew on at 8,000 feet. The first cloud break proved to be over open water. Forty-six minutes later, with the short Arctic day ending and twilight fast approaching again, they spotted a second hole and the glow of a glacier. Diving through, they buzzed a wide, flat bowl covered with fresh snow. Turning for a closer look, the left inboard engine coughed, thirsty for fuel. Time was running out. If they didn't make a choice soon, the choice wouldn't be theirs to make.

"Prepare to ditch," Arnett called.

Hatches were opened and a biting, cold wind and roaring noise flooded the *Kee Bird*.

First Lt. John Lesman, the dead-reckoning navigator, lay prone in the narrow tunnel connecting the forward and aft cabins, bracing his feet on the forward upper turret.

S.Sgt. Ernie Stewart, strapped in his right rear seat, prayed that the *Kee Bird* wouldn't catch on fire and that if it did, that they would all die painlessly. *My poor mother*, he thought. *I hope they don't send her a telegram too quickly and worry her.*

Cowan wrapped his sextant in his pants, sat next to Luedke, his backpack parachute against the bulkhead behind the pilots, and braced his feet on the turret.

Other than keeping his wheels up, Arnett flew a normal landing pattern, full flaps out, 130 miles per hour. *This is no dream,* co-pilot Jordan thought. *You're in trouble now.* And Jordan was angry. *This isn't my fault!* he thought. *I'm going to die for something that's just an accumulation of little stupid events! Just accept it and face the facts.* Ten seconds before impact, Jordan reached behind and tapped Cowan. Upon that signal, Cowan cut the fuel-mixture controls as Luedke hit the fuel valves and the master power switch, cutting all power and fuel to the engines. The tail touched, dragged fifty feet, and then the *Kee Bird* bellied down, sliding 900 feet across ten inches of fresh powder. From his seat, Adams watched huge sprays of snow wash across the window. Radio operator Bucky Leader thought it felt like sliding across a greased skid. It was the softest landing Jordan had ever felt.

It was 10:10 A.M.; the final flight of the *Kee Bird* had lasted nineteen hours and forty minutes.

Jordan, leaping through the hatch above his seat, was the first one out. Stewart couldn't get out of his seat belt. "Hey," said M.Sgt. Lawrence Yarborough, "just calm down." Stewart took a breath, inhaled slowly, and unhooked his belt. S.Sgt. Paul McNamara jumped out, kneeled on the snow, and made the sign of the cross. "I thought this only happened to other people," he said. Lucky Luedke, well, he was exhilarated. *This is what I'm here for,* he thought. *I just hope we don't get rescued too soon.*

Oil was pouring from the number-three engine and all four props were bent from hitting the ground on the wheels-up landing, but otherwise the *Kee Bird* looked undamaged. Immediately, they all noticed that the tail skid, a wheel-less piece of metal that protected the tail of the plane during landing, was dangling from the end of the plane. Failing to retract on takeoff, its extra drag accounted for the plane's poor flying performance and faster than normal fuel consumption. It was fifty degrees below zero and getting dark fast. They hustled their emergency cans of food, sleeping bags, tents, and heavy boots out of the plane. In the darkness, Cowan finally took a fix with his sextant, placing them somewhere on the 80th parallel, or on a latitude fifteen degrees and 900 miles north of Fairbanks. But where? He didn't have a clue. Before flying, Cowan had cut from his map all but the area of his flight path, and he hadn't brought the regulation emergency kit containing maps of Siberia, Greenland, Canada, and Alaska. Looking at the *Kee Bird*'s skid marks, Jordan knelt and brushed away the snow. A chill went through him: *Was this hard gray stuff concrete?* Before he realized it was ice, he had the panicked thought that he was on some emergency runway in Siberia.

Huddled around a fire made from burning parachutes, Luedke fashioned a lamp out of oil and gas in a can using a strip of cloth as a wick, with which he warmed the little two-stroke auxiliary power unit in the rear of the plane. After two hours of yanking on a rope wrapped around the flywheel, the APU burped to life, and Leader cranked up the radio.

At Ladd, rescue operations were already underway. Maj. Maynard White, commanding officer of the 46th, had been awakened in the night, shortly after receipt of the last message from the *Kee Bird*. And although the plane's crew didn't know it, Ladd's radio operators had in fact gotten a bearing, placing the plane on the 46th meridian, some 1,800 miles east of their intended destination. Within hours, seven B-29s were scrambled, searching in ever-widening arcs. Four hours after crashing, Leader made contact with a B-29 nearing Borden Island in the Canadian archipelago, where the *Kee Bird* was believed to have crashed. Using Burl Cowan's coordinates, the searching B-29 placed the *Kee Bird* in northern Greenland, somewhere a few hundred miles north of Thule, where an airfield and weather station had been built in 1946 next to an Inuit village. The first wave of rescue planes were running out of fuel, and darkness was setting in again. Tomorrow, the plane radioed, we'll find you. Howard Adams slid into two down mummy sleeping bags inside the bomb-bay tunnel. Ernie Stewart curled into a bag beneath the left wing. Russ Jordan finally squeezed into his bag next to Stewart. He'd been awake for more than forty hours and he was exhausted;

but in the biting cold he was afraid to fall asleep, afraid that if he did he'd never wake up again.

On February 22, 1st Lt. Bobbie Joe Cavnar, utterly unaware of the *Kee Bird's* crew sleeping on the Arctic ice, was flying south, down the Davis Straights between Newfoundland and Labrador, heading from Thule, Greenland, to Westover Field in Massachusetts. Suddenly, his radio crackled: Was Bobbie Joe Cavnar inbound on the *Red Raider?* Lt. Gen. William Tunner, commander, Air Transport Command, U.S. Army Air Force, wanted to know.

An ambitious, straight shooter from Oklahoma, Cavnar was just twenty-two years old, but in the Arctic he was already a star. Raised in the dust bowl, he qualified for a pilot's license at sixteen and enlisted in the Air Corps the day after he turned eighteen. In basic training he was promoted to cadet colonel over 44,000 other cadets and won a spot at a U.S.-based Royal Air Force flight school, where he trained to fly Spitfire fighters. But then, with the war ending, he was assigned to fly big, four-engined C-54 transports. By the time the *Kee Bird* went down, Cavnar had more than fifteen hundred hours flying in the high Arctic and was responsible for getting supplies to a growing number of bases and weather stations in Greenland and far-northern Canada. He'd flown the first airplane over Thule, in May 1946, had landed the first plane at Thule that September, had landed on ice and snow and everything in between from Alert to Baffin Island to the whole west coast of Greenland. Almost no one had as much experience navigating and landing in the Arctic as Bobbie Joe Cavnar.

He was crossing the Saint Lawrence River when that first coded message reached his C-54. *Roger,* said Cavnar, *this is Lt. Cavnar and I'm inbound on the* Red Raider.

Report to General Tunner the moment you hit the ground.

Oh boy, thought Cavnar, *I must have really messed up.* But six hours after landing, he was airborne again, and headed back to

Thule, via Bluie West Eight, the name for the American base at Sondre Stromfjord, 850 miles down the coast. Somewhere north of Thule, he'd been told, the *Kee Bird* had disappeared, and he better get north in case a rescue was needed.

At the crash site, it was numbingly cold and the crew huddled around a smoky fire of parachutes and oil burning in an engine cowling. Lucky Luedke went for a hike carrying an over-and-under combo gun—a .22 Magnum rifle over a .20-gauge shotgun—in hopes of bagging an Arctic hare or a fox. He didn't see another living creature. Radio operator Robert Leader tried Ladd on the radio and picked up the B-29 *Boeing's Boner* headed their way. While the *Boner's* radioman talked, Leader listened to the signal's strength. Whenever it improved, Leader told the *Boner* to hold its course. Soon the *Boner* swept low over the *Kee Bird*. Dozens of barrels packed with everything from life rafts to Chiclets to Spam to flares and a girlie calendar rained down on them. The calendar was scrawled with messages:

"This is in case fellas like McNamara get a little lonesome."

"What's the matter, boys—having a little difficulty?"

"Why the hell can't you girls get in the air and stay there. . . . Ha, ha. Have a good camping trip and we will take care of things at home for you."

"Say, Arnett, how about bringing me a polar bear back—not in the family way, either."

Cavnar refueled at BW 8 and headed toward Thule, which was manned in the winter by a small band of Danes. With rescue still possibly days away, he was to drop additional survival equipment at the crash site and then return to Thule to await further instructions, nothing more. En route he made radio contact with *Kee Bird* copilot Russ Jordan, who reported that the ice was hard and the snow firm enough to support a landing at the crash site. "Mark a runway," Cavnar said with his usual self-confidence. "I'm coming to get you." Then he radioed General Tunner.

Outbound from Ladd, a C-46 towing a glider was already heading toward the *Kee Bird*. Maynard White's plan was to drop the glider, load it with the crew and then snatch it off the ice. Meanwhile, as a backup plan, a C-54 loaded with a Coast Guard helicopter from Elizabeth City, North Carolina, was scrambled to Goose Bay, Labrador.

But Cavnar made a compelling case. "I have complete confidence," he told Tunner. "I've landed in the most adverse conditions in the Arctic and this is nothing."

"Do it," Tunner said, and the glider was recalled.

At Thule, local Inuits hand-pumped just enough fuel from fifty-five-gallon drums for Cavnar to make the five-hundred-mile round-trip to the *Kee Bird* and back. Cavnar connected the *Red Raider*'s eight wing-mounted, jet-assisted takeoff (JATO) bottles—eight small rockets that fired for forty-five seconds—and headed north.

At the *Kee Bird*, the crew poured red hydraulic fluid to create a marker at the spot where Cavnar should touch down. And then they waited.

Though morning, it was barely light as Cavnar's *Red Raider* swept over the *Kee Bird*. Cavnar could hardly see the hydraulic fluid, but bright yellow flames jumped and flickered from the campfire by the *Kee Bird*'s tail, thick black smoke rising into the dawn, the *Kee Bird* a silver bird belly-flopped on snow black with viscous oil. Eleven small figures jumped up and down and waved. *What a beautiful sight*, thought Stewart, watching the *Red Raider* fly over. Adams started to cry.

Cavnar made one pass, landed on the lake, and skidded onto shore, bouncing roughly. He taxied a few times back and forth to smooth and pack the snow for takeoff before pulling up next to the

Kee Bird. In 16-millimeter film shot by Cavnar's crew, the *Kee Bird* survivors look like children, grinning wildly, their faces black with soot, their hats at jaunty angles in the forty-below temperature. The two crews posed together beneath the *Red Raider*'s mascot—Bugs Bunny sweeping down a hill on skis, his red bathrobe and long ears flat behind him in the wind. Cavnar tossed out the *Raider*'s emergency sleeping bags and mukluks and rations. "We need to be as light as possible," he told the crew, "so don't take anything." Despite the warning, Robert Leader pulled the *Kee Bird*'s clock out of the cockpit and stuffed it in his pocket. Howard Adams yanked the clock from his radar panel. Lucky Luedke shoved the over-and-under gun down his pants leg. Ernie Stewart tucked the girlie calendar in his jacket. And with that, the eleven men of the *Kee Bird* climbed into the *Red Raider*.

Bobbie Joe Cavnar ordered all of them into the rear of the plane. Then he stood on the brakes and jammed the throttles up to full power, an emergency sequence that would be almost identically repeated in the same place a half-century later. The props screamed. When the locked tires started skidding forward, he released the brakes and the plane leaped across the frozen lake. At fifty knots he hit the JATO control button on his steering yoke, activating the eight rockets. *Boom!* In an explosion of smoke and snow (for a moment, as seen from a B-29 circling above, the *Red Raider* looked like it blew up), Cavnar catapulted to eighty knots and took wing. Two hours later, in Thule, Cavnar radioed two words in code to General Tunner: "Mission accomplished."

After a quick steak dinner, Cavnar and the *Kee Bird* crew refueled the *Red Raider* and took off for Westover Field in Massachusetts. Ten hours later, after four days without sleep, Cavnar popped out of the clouds 4,000 feet over Westover to a sight that stunned him. Thousands of people crowded the ramp. His mission was supposed to have been top secret; all his communications had been in code. But the U.S. Army Air Force, sensing a public-relations coup, had gone public. When he and the crew stumbled from the plane,

5,000 people cheered them. Flashbulbs exploded. Cavnar's family had been flown to meet him. ELEVEN AIRMEN RESCUED IN ARCTIC BY DARING ARMY RELIEF FLIGHT, blared the front page of the *New York Times*. The next day, Wednesday, February 25, 1947, Carl Spaatz, commanding general of the Army Air Force, decorated Cavnar with the Distinguished Flying Cross. ARCTIC RESCUE BRINGS PILOT SPEEDY HONORS, trumpeted the front page of the *Washington Post*. That Thursday, President Truman honored Cavnar and his crew at the White House. "It was strenuous," Cavnar said to radio interviewers that day, "and I wasn't scared until I realized what I'd done."

Cavnar became the youngest colonel in Army Air Force history and went on to pilot B-36 bombers armed with hydrogen bombs. He turned down a promotion to brigadier general and now heads a community of born-again Christians in Texas.

The crew of the *Kee Bird* was shipped back to the 46th at Ladd Field and dispersed, never to fly together again.

Ernie Stewart crashed soon after in another B-29. While recovering from burns and a broken neck in the hospital, he met and married his nurse. He lives in Connecticut.

Pilot Vern Arnett crashed his third B-29, in Alaska, soon after returning to Ladd Field. Hiking to an Inuit village in search of help, he died of exposure.

Copilot Russell Jordan lives quietly in California.

Navigator Burl Cowan died in 1994 and asked that his ashes be scattered at the *Kee Bird* site in Greenland.

Radar operator Howard Adams piloted RB-47 reconnaissance planes over the Soviet Union and served as chief of covert operations in Laos in 1968. In 1970, after working four years with the Joint Chiefs of Staff, he retired from the military. He lives outside Washington, D.C.

Lucky Luedke lived up to his nickname. He walked away from his third crash soon after returning from Greenland. Today, in his seventies, he operates a building-demolition and salvage company in Denver, Colorado. He recently donated the *Kee Bird*'s survival gun (the over-and-under he stuffed down his pants leg) to Maj. Maynard White's son, who plans to give it to the Strategic Air Command Museum in Omaha, Nebraska. He still goes by the name Lucky. "I didn't want to be rescued so quickly," he says now, a sturdy, ruddy-faced man with long silver hair and a ready laugh, "but you wonder sometimes: What would have happened if we hadn't been found? How hungry would you get? Would you or wouldn't you? Who would have been the first to go?"

And the *Kee Bird*? The B-29 might have been the most complex and expensive weapon produced in World War II, but its airframe, piston-engines, and propellers represented prewar technology. By 1945, Germany, Britain, and America were flying jets. In October 1947, just eight months after Vern Arnett belly-landed the *Kee Bird*, Chuck Yeager broke the sound barrier. B-29s, once big and powerful and high-tech, were suddenly considered slow and lumbering, and obsolete for war. The *Kee Bird* was abandoned at the top of the world, just one of thousands of similar relics.

As the years passed, the airplanes that won World War II gradually disappeared. Of the 3,895 B-29s built, only thirty-two were left by the 1980s, and only one was still flying. Not a single one of them was a stock, armored and armed, war-ready airplane like the *Kee Bird*. In a single generation, the forty-five tons of scrap metal called the *Kee Bird* had become precious treasure.

THREE

—

SUPERFORT ON ICE

Daugaard Jensen Land, Greenland; August 1993

That the crew of the *Kee Bird* had been found and rescued so quickly in an era without satellite global-positioning systems or in-flight refueling was remarkable. Even today, travel in Greenland presents a logistical nightmare requiring deep pockets or great ingenuity to navigate. Earth's largest island, it is 800,000 square miles of ice and rock, with a population "density" of seven people per one hundred square miles. You can't drive; there are barely any roads. You can hardly fly from town to town by airplane: there aren't very many scheduled flights, or even places to land, especially up north or inland. Even worse, the weather is fickle. It's clear one moment, raining the next, snowing that same afternoon. Chilled winds whip off the ice cap, and if there's snow, all you can do is hunker down and wait, and hope you don't freeze to death while you're at it. There was a reason, after all, that Bobbie Joe Cavnar was declared a hero for his flight in and out of the *Kee Bird* site.

This was becoming increasingly clear to Tommy Hauptman, Darryl Greenamyer's easygoing, slightly paunchy helicopter pilot from Hawaii. It was August 8, 1993, forty-six years after the *Kee Bird's* crash and two years before Darryl would try to fly her again. Tommy, Darryl, Rick Kriege, and Gary Larkins were high on the ice cap in the middle of nowhere, and Tommy couldn't get his helicopter off

29

the ground. Rick had just hand-pumped 160 gallons of fuel into the olive-drab UH-1 "Huey" helicopter from five fifty-five-gallon drums they'd left on the ice a few days earlier, one of a string of fuel caches they'd laid every eighty miles. The fuel added nearly 1,100 pounds to the already overloaded bird. Rick climbed over the stack of equipment piled in back and wiggled in. There wasn't much room. A folding aluminum ladder and two twenty-ton jacks were tied to the skids. A fifty-five-gallon drum of fuel, twenty-five cases of Army MREs (meals ready to eat), two generators, two sixty-ton jacks, lubricating oil, tool boxes, a shovel, two VHF radios, a tent, clothes, cargo straps, and odds and ends were piled nearly to the ceiling like an overloaded family station wagon, leaving a one-foot space on top for Rick Kriege and Gary Larkins to perch. Seat belts were an expendable luxury. The rotor blades still turning, Tommy stuffed Rick's feet in, but the door jammed on the overflowing cargo. He pushed some more, squeezed the door shut and slid back into the pilot's seat.

Gary Larkins was getting irritated. He thought of himself as the leader of the expedition—all the permits were in his name, and he'd known Tommy longer than Darryl had—but there was Darryl, right up front in the copilot's seat next to Tommy, while he was crammed in back on top of all the junk. He'd only been traveling with Darryl for a few days but already Darryl was like a mosquito he couldn't keep from biting him and buzzing in his ears. Quickly, however, his irritation evaporated; he was too excited to let little things like that bother him.

Steadying the controls, Tommy throttled up. The Huey rose a foot, its single turbine screaming, shook and rose no more, swaying in the air like a kite on a string. By the rule book, the Huey's gross takeoff weight wasn't to be more than 8,500 pounds, but this Huey weighed thousands of pounds more. Taking off from Thule's 10,000-foot runway, there'd been plenty of room to drag the skids and pick up enough forward airspeed for the force of lift to kick in. And Thule was in the dense air of sea level. But the ice cap was 2,000

feet higher, and each time they refueled they added more equipment until suddenly the helo wouldn't fly. *No problem,* thought
Tommy, who never did anything by the book.

"Gary out!" he yelled, bumping onto the ice again and eyeing
the steep slope of a crater a hundred yards away.

Gary scrambled out and Tommy spooled up. *Bump, bump,* the
Huey rose a foot, fell onto the ice, rose, twirled around and fell
again. Still too heavy.

"Rick out!" Tommy shouted.

Rick slid out and, now, nearly four hundred pounds lighter with
the two men left on the ground, the Huey rose ten feet above the
ice cap, dazzling in the bright August sun, and wobbled over the
glacier to the crater's edge. Tommy set the Huey down and Rick and
Gary ran over and piled back in. Below the Huey's nose the glacier
fell away in a mile-wide bowl. At the bottom, five hundred feet below, shimmered a blue lake. Rising from the other side was a rugged
brown wall topped with a rim of ice. Tommy lifted the Huey slightly
off the ground and eased the control cyclic forward. The Huey tilted
nosedown and plunged over the crater's edge, its skids sliding down
the snow like runners on a sled. The gathering speed sent air faster
over the churning rotor blades until the Huey lifted off the ground,
albeit still plunging toward the lake.

I know Tommy's good, Gary thought, *I just hope he's great.* Near
the bottom of the crater, the Huey found its wings and, its engine
screaming, Tommy climbed sharply. "Whoa!" he shouted, barely
missing the ridge, thinking, *This is insane!* The normally taciturn
Rick grinned from ear to ear; they all began to laugh uncontrollably.
"Isn't it strange how when you're about to die you always laugh?"
Rick yelled. *This is great,* thought Gary, who'd been dreaming about
this trip for seven years. Tommy settled into his seat, turned the
controls over to Darryl, who didn't have a helicopter pilot's license,
and the Huey hurtled north at one hundred knots, skimming over
the rock and ice.

To a casual observer, the Huey and its crew probably would

have looked like a bunch of middle-aged yahoos on a camping trip whose RV had suddenly metamorphosed into a helicopter. Tommy Hauptman was a round-faced father of six, dressed in a T-shirt and a nondescript brown-leather flight jacket. Darryl Greenamyer was small, unshaven, dressed in an oversized Air Force–issue green polyester parka, a Russian-style fur hat pulled over his ears. Rick Kriege's blue jeans, black T-shirt, and perpetually grease-stained fingers were more appropriate in a biker bar than the high Arctic. Gary Larkins had jet-black hair, dark, thick eyebrows, a legacy of his great grandfather, a Cheyenne war chief, but in his jeans, Air Force mukluks, and odd, oversized, rimless glasses, he hardly looked like a swashbuckling, romantic character. And the Huey was dented and oil-stained, its insulation falling from the ceiling, a ragged survivor clinging to life.

When they had emerged from an Air Force C-130 cargo plane at Thule Air Base a week earlier, the base commander and his lieutenants had been appalled by this ragtag gang and their beleaguered helicopter. But looks can be deceiving. They were, in fact, a remarkable collection of talent.

Tommy Hauptman was one of the best helicopter pilots in the world. He'd survived two tours in Vietnam flying Hueys and small, agile OH-6 choppers used to scout enemy troops, usually by drawing fire. He'd been shot down three times. In the early nineties he'd won the world's first and only helicopter pylon race in his own Hughes 500 (the civilian version of the OH-6), beating factory-sponsored teams with deeper pockets and the latest equipment from the likes of McDonnell Douglas. The owner of a charter helicopter service on the Hawaiian island of Maui, he was a veteran of over 20,000 flight hours. When he flew a helicopter he wasn't operating some alien machine. It was an extension of his body, the rotors and turbines and gauges an integral part of his arms and legs and brain.

A year earlier, three cameramen shooting a Sharon Stone movie had tried to get footage from within the active crater of the

Kilauea volcano. But when they encountered zero visibility inside the smoking crater, their helicopter crashed and they were trapped on a ledge. Over a period of two days, helicopters from the Coast Guard and Air Force rescued two of the men but failed to get the third. Finally Universal Studios called Tommy Hauptman. He swept in flying a diminutive Hughes 500 dangling a seventy-five-foot-long rope and net. The helicopter is too small, said the Army and the Coast Guard. Wrong, said Tommy, it's just perfect. He hovered over the spot where, below, hidden in the smoke, the filmmaker huddled. When the net got near him, the filmmaker grabbed it. Tommy couldn't *see* the guy, but in the little helicopter he could *feel* the pull and he knew to hover exactly overhead until, again, he could feel him climb into the net. And that was the crux: Tommy wasn't just good, he was, Gary Larkins put in, "crazy enough to fly out there and to violate all the rules doing it."

Among pilots, Darryl Greenamyer was another legend, a fearless flyer who would rather make rules than follow them. In 1961, when he was twenty-five years old, he was flying test flights for the Lockheed F-104 Starfighter, the fastest production fighter in the world. Just two years later he became a test pilot in Lockheed's famed Advance Development Projects division, known as the "Skunk Works." Though a civilian, he graduated from both the Air Force Aerospace Research Pilots School and the Navy's Top Gun School. He flight-tested U-2s and the hottest airplanes in the world, the CIA's Lockheed A-12 and the Air Force's SR-71 Blackbird. In 1965, Darryl won the National Championship Air Races at Reno, Nevada, in his World War II–era Grumman F8F Bearcat fighter, his first of seven first-place victories in eleven tries, a record still unmatched thirty-five years later. In 1969 he broke the world absolute propeller-driven speed record, which had been held by Germany since 1939. In 1977 he snatched the world low-altitude speed record from the U.S. Navy in a hand-built Starfighter, streaking across a one-kilometer course four times at an average speed of

988 miles an hour, thirty feet above the ground. (His record remains unbroken at the time of this book's publication.) Greenamyer made a small fortune wheeling and dealing in surplus airplanes, often recovering them by flying them out of places like Panama or the Pacific atoll of Kwajalein. Darryl liked to think there wasn't a plane in the world he couldn't fly.

Gary Larkins had a pilot's license, too, but he wasn't known for his ability to fly airplanes so much as for his ability to recover them once they'd crashed. Over twenty-two years the self-described "Air Pirate" had salvaged fifty airplanes from the world's most exotic nooks and crannies. To get them he'd dodged machine-gun fire from Communist guerrillas in the Philippines, had hid from pirates in the Sulu Sea, and only months before had spent ten days in a perilously unshored cavern some twenty-six stories under Greenland's ice cap. Believing the old saying "It's better to beg for forgiveness than ask for permission," he had illegally crossed into the jungles of Burma with teak smugglers and been incarcerated in a four-foot-square metal box in the Solomon Islands. He had been to New Guinea twelve times, Greenland twice, and Alaska too many times to count. He liked to say he had "dived in every sump hole from Maine to Manila," from which he returned with some of the rarest airplanes on earth: Wildcats and Hellcats, Corsairs and SBD Dauntlesses, B-17 Fortresses and P-39 Aircobras, even a Sikorsky flying boat and the world's last 1935 Bellanca Aircruiser. They graced exhibit halls from the Museum of Flight, in Seattle, to the National Museum of Naval Aviation, in Pensacola, Florida. Hundreds of thousands of people admired them every year without ever knowing where they came from or what it took to get them there.

Rick Kriege was an FAA-licensed airframe and powerplant mechanic, a thirty-eight-year-old former Wyoming oil-field roughneck Darryl had met in 1987 when Kriege had plucked him out of a plane crash.

And the Huey? The UH-1 was a big, powerful military helicopter, the backbone of the U.S. Army in Vietnam. Worth

$200,000, it was hardly the kind of craft civilians usually tooled around in, especially in a place as remote as northern Greenland.

Seven hours after departing Thule, and thanks to his fearless pilot-ing, Tommy Hauptman veered off the ice cap and popped over a ridge. Below lay a large lake, luminous blue in a world of dull brown. On the far side of the lake, a silver dot gleamed in the sun. Tommy skimmed toward it at a hundred knots, a hundred feet over the wa-ter. They'd been dreaming about this moment for months. They'd all seen photos, some taken in the dead of winter showing the *Kee Bird* heaped with snow, a few taken in the summer. It looked to be in great shape, but you couldn't really tell from photos. This short reconnaissance trip would reveal whether or not the plane was worth trying to salvage. Quickly, the dot grew and then there it was, a B-29 bomber, great long wings outstretched, resting in still water. Tommy buzzed it, whipped around for a second look, headed straight for the nose and zipped along past the left side. *Shit,* Darryl thought, seeing what looked like ripples along the bottom of the fuselage, *we've come all this way and it's twisted.*

Tommy set the Huey down with a bump and they piled out, scrambling from the shore into the ice-cold knee-deep water around the *Kee Bird.* "God! Look at that thing," Rick said.

"She looks like she rolled out of the factory yesterday," Tommy said.

Cans of C rations, snowshoes, old mukluks littered the lake bot-tom. Gary and Rick squeezed through the open rear door and were the first inside. Bundles of parachutes lay where radar operator Howard Adams had spent a cold, restless night all those years ago. A coffee cup and a notepad sat on navigator Burl Cowan's desk. In the flight engineer's and navigator's compartments, away from the cockpit's harsh sunlight, the green paint covering the walls was vi-brant, unflaking, the cotton insulation still perfectly white, the glass over the gauges clear.

"This is fantastic," said Gary, who was used to finding airplanes with barely salvageable airframes. "It's like the goddamned Holy Grail," he said, lighting a cigar in celebration.

Darryl walked around the plane, studying what he could see of its wings and fuselage. The black paint under the wings shined. He couldn't see a single spot of corrosion or rust. The twist he thought he'd seen in the fuselage had just been a reflection from the water.

After all the talk and dreams of so many other warbird fanatics and wanna-be collectors, Darryl and Gary were actually there with their own helicopter and salvage tools. And the *Kee Bird* surpassed their wildest hopes.

If I search for the rest of my life, Gary thought, *I'll never find a plane as perfect as the* Kee Bird.

FOUR

—

WARBIRD FEVER

The Midwest, U.S.A.

Most valuable objects have value because they're rare, and usually they're rare because there weren't very many of them in the first place. Gold and diamonds and van Goghs and literary first editions and Spanish treasure come to mind. World War II airplanes are different, because there were once so many of them that they were long considered to be worthless. In fact, you might even say that warbirds are now so valuable *because* they were once so ubiquitous.

To understand how that happened, I called Walter Soplota, a renowned eccentric with what was reported to be a remarkable collection of rare airplanes in his backyard. I got Mrs. Soplota. "We're not interested in any visitors," she said.

"I understand," I said, "but—"

Click. She hung up the phone.

I wrote the Soplotas a letter and called again. No luck.

Finally, Darryl Greenamyer called Soplota for me. "He *might* talk to you," Darryl said.

I called again and this time Mrs. Soplota sighed and turned the telephone over to her husband. "Too many visitors," he said, "and the neighbors will complain. We're not open. Now everybody wants my airplanes. Millions of dollars they're offering me, but I'm not selling anything." He had a nasal-sounding voice and the trace of a stutter; I pictured a stooped gnome sitting atop a pile of treasure.

I listened for an hour and promised not to reveal his whereabouts. "Okay," he said, "come on by." The directions to his house filled a page.

I flew to a city in the Midwest. Thirty minutes from the airport I exited the highway, cruising past the engines and by-products of the roaring turn-of-the-century economy. Starbucks. Old Navy. The Village Square Mall. Blond moms in Range Rovers. Keeping an eye out for Soplota's road, I passed the polo grounds and rambling estates with names like Windwood and Greenledge nestled in the trees. I hung a left onto an unmarked paved road, then onto a gravel road, passed a lake, turned again, onto dirt this time, and threaded my way through "a set of gullies," as he'd directed me. Surrounded by thick woods at the end of a muddy road stood a white clapboard house. Sweet-smelling wood smoke curled from its chimney. The house was an atoll surrounded by an ocean of junk.

I squeezed past a rusting Dodge van sinking into the mud, filled to the roof with *National Geographic* magazines and *Streets Baseball News.* I threaded past a corncob of cylinders, a big piston radial engine resting in a wooden cradle partially covered with a torn blue tarp. I edged by a three-foot-long jet engine small enough to be some kid's science-fair project. Children's bicycles, stacks of wood, upended electrical component racks, piles of corrugated tin, a pot of fluorescent-yellow plastic tulips, a bright blue wingless AT-6 World War II trainer, an odd, twin-engine floatplane, several more engines, airplane wings piled like cordwood, stacks and piles of stuff reaching over my head. I followed a well-trod path. The front porch was filled to the ceiling. The front door looked like it hadn't been opened in decades. I peered in through the smudged glass. More debris, filling every square inch of the room. "Hellooo," I called.

A dog barked. A *big,* resonant *whoof, whoof.* "Who's there?" came a muffled woman's voice from around the side of the house.

I headed toward the sound, squeezing past a ten-foot-high piece of ragged fuselage, dangling wires, part of a giant British Victor bomber.

Suddenly a shaggy junkyard dog crashed around the corner, dragging a short woman in black rubber boots at the end of a frayed rope. The dog wanted to rip my throat out, but she held on fiercely, eyeing me from under a faded black Easter Sunday hat with a big satin bow. "Walter's out back," she said. "Wait here."

She returned a moment later, this time with the dog on a proper leash. He acted like he'd just had a lobotomy—now he wanted to nuzzle me to death. I reached out a hand to cement our new friendship. "Better not," she called back to me, heading into the junk, dragging the dog in her wake. We crawled under wings, edged around a blue 1957 Chevrolet panel truck filled to bursting with toy airplanes and water-stained aviation magazines, climbed over landing gear and upside-down fuselages. And every so often I caught a glimpse of whole planes, rare planes collectors would die for. Was that a Chance Vought Corsair under the A-frame of two-by-fours and corrugated tin? A North American B-25 Mitchell wrapped in old road signs?

"Walter," she called, in a sweet singsong voice, crunching through the leaves and stray pieces of aluminum. We edged out of the pile into the woods. "Walter? Hon, that writer man is heeere."

Walter Soplota emerged from the brush carrying a plastic bucket filled with kindling. He still had that stutter and nasally voice. But even though I knew he was seventy-six years old, he looked twenty years younger. He was slender and straight, with piercing green eyes flecked with gold beneath wild, Einsteinian eyebrows. His face was handsome, weathered and tanned and covered with gray whiskers; a full head of gray hair lay beneath his red wool stocking cap. He was dressed in green Dickey work pants, white sneakers, and a ragged gray sweater. He limply shook my hand and took off into the debris. I followed, his wife skittering ten feet behind, yanking the mutt along while frantically scratching notes on a small pad as he talked. *Who was she keeping tabs on? I wondered. Me? Or Walter?*

"This here's a Grumman TBM Avenger," he said, patting an intact airplane standing on its landing gear, its wings folded as if stowed on an aircraft carrier. "Same kind of torpedo bomber President Bush flew. Carried one torpedo or twelve bombs. Biggest single-engine plane we had in the war. Saved her from the smelters in Rising Sun, Maryland. Paid fourteen hundred dollars for her but, man, oh man, she's valuable now. Guy offered me fourteen thousand just for the bomb-bay doors the other day. Took me four trips over seven mountain ranges in my '57 Chevy and trailer. There's hardly any of them Avengers left. The government destroyed them all. It breaks my heart what the government did to our heritage."

When the Nazi blitzkrieg punched across the Polish border in 1939, Soplota was nineteen, and much of that aviation heritage hadn't even been conceived yet. Although the advent of war was hardly a surprise to the Allies, what was unexpected was the scale necessary to win it. "For almost all of the twenty-one years immediately following the end of World War I," writes aviation historian Walter J. Boyne, "conscientious statesmen, politicians, newspaper editors, and the general public believed it not only possible, but probable, that the next war might be won in a few days by the terror bombing of helpless cities. Fleets of aircraft were to stream in to drop tons of bombs, making London or Paris uninhabitable; the frightened, demoralized populace would flee, demanding surrender from its governments."

It was a simplistic, erroneous belief based on an unrealistic understanding of the capability of 1930s-era technology. Airplanes simply couldn't fly far enough, fast enough, carry a big enough load or target it accurately enough to wreak the kind of wholesale havoc necessary to bring nations to their knees. The top-of-the-line fighter at the outbreak of the war, the German Messerschmitt Bf-109E, produced 1,050 horsepower, and could fly just 340 miles at a speed of 365 miles per hour. Britain's new Hurricanes were fifteen miles per hour slower and used fixed-pitch wooden propellers, barely different from those used on World War I fighters. Germany's top bomber, the Heinkel He-111P, had two engines, flew 247 mph, and carried just 2,200 pounds of bombs. And even such relatively simple airplanes as these usually took four years to make from design to completion.

In 1939, the great powers all believed that a top-of-the-line air force should consist of 5,000 aircraft, one-third of which would be frontline fighters and bombers. Attacking Poland on September 1, 1939, Germany deployed 897 bombers and 210 fighters. Hermann Göring, head of the Luftwaffe, planned to destroy Britain's Royal Air Force in four days. To do so he rounded up 2,550 bombers and fighters. In 1940, Japan built 4,768 airplanes, the United States 6,000. That same year, the U.S. military had 8,000 pilots, barely more than it had during World War I.

In hindsight, the numbers seem absurd, given the vast distances fought over, the voracious appetites of the Axis leaders, and the technology available to them. But all-out war is a great motivator and the United States and England realized much earlier than Germany or Japan, writes Boyne, "the gigantic scale of effort necessary to exercise airpower." In just four years, aviation technology surged decades ahead, the piston engine and its propellers approaching their physical limits. The Curtiss P-40 Warhawk, first built in 1939, flew 364 mph, with a range of 610 miles. The Navy's Grumman F-4F Wildcat, built in 1940, hit all of 318 mph, with a range of 925 miles. Under the pressure of war, the Grumman F6F Hellcat went from drawing board to battle in twenty-five months and buzzed over 400 mph for nearly 1,800 miles. The North American P-51 Mustang went from design to rollout in 102 days; it had a range of 980 miles and could race through the skies at 440 miles per hour and fly at an altitude of 41,000 feet. The Chance Vought F4U Corsair, known to the Japanese as the "Whistling Death," flew at 446 miles an hour with a range of 1,005 miles. Today, Mustangs and Super Corsairs remain among the fastest propeller planes in the world. The mighty B-29 Superfortress went from design to rollout in nineteen months.

The real miracle came in the numbers. During the war years, millions of Americans, many of them unemployed farmers and housewives who had never before worked in factories, built some 304,000 airplanes—almost 100,000 in 1944 alone. While today's U.S. Congress waffles over the building of a few hundred F-22 fighters, between 1940 and 1945 this country built 18,000 B-24 Liberators, 12,000 B-17 Flying Fortresses, 9,800 B-25 Mitchells, 5,000 B-26 Marauders, 7,200 A-20 Havocs, 3,895 B-29 Superfortresses, 9,500 P-38 Lightnings, 15,500 P-47 Thunderbolts, 15,000 P-51 Mustangs, 12,600 Hellcats, and 12,571 Corsairs.

Each B-29 alone required 45,540 parts and one million rivets. At any hour, 15,000 men and women were assembling them in Boeing's Wichita, Kansas, plant. Shifts lasted ten hours a day, seven days a week, with every other weekend off. During one three-week stretch in 1944, the Wichita shifts worked twenty-one consecutive ten-hour days. Twenty percent of the workforce was composed of riveters, the majority of whom were women.

Imagine the numbers of parts and the hours of labor that went into every type of plane being built—the scale is mind-boggling. Then match the number of airplanes with the number of pilots and navigators and bombardiers and gunners needed to operate them. Between Pearl Harbor and the victory over Japan the United States trained over 300,000 pilots, 347,236 gunners, 493,000 engine mechanics, 195,422 radio mechanics, 50,976 navigators, and 47,354 bombardiers. Although 50,000 Americans died in Vietnam, nearly that many aviators of the Eighth and Fifteenth Air Force alone died in World War II. Hardly a family in America didn't have some direct, personal connection to the warplanes being churned out and the air war being fought.

Barely a decade after Charles Lindbergh dazzled the world by buzzing at one hundred miles per hour from New York to Paris, just a few years after the despair and joblessness of the Depression, the country was dedicated to designing, building, and flying airplanes that were revolutionizing technology, industry, and warfare. These new airplanes were also romantic symbols of American inventiveness and daring, the battles and exploits fought in them easily remembered, like the famous 1942 raid on Japan, carried out by air racer Jimmy Doolittle's squadron of sixteen B-25s launched from the aircraft carrier USS *Hornet*, 825 miles east of Tokyo. The launching of the heavily laden bombers, the largest planes ever to take off from a carrier, had to be timed perfectly with the wind and the rise of the ship. Though they did little in the way of physical damage, the first U.S. bombing of Japan was a huge psychological lift for American forces, which had been repeatedly pummeled in the Pacific. And then there was the Palm Sunday massacre in 1943, in which four squadrons of P-40 Warhawks shot down seventy-one German planes over the Mediterranean in a single action, with just seven Allied losses. And the hundreds of thousands of sorties of the B-17s of the Eighth Air Force, escorted by Mustang fighters, that dropped millions of tons of bombs on Germany.

Then one day the war was over. Overnight, there were too many planes, planes that had no purpose in a civilian world. A four-engine B-29 Superfortress that guzzled four hundred gallons an hour and didn't have any room for passengers? A Mustang fighter that carried a single pilot at 440 miles an hour? "You needed your own gas station to fuel 'em," is the way Soplota put it. There were tens of thousands of fighters and bombers, and what good were they? In a process almost as efficient as their production, the planes of World War II were declared surplus and destroyed.

Brand-new planes were tumbled over cliffs, pushed off aircraft carriers, plowed into landfills. In the late 1940s, a pilot named Paul Mantz bought 475 surplus planes, including 228 B-24 Liberators. He paid $55,000 for the lot. B-29s sold for $350, a P-38 Lightning for $150. Sometimes the fuel left in their tanks was worth more than the planes themselves. The Army Air Force sold huge lots of airplanes for scrap: the largest bunch involved 21,800 tactical planes sold for two-tenths of a cent on the purchase dollar. Planes were blown up with TNT, strafed and bombed for target practice at California's China Lake Naval Weapons Center and Maryland's Aberdeen Proving Ground, chopped into pieces by huge portable guillotines, melted into ingots by portable smelters. The Bachman Brothers of Rochester, New York, bought $100 million worth of B-29 parts for $1 million (which they sold back to the government during the Korean War for $5 million). In Mojave, California, a smelter named Rhino Bill stacked cordwood around a B-29, dug a series of trenches, and melted it into chunks that he carried by mule to his furnace. The destruction was wholesale and complete, especially with less-successful planes that had been built in smaller numbers. No one thought to preserve one or two of every type; today, for instance, not a single TBD Devastator survives.

Walter Soplota was horrified. The penniless son of Czech immigrants, Soplota became obsessed with saving airplanes from the smelter. "When I saw the government destroying our heritage, I cried myself to sleep," he said, looking starry-eyed at a rare Grumman Tracker fuselage upside down in the weeds. "They wouldn't stop until the last one was chopped up. How could they do that? My wife, she's a good woman. She said, 'I don't care what you bring home as long as it's not another woman.' " During the week he worked as a union carpenter and every Friday night he took off in a succession of dilapidated vehicles towing a creaky wooden trailer that he rebuilt four times from the wheels up. "I'd sleep in the vehicle, disassemble the plane, and come back Sunday night. Man, oh man, I was tired. It'd take me two weeks to recover. The state highway patrol took four of them cars away from me, condemned 'em," he said. Once, he was stopped in his 1945 school bus, a plane sticking fifty feet out the end. He was cited for 145 violations, and the state trooper, who'd heard of Soplota, told him to get on home and to never, ever, drive the school bus again. When he finally dragged the pieces into the yard, he'd pose his four daughters and one son atop them like trophy hunters over a freshly killed lion. The black-and-white photos are pasted edge to edge, twenty to a page, in a wallpaper sample book: "SAVED," written over and over again in scratchy blue ink beneath photos of dark-haired, pretty girls in gingham dresses perched atop wings and engines and fuselages. (One of his daughters entered a convent on her eighteenth birthday. Around the same time Lt. Comdr. Dick Oliver, a Navy Blue Angel, crashed his F-4 Phantom jet, and Soplota carted home all that was left: a single stabilizer and a twisted, bent engine. That night, Soplota was weeping over his daughter's marriage to God when, he says, none other than the recently deceased Dick Oliver appeared next to Soplota's bed, his face nothing but a bright glow. " 'What are *you* crying for,' Oliver says to me. Then he told me to take good care of his airplane and, *poof!* He was gone and never came back. My daughter wasn't surprised. Apparently when someone enters a convent God sends someone special down to thank you.") "If I had money in them early days I really could have saved some planes," Soplota said, slapping the sample book shut and striding into his aluminum zoo.

In 1950 he paid $500 for air racer Cook Cleland's Super Corsair, winner of the 1947 National Championship Air Races, in Cleveland, Ohio. Only ten of the Super Corsairs had been delivered late in the war to intercept Japanese kamikaze suicide bombers, and the eighteen-cylinder, 3,500-horsepower fighters were the fastest, most powerful single-engine planes in the air. When Cleland blew the plane's engine in 1949, he abandoned it. Soplota snatched it up.

That same year Soplota also dragged home a standard Corsair. "For three years it had been this war memorial at the Cuyahoga, Ohio, airport," he said. "But the area was really exclusive and the mayor said it was an eyesore. He told me scrappers said they'd give him three hundred dollars for it and I could have it for two hundred."

We ducked under a wing, stepped over rusting scaffolding, and came upon an intact plane covered in old road signs. His wife scuttled after us, scribbling fiercely. "Here's a B-25 I got from a scrapper in Franklin, Pennsylvania, in 1966," Soplota said. "Paid twelve hundred dollars. Took me twenty-five loads to get that home in my '57 Chevy—the truck's enshrined in the building there, I'll never scrap her, she's my airplane hauler—and they wouldn't let me on the turnpike." Spread across the back of the lot, patched with sheet metal and reinforced with two-by-fours, was his oddest airplane, a postwar B-36 Peacemaker, the largest bomber ever made. It weighed 98,000 pounds and had a 236-foot wingspan. Salvaging it from the smelters took Soplota twenty-five trips.

Soplota was obsessed. He spent every cent he had on airplanes that were considered worthless, outbidding aluminum scrap dealers. "I hate aluminum siding, aluminum doors, anything made out of aluminum but airplanes," he said, running his hand on a Douglas Skyraider, a prototype still wired with sensors from its test-flight days. "I hate that aluminum is valuable, I hate it because these airplanes are made of it." To save it from the smelters he made a few sacrifices. He didn't go on vacations, he didn't fix up his house, he didn't buy new clothes, and sometimes, he said, "I couldn't even put food on the table."

But Walter Soplota was a nut mostly because he was so ahead of his time.

It's hard to say exactly when the warbird boom hit. By the late 1970s and early eighties, collectors got a hankering for the planes they'd flown, or that their parents or grandparents had flown. Maybe just enough time had to pass to erase the pain of the war, or the world had to grow complicated enough for the days of World War II to seem simple. Or maybe all those transistors and nearly microscopic computer chips and their binary, digital gate-

ways suddenly illuminated the beauty and wonder of a piston engine and its finely machined and tuned moving parts exploding in
harmony. World War II got romantic. A growing number of aviation museums suddenly realized that they had few, if any, airplanes
from the most important period in aviation history. But by then
most of the planes were gone. And people want what they can't
have. Using more modern surplus airplanes (usually transports that
could be refurbished and sold to air-freight companies, or smugglers
or Third World guerrillas) as currency, the U.S. Air Force and the
U.S. Navy began actively building their collections, contracting
with salvors like Gary Larkins and Darryl Greenamyer. They traded
Lockheed C-130s for B-17s and B-26s in 1981, a C-130 for a P-51
Mustang and a de Havilland Mosquito in 1982, two C-123s for
three F-104 Starfighters in 1986. At the same time, private collectors with lots of money started lusting after them and driving their
price up. To own a warbird was to own something that no one else
had, the ultimate toy to show off. Don Whittington, who served
time in federal prison for tax evasion, reportedly became the first
person to pay $250,000 for a plane, $350,000 for a plane, and
$500,000 for a plane.

These days, warbirds seem to drive people crazy. "It has gotten
completely out of hand," said Ascher Ward, a plane dealer in Van
Nuys, California, who wheeled and dealed with Darryl Greenamyer
for years. "There's just so few of them that people have to have
them," he said. "When I started in this business you could get
planes for ten cents a pound, but it's out of the hands of the little
guys now."

Kermit Weeks, a collector in Florida, has 140 planes, a collection worth tens of millions of dollars. Fantasy of Flight, his inter-
active museum in Polk City, Florida, draws 100,000 visitors a year at
twenty-one dollars a pop.

Until he recently began selling his collection, Minnesota crane
mogul Wally Fisk had dozens ready to fly at a moment's notice

should he get the urge; they were housed in a string of hangars so spotless you'd think nothing of letting your naked toddler slither across their floors.

Helicopter crane and logging tycoon Jack Erickson has twenty-five, and has spent a small fortune sending Gary Larkins into the wilderness to bring more home.

Arizona collector Doug Champlin spent $75,000 just to learn the location of an airplane 600 feet under the Atlantic Ocean.

In 1981, Pat Epps, the owner of a flight service and charter operation in Atlanta, Georgia, embarked on a quest to find and recover six P-38 Lightnings that crashed on the Greenland ice cap in 1942; by the time he got one of them, crushed and in far worse condition than many of the planes Soplota had saved, he'd spent millions.

A Florida underwater salvor named Peter Theophanis ignored U.S. law and spent thousands of dollars to fish a wingless, engineless Wildcat out of Lake Michigan. He wound up in Federal Court, charged with theft of government property. (The U.S. Navy claims title to all Navy property, in any condition, anywhere in the world.) "Private collectors and museums are the same," said Theophanis. "They're both greedy."

And the gung ho guys creating the Quonset Air Museum, in North Kingstown, Rhode Island, just got a little too excited when they discovered a Hellcat off the coast of Martha's Vineyard and recovered it against the explicit orders of the U.S. Navy. They, too, found themselves facing federal charges as a result of their passion.

Machines built expressly for killing have become synonymous with a golden age, a time when, as Quonset's Mark Newton put it, "guys from the farm fields of America turned this country into the greatest power the world has ever known." Today's jet fighters and bombers are far more powerful than any plane from the 1940s. But looking at a gull-winged Corsair sweep through the sky, hearing its massive radial engine growl, sends chills through men's (and a few women's) hearts. "In America," writes David E. Nye in his book

American Technological Sublime, "technological achievements became measures of cultural value ... technical can-do proof of the nation's inventive and productive genius—an outward and visible sign of an ideal America." Jets and rockets may be infinitely more powerful, but they're also infinitely more complex, their systems and principles beyond the reach of most ordinary tinkerers.

Walter Soplota couldn't agree more. He celebrates the Fourth of July by cranking up the wingless AT-6 a few feet from his front door, as he has for decades. The exploding pistons of 600 horsepower are better than any fireworks display. "I chain up the tail to one of them old vans and off we go," he said with a gap-toothed grin.

With warbirds so popular, Walter Soplota is now under siege. Not long ago a well-known warbird magazine publisher pulled up to his house in a white Cadillac and scolded Soplota for not doing anything with his collection. "You're ruining them!" he yelled. "These things ought to be in a museum or flying through the sky at air shows!" Soplota shook his head at the memory. "For twenty years I had 'em and everyone said 'Why don't you scrap this worthless stuff,' and now they're telling me I've got no business owning it because I'm not preserving it or making it flyable. But everything here was going to the smelter before I saved it!" Everybody wants his warbirds; when he finally couldn't manage the minimum payments on his credit cards, he sold two: his Super Corsair, for $800,000, and his F-82 Twin Mustang, for $475,000. Dave Arnold, who bought the Twin Mustang—only a few hundred were built and only four survive today—turned around and flipped it to crane mogul Wally Fisk for close to $1 million.

Now Soplota is protecting his planes from the warbird buffs. He doesn't want to see his planes restored to flying condition, and then possibly ruined in a crash, their ultimate fate the same as if they'd gone right to the smelter. For Soplota the planes are monuments in and of themselves, just as they are. "I got a buyer for everything here, tons of money. I got a dozen guys who want to give me three hundred fifty thousand dollars, cash, for my Corsair. Another guy said he'd give me three million for everything in the yard. They're begging me. But I don't want to sell 'em. I didn't do it for the money. And I don't want to see 'em fly."

Soplota opened the doors to his basement, garage, sheds, and trailers. Stuffed, all of them, with rare old wings and fabric-covered flight controls, an intact DC-7 flight simulator ("She's got ninety-six instruments on her"), cockpit canopies, a T-33 fuselage, gun sights, and who knew what else. Now he was turning away visitors, defensively hoarding his collection. He was afraid of the Internal Revenue Service. Afraid of the Environmental Protection Agency. Afraid even of the state department of human services, which had recently shown up to see if he and his wife were sane, and left worried that the house might collapse under all the weight. "They said it was overloaded," he said, shrugging. "I got every room filled!"

Finally he paused in a clearing, choked back a tear, and then bent down on his hands and knees, clearing leaves and weeds from two small, rounded concrete humps. One had the impression of a tire in it, like a fossilized pterodactyl footprint. "This is where my Super Corsair was for over forty years," he said, "and I think these'll be my tombstones."

I asked Soplota if he had any favorites, now that the Super Corsair and Mustang were gone. He stood up, scratched his head, and softly brushed the concrete with a toe. "They're all listening, so I wouldn't want to hurt their feelings. I love every one of 'em. I never dreamed they'd be this valuable. Never. I used to love 'em more than the wife did, but now it's the other way around." Mrs. Soplota was leaning on a wing, ten feet away, scribbling like a court reporter on speed. I never did discover what she was writing. But for the first time all afternoon, I thought I saw her smile.

FIVE

—

FIRST COME, FIRST SERVED

Daugaard Jensen Land, Greenland; August 1993

For all its romance, treasure hunting mostly consists of back-breaking physical labor and elbow grease, and that's especially true with recovering airplanes. Magic wasn't going to bring the *Kee Bird* back to life like the mythical Phoenix. After Darryl Greenamyer and Gary Larkins got over how incredibly well preserved the *Kee Bird* was that summer in 1993, Darryl darted into the cockpit and Rick Kriege and Gary put on their rubber hip waders and slogged into the lake. On this scouting trip they hoped to stand the plane on its landing gear and maybe even start an engine. That meant raising it high enough with a short set of twenty-ton-capacity jacks to squeeze a taller set of thirty-ton-capacity jacks in place, all to lift the *Kee Bird* enough to swing its wheels down. And to do that they had to start digging.

"Man, this is cold," Rick said, squatting in the near-freezing water.

"You should have seen that big old hole under the ice cap I was in," Gary said, shoveling heavy gobs of mud.

Just the month before, Gary had been hired by Atlanta businessman Pat Epps to dismantle a P-38 Lightning in southern Greenland. Epps had spent years searching for the plane, which ground-penetrating radar had finally located buried under 265 feet of shifting glacier. After melting down through the equivalent of twenty-six storeys into the ice, he'd carved out an ice room around the plane with steaming hot water. Although badly damaged, the Lightning remained intact and salvageable, and it had been Gary's job to figure out how to take it apart and get it to the surface.

"I was down there for ten days straight," Gary said, pitching another shovelful behind him. "I was soaking wet and the hydraulic fluid ate right through my dry suit. It was nasty. They'd pump all the water out of the hole and by the end of the day it would be up to my waist. I was just waiting for the whole goddamned cave to collapse on me."

The jacks weighed hundreds of pounds each and it took hours for Gary, Rick, Tommy, and occasionally Darryl to drag them into place through the mud and the ice-cold water. They laughed, ribbed each other, and dug some more, pausing every so often to take a break. When they did, the place was eerie. The ground around the lake was khaki brown, dotted with clumps of olive-green lichen. At eighty degrees north latitude, nearly twelve hundred miles above the Arctic Circle, the lichen was the only sign of life. Nothing moved or made a sound or broke up the landscape. Not a bird or a rabbit or a fly. Not a tree or a shrub or a power line. Nothing at all, and that made the hair on the back of their necks stand up. Nothing distracted from the 141-foot-long silver wings resting in the western corner of the blue lake, the names "Polly," "Ida," "Norma," and "Pat" hauntingly painted in yellow on the cowling of each engine.

It doesn't get any better than this, thought Gary. When he set out in pursuit of an old warbird, he wasn't just hustling pocket-lining treasure or embarking on a grand adventure. He was pursuing a lost memory, clawing at the doors of time, trying to live all those moments when the fate of the world hung in the balance. It was one thing to find a plane busted up in the jungle, or coral-encrusted on the bottom of the ocean, or even partly disassembled and covered with cobwebs in some old guy's barn. That always gave him a momentary period rush. But out here in the middle of nowhere, time and distance dissolved into a blur. The *Kee Bird* looked like unfinished business, a mid-flight pause rather than a final journey. Gary and Darryl knew that if they could get it started and maybe even flying, then fame, glory, and money would likely be theirs. But more important was something intangible. With every crack of a piston and every turn of a propeller they'd erase forty-six years of time.

If you were flying in an airplane that was completely authentic, from its wires to its pistons to its props, you were experiencing the 1940s. You were there; then was now. The wind, the sounds, the movement of the aircraft, the flying skills required to keep it up there, the temperatures, all those were virtually identical to when, say, Vern Arnett was flying the *Kee Bird* or Paul Tibbitts was flying *Enola Gay*. Up there in the clouds the experience was pure, and who's to say whether it was 1941 or 1947 or 1999?

Man, thought Gary, puffing on a cigar while poised over his shovel, *I've stepped through the frame of an old Kodak print.*

That same feeling touched everyone who saw an old warbird—especially the *Kee Bird*—and Darryl and Gary were hardly the first to find it compelling, or to imagine bringing it home. In fact, they weren't even the first ones to visit it since its crash in 1947.

Two months after the *Kee Bird* crashed, Col. Lloyd Nuttall, flying out of Thule, managed to land his C-47 next to the plane. He snapped a few photos and left.

In April of 1947, Preben Morland, a Danish doctor, set off from Thule by dogsled to find the *Kee Bird* and recover its radios. He returned empty-handed two months later, having failed to reach the plane.

As remote as the *Kee Bird* was, it was also just 240 miles north of Thule. For years the Air Force and Navy pilots who flew out of the base (which expanded as the Cold War progressed) couldn't keep away from it. Overflying the bomber was a rite of passage and an Arctic navigation lesson for new pilots assigned to the base, a poignant monument to human error in the far north. In 1978 a photo of the abandoned curiosity appeared in *Air Classics* magazine. Thousands of readers, no doubt, gazed at the *Kee Bird* with longing or fond memories. But Gary Larkins saw the photo and fired off letters to the Air Force and the government of Denmark. He wanted that plane. All files relating to the *Kee Bird* were classified, responded the Air Force. Denmark didn't answer at all.

Then Giles Kershaw landed at the *Kee Bird* site. A commercial airline captain for Britannia Airways, Kershaw was temporarily on contract to the U.S. Navy, supporting three ice stations in and around the North Pole. He flew a one-of-kind DC-3, a ski-equipped "strange and wonderful creation," as he put it, its two piston engines replaced by three turbines, one of them in the nose. Kershaw was returning to Thule in April 1985 when he decided the weather was perfect for "an unofficial look" at the *Kee Bird*. His account of the plane's near-perfect condition and his haunting photographs of the snow-filled cockpit were published in *Aeroplane Monthly* in 1987. (A few years later, Kershaw was killed in a plane crash in Antarctica.)

By 1987, prices for warbirds were escalating. To the growing community of people lusting after the airplanes, Kershaw's description and photos were like evidence of Noah's Ark. Guys were pawing through jungles and digging under the ice for crushed or corroded or broken-up airplanes and here was an intact B-29, one of the rarest of them all. By this time, forty years had passed since the *Kee Bird*'s crash, and its files were finally declassified. The Air Force made no claim to it, nor to any other U.S. Air Force or Army airplane that crashed before 1962. But Denmark was another matter. The Danish government referred a growing number of inquiries about the *Kee Bird* to the Ministry of Foreign Affairs, which refused to grant salvage rights.

Still, the race was on. In the spring of 1989, Bob Ellis, the director of the Kalamazoo Aviation History Museum, in Kalamazoo, Michigan, flew to Resolute, Canada. In a chartered de Havilland Twin Otter equipped with skis, Ellis then flew to the village of Grise Fjord and finally over Baffin Straight to the *Kee Bird*. "We flew hours and hours," remembers Ellis, "and I started thinking we'd never find it, that maybe it was buried in snow. But finally there it was." Ellis had been skeptical. People were always coming to him with glowing reports of winged treasure. Usually, if they were there at all, the planes were riddled with corrosion or stripped of crucial parts. "Believe me," he said, "I know what airplanes look like that have sat out in the weather for decades." Ellis peered inside the cylinders of the engines using fiber-optic boroscopes. "I was amazed. They were as shiny as if they'd been made yesterday." After examining the plane for eight hours, Ellis returned to Michigan with visions of flying the *Kee Bird* off the ice. "I don't like to talk about dollars," Ellis told me later, "but the rarity of B-29s, its history as a plane that was part of the very first mission of the Strategic Air Command, the rescue of the crew—the *Kee Bird* was a real prize." To get it, Ellis figured he'd hire a few natives from the village of Qaanaaq "to keep us alive," build a big tent over the plane to work on it in relative comfort, and at last "put our little museum on the map." He ran a few numbers. All he needed, he calculated, was a half-million bucks.

Back home in Michigan, Ellis acquired a set of new Curtis Electric propellers for the plane. But then reality set in. Half a million was a lot of money, and the Danish government still wouldn't grant salvage rights. And it was one thing to fly up there in a chartered Twin Otter for eight hours, another to build a thousand-square-foot tent in the middle of nowhere. Finally, the recovery seemed too risky and too unlikely to succeed.

In 1989, William Schnase, a retired Air Force major living in St. Petersburg, Florida, hatched the Snow-Bird Project. In phase one, he and none other than the *Kee Bird*'s original flight engineer, Lucky Luedke, would fly to the *Kee Bird* via Resolute and Thule on a chartered airplane, raise the fuselage and lower the landing gear by inflatable lift bags, and try to start its engines. If successful, they would return for phase two: installing new props and flying it out. Schnase planned to buy the props from another old *Kee Bird* name, Maynard White, the former commanding officer of the 46th Reconnaissance Squadron in Alaska. Schnase received written permission from the director of operations at Thule to use the base, but permission from Denmark lagged. Finally, in May of 1990, Schnase was ready to go anyway. He informed the Danish Ministry of Foreign Affairs that he was proceeding with his plan. Two days before he was to arrive in Thule he received an urgent telex: the Danish Ministry of Foreign Affairs, it said, was "engaged in a legal assessment of the matter" and "any question of granting salvage rights to any of the several persons/organizations who have shown an interest in the aircraft cannot yet be considered." Schnase, the telex stated unequivocally, was not authorized to visit the *Kee Bird*. He wrote Luedke in October, postponing phase one until May 1991. And then he promptly disappeared, never to be heard from again, his telephone disconnected, his address a mystery. "It's weird. I'm telling you," said Luedke, "he just vanished."

Gary Larkins was different, a romantic who was bottle-fed on warbirds. His father, a chief line inspector at Douglas Aircraft, would accompany a pilot on the test flight of new B-17s coming off the assembly line. (The B-17 was originally designed and built by Boeing, but, like many warbirds, was licensed to and produced by other manufacturers to increase war production.) Eventually his father ended up fighting in the jungles of New Guinea before finally flying as a B-17 flight engineer. Gary's earliest memories include the framed color photos of his dad's B-17 in the living room and hall of their house, and hearing his father's war stories.

Even more important to his developing fixation, the Sierras, where he was raised, were firefighting country. Retired B-17s and B-25s were ideal water tankers: rugged, powerful, and cheap airplanes perfect for swooping in low with a heavy load of slurry to drop on raging forest fires. Almost every one of those planes existing today survives because it was used for that purpose. Gary's house was near a fire-bomber base. In the winter, off-season, the planes would be parked far from the hangar. From the time he was about twelve, Gary would frequently ride his bike to the base at Grass Valley, climb the fence, and sneak into a B-25 Mitchell. Sitting in the cockpit, hands on the throttle and yoke, Gary was Spencer Tracy in *Thirty Seconds over Tokyo*.

One afternoon when Gary was seventeen Ralph Ponte caught him. A rough, taciturn World War II torpedo-bomber veteran and firefighting pilot, Ponte gave Gary a choice: he could get the hell out of the B-25 and never come back, or he could grab a wrench and get to work. Gary worked for Ponte, off and on, for nine years, and Ponte taught him to fly and how to work hard, for long hours, seven days a week, until the job was done.

In 1971, while working both for Ponte and at his dad's glass shop, Gary spotted an Allison aircraft engine up for auction. Also into hot rods at the time, he thought the engine would power a very fast car. Gary drove to Salt Lake City, bid $500 on the engine, and trailered it home. The Allison turned out to be the rare left engine of a P-38 Lightning (the propellers on a twin-engine P-38 rotate in opposite directions) and within a few months he had sold it to a collector for $3,500 cash.

Soon after, he heard of a big, twin-engine transport airplane called a Lockheed L-18 Lodestar that had long sat abandoned at an airport in Auburn, California, and was being auctioned off by the city. The auction required a minimum of three bidders. Gary went and there were only two other bidders, two scrap dealers working in cahoots. "Listen, kid," they said to the twenty-one-year-old Larkins, "we need you to bid twelve hundred fifty on that plane." No problem, Gary said, fingering the $3,500 in his pocket. And sure enough, when Gary hit $1,200 one of the scrap dealers offered $1,500 to wrap up the deal. But then Gary bid it up to $1,735. The Lodestar was his.

Gary hurried over to Ponte's. "I just bought an airplane," he said. Ponte pictured a little single-engine Cessna. "No," said Gary, "a *real* airplane."

"Yup, she's a goer," Ponte said when he saw the plane. "You done real good."

Four weeks later they had the Lodestar flying and sold it to a skydiving company for $35,000.

Next, for $25,000, Ponte and Gary purchased the same B-25 that Larkins had played in; in short order they polished it up and traded it and a single-engine Stinson L-5 spotter airplane to the Air Force for a giant KC-97—known in the civilian world as a DC-10—along with five engines and a pile of parts. At the Air Force boneyard at Davis-Monthan Air Force Base in Tucson, Arizona, Ponte and Gary went through one KC-97 after another, trying to pick one they wanted. But then they spotted a "cherry" four-engine DC-6. Ponte fell in love with the plane and the Air Force said they could have it instead. Larkins and Ponte towed it off the base behind Gary's 1966 Chevrolet Suburban and immediately set to work.

In the blazing heat of the Arizona desert they worked from sunup to sundown, seven days a week, sleeping in an eight-dollar-a-night motel. Gary had a wife and a new baby girl, but Ponte kept them at it for weeks on end. One day, Gary didn't look too happy.

"I know what's bugging you," Ponte said.

Thank God, thought Gary, *we're going home for a break.*

But Ponte said, "This cost of this hotel is killing us. Let's move into the plane."

And that's what they did, eating hot dogs and beans and working straight through Thanksgiving and Christmas. A few months later they sold the plane to an Alaskan cargo company for $225,000.

At this same time, the United States Air Force Museum in Dayton, Ohio, recognizing its lack of historically significant planes, initiated the Heritage Program. Under the program the Air Force would trade surplus U.S. Air Force airplanes for planes it wanted in its various museums. With this program in mind, Gary spent a year tracking down a B-17, a P-38 Lightning, a P-47 Thunderbolt, and a B-26 Marauder—all planes either gathering dust in the stables of a few early collectors or being used as tankers. He offered them to the Air Force Museum in exchange for two giant, four-engine surplus C-130 cargo planes. The warbird boom hadn't really hit yet and there were still a few old planes around, and they were still relatively inexpensive. The trick would be financing: Gary had no money (he'd had to split the DC-6 profits with Ponte and a third investor) even as he brokered the deal promising to deliver the four warbirds. With Air Force contract in hand, he persuaded a couple of San Diego real estate brokers to pony up $1 million. In 1981 Gary acquired the four planes, got them all flying in a frantic month, and delivered them as promised to four different locations across the country. Thereupon, he found himself one of the first civilian owners of two C-130s, which he got flying and sold for over a million dollars each.

A few years earlier, turning wrenches under Ponte and working for his dad, Gary had been making $3.50 an hour. Suddenly he was sitting on a hundred thousand times that. "I should have stopped right then and there and put that money in T-bills," he told me over a whiskey in the Alaskan bush twenty years later. "But warbirds are like an addiction. You can't stop yourself."

Like Kalamazoo's Bob Ellis and the Snow-Bird Project's William Schnase and others, Gary Larkins had been hounding the Danish government for the *Kee Bird*'s salvage rights since he had first seen its photo in 1978. But unlike the others, Gary went to the trouble of hiring a local agent in Copenhagen to press his case. And in 1992 the Danish Ministry of Foreign Affairs ruled that the government couldn't claim title to the *Kee Bird*. Whoever took physical possession of the plane first would own it.

The plane was Gary's—if he could get to it before anyone else.

Therein lay the problem. Though historically priceless, its market value was unknown. Two million dollars seemed a reasonable guess, but a collector's item is worth only what someone will pay for it. Recovering the *Kee Bird* had to turn a profit for whoever bankrolled the project. And the plane was about as far away from civilization as possible. As Bob Ellis had demonstrated, it wasn't all that difficult to charter a Twin Otter and set down next to the *Kee Bird* for a few hours, at a cost of about $15,000 for the single round-trip flight. But a Twin Otter's maximum load, after the pilots and the Otter's fuel, was only about 2,500 pounds, nowhere near enough for a handful of people and their food, plus the tools and equipment necessary to work on the plane for several weeks. Fuel alone for the *Kee Bird* and the generators weighed nearly seven pounds a gallon. Add the dozens of flights necessary to bring everything in and the costs started spiraling out of control. There were few other airplanes available that had the range to get to the *Kee Bird* and the ability to land and take off on the snow or dirt in a confined space. You might charter a four-engine C-130 transport, but that would cost hundreds of thousands of dollars per flight. Bob Ellis's plan for a huge tent over the *Kee Bird* was a fantasy.

Once there, the question remained how to get a plane weighing 90,000 pounds back to the United States. You could disassemble the plane into more manageable pieces—an enormous job in a warm hangar with all the right tools—but they still might be too bulky to fit inside even a C-130. You could fly the pieces out by heavy-lift sky-crane helicopter, but such helicopters can only lift 25,000 pounds and have a range of only 125 miles. Plus, they have a voracious thirst for fuel, none of which existed near the *Kee Bird*. And a sky crane wasn't cheap.

No, if the *Kee Bird* was in the good shape Kershaw reported, the only answer was to fly it out. The idea was crazy, though; the *Kee Bird* had forty-five thousand parts and a million rivets, all of which had suffered some of the harshest winds and temperatures in the world for more than forty years. Even if it *looked* good, there was no telling the condition of its miles of wire and hydraulic systems. And if *they* turned out to be preserved, the feat required, at the very least, four new sets of propellers—four eight-foot-long steel blades to a set—weighing nearly a ton each, along with thousands of pounds of fuel, tools, food, supplies, all still needing, somehow, to be flown in to a site nearly 500 miles from the nearest civilian airfield in the high Arctic. It was a daunting prospect.

Although the Danish Ministry of Foreign Affairs had ruled the first team to get the *Kee Bird* could have her, any expedition still required permits from the Danish Polar Center to operate in Greenland. Gary applied for and received the permit, good from June 1, 1993 to October 1, 1993. So, too, did another American, a warbird collector named Davis Tallichet. Gary didn't know if Tallichet had the ability and financial backing to get to the airplane. And he couldn't chance waiting to find out.

For years Gary had been recovering airplanes for Jack Erickson, the Oregon-based multimillionaire owner of Erickson Air Crane. Erickson's warbird collection numbered nearly two dozen, all of which were nested at the Tillamook Naval Air Station Museum in Tillamook, Oregon. Not only did Erickson have the money necessary to bankroll a *Kee Bird* expedition, he could supply helicopters to accomplish the task. But Erickson, like most rich collectors, could be mercurial. When Larkins finally had the permits in hand, Erickson declined to participate. "It was too big, too complex," Erickson said.

Gary flew to Florida to see Kermit Weeks, another wealthy collector. But Weeks already had one and a half B-29s that he hoped to assemble into a flyer someday.

The Lone Star Flight Museum in Galveston, Texas, offered Gary "a substantial amount of money for the *Kee Bird*," says the Museum, if he could deliver it to their door in flying condition. But to get the *Kee Bird* back Gary figured he needed at least $350,000 up front. Someone who didn't mind a little risk was going to have to step forward.

Then one day in April 1993 the telephone rang. It was Darryl Greenamyer. He had heard about Gary's problem.

Like Gary, Darryl was a native Californian whose father had worked for Douglas Aircraft during the war. His dad also had had an independent streak that now ran deep in his son. Darryl was small, and early on he developed a passion, as he put it years later, "to show those bastards"—those bastards being just about anyone who ever said "No" or "It can't be done" to Darryl Greenamyer.

After graduating high school in 1954, Darryl joined the Air Force. But military life was too rigid for him, and after a year and a half on active duty he was discharged. He enrolled at the University of Arizona and joined the Arizona Air National Guard. By the time he graduated with a degree in mechanical engineering in 1961, Darryl had 1,000 hours flying time in F-86 and F-100 jet fighters. And he'd developed a passion for "hauling ass."

If you wanted speed in jets in the 1950s, there was one place to be above all others: Lockheed Aircraft Corporation, which was then developing the hottest airplanes in the world. In 1961 Darryl was hired to fly "chase and target" in the F-86. He wasn't exactly a test pilot—he flew the plane the test pilots were pretending to shoot down, or he flew alongside test flights as an escort—but at least he was in the game, without having to spend years working his way up through the military. One night in the early 1960s shortly before Christmas all the great Lockheed test pilots, guys like Herman "Fish" Salmon, Tony LeVier, Brack Harrell, and Harold Kitchens, had a party. Around Mojave and Edwards Air Force Base these flyers owned the world. They went wild that night, getting kicked out of one bar after another, getting ever drunker and wilder, until they ended up at a Lockheed hotel suite. They trashed it like prima donna rock stars. Then, barely able to walk, Harrell and Kitchens climbed into a Lockheed 10 and took off for Vegas. They crashed, and their deaths opened up a place for Darryl in the F-104 test program.

Nicknamed "the missile with a man in it," the F-104 Starfighter had a needle-like fuselage with thin little wing stubs (the leading edge was just one-sixteenth of an inch thick) that stuck out just four feet on either side of the fuselage. It was the fastest production jet fighter-interceptor in existence, the first fighter to exceed Mach 2, twice the speed of sound. It flew faster than the shells it fired and a careless pilot could shoot himself out of the sky with his own bullets. Many American pilots feared the plane, but Darryl loved the Starfighter for its raw speed, and he spent six months in Italy on contract to Fiat, which was then building its own versions under license from Lockheed.

After "pleading and begging" with Lockheed when he returned home, Darryl got the company to send him to the U.S. Air Force Aerospace Research Pilots School at Edwards Air Force Base. Upon graduation he scored the ultimate plum, getting assigned to Kelly Johnson's Skunk Works division at Lockheed. Over the next decade, Darryl flew experimental and developmental test flights on the super-secret Lockheed A-12 and SR-71 Blackbirds, the fastest, highest-flying jet planes ever made, flying more than three times the speed of sound and as high as 90,000 feet. Among experimental test pilots it was hard to get more elite than Darryl Greenamyer. While the rest of America was listening to Grand Funk Railroad or sputtering around in their Ford Falcons, Darryl was hurtling from California to Florida in fifty-eight minutes.

His escapades outside of Lockheed really set Darryl apart. He loved speed and he had an intuitive aerodynamic and mechanical understanding of how to get it. He'd been schooled in its complexities by the best aviators and aeronautical engineers in the world and was a natural competitor when the National Championship Air Races were revived in 1964 at Bill Stead's Sky Ranch in Reno, Nevada.

Darryl entered that first race, flying a Grumman F8F Bearcat, a stubby, powerful Navy fighter introduced at the end of World War II. He replaced its cracked cockpit canopy with the tiny searchlight cover off a Lockheed P-3 Orion, but did little else to increase the speed of the plane. Darryl streaked to victory in the second of four heat races but was disqualified for landing at a different airport when he decided that he couldn't safely set the Bearcat down on the narrow, sand-covered metal mat runway surrounded by spectators at the Sky Ranch.

To wring more speed from the airplane the following year, Darryl and Lockheed Skunk Works engineers Pete Law and Bruce Boland radically modified the airplane and engine, clipping its wings, streamlining the cowling around the engine, installing a water-boiling cooling system, and adding an oversized propeller hub from a Douglas Skyraider. Over the next thirteen years he won the Reno Unlimited division seven times, and set the absolute piston engine speed record of 483 mph in the Bearcat in 1969. During the years he reigned at Reno, Darryl was nearly unbeatable.

Even back in those days, Darryl had the ability to cut a wily deal. To get the Bearcat in 1964, he convinced the two Connecticut doctors who owned it to lend him the plane with the idea that he would, as he put it, "run up its value." Then they'd all sell it or donate it to a museum (taking tax write-offs in the latter case). Increase the value of it he did: Darryl used the plane during his legendary winning streak at Reno, and then shattered the speed record with it. When the doctors "donated" it to the National Air and Space Museum in 1969, they each got a five-figure write-off, while Darryl took in trade another Bearcat and a Grumman Widgeon seaplane from the Smithsonian.

After leaving Lockheed in 1976, Darryl began dealing in planes with Ascher Ward, a former drapery salesman working out of a small office at the Van Nuys Airport, in L.A.'s San Fernando Valley. Theirs was a sticky business filled with odd characters. Done right, there was a lot of money to be made quickly, but you could lose everything just as fast. In the basic scheme, Darryl and Ward would salvage an aircraft the Air Force wanted and trade it for surplus military aircraft, which Darryl and his mechanic Rick Kriege often had to repair and fly out of unlikely places, enabling Ward to sell or trade the aircraft again. This wasn't baseball cards or vintage automobiles, but expensive warplanes, and the salvages, trades, and sales were complex deals involving hundreds of thousands of dollars and everything from foreign governments to various military agencies, private collectors, and museums, both public and private.

In one trade in 1986, Darryl received seven de Havilland Caribous—a cantankerous twin-engined short-takeoff-and-landing cargo plane built for use in the Vietnam War. Darryl, Rick Kriege, Matt Jackson, and Darryl's old friend Al Hanson spent two weeks in the tropical sun on the Pacific island of Kwajalein getting the stored planes running, and then flew them back to California, where Ward sold them.

In 1989, before the Berlin Wall fell, Darryl traveled to Hungary in pursuit of two MiG-21s for the Air Force Museum. "It was an airfield south of Budapest," he told me, "and these three MiGs had been flown in the day before. Everything had been arranged and the price was agreed upon, and I was just supposed to see the planes. No money was supposed to exchange hands until they were out of the country. The planes were gorgeous, brand-new, with full radar systems, guns loaded and operational, absolutely fucking beautiful. . . ." The third plane was a surprise. "We went to have lunch with the base commander and the squadron commander and everyone got drunk and suddenly they said they wanted thirty thousand dollars in cash up front to get the deal going. Two were supposed to go to the Air Force museum, but I wanted the third for myself and I was trying to think how I could get permission to get it into the country. We haggled all night in this room with the TV turned up really loud because of the bugging. But finally the deal was off. They went home and I went to bed. But the next morning the deal was on again for the original terms, but I couldn't get the third one." Darryl won't say what he paid for the MiGs, or how exactly the deal came about, but one went to the Air Force museum in Dayton and the other went to McClellan

Air Force Base near Sacramento. For brokering the deal, which speci-fied that the MiGs "be delivered . . . complete (with guns) and fully operational," Darryl got four T-39 jet trainers worth $100,000 each.

Gary and Darryl weren't friends, but, as Darryl put it, they'd had "multiple dealings" with each other. Shortly after Darryl's call, he and Gary Larkins met in Ascher Ward's office at the Van Nuys Air-port. Gary was wary of Darryl; he didn't trust him and felt it had taken too long to get paid on a previous deal with Greenamyer. For his part, Darryl didn't respect Gary, who'd never been to college, hadn't flown at a fifth of the speed he had, and in his eyes earned his living salvaging wrecks. But this time there wasn't any way around it: both wanted what only the other could offer. It didn't take long to strike a deal. Gary had the permits; Darryl and Ward had recently bought a load of surplus Hueys from the Norwegian army. Both knew the perfect helicopter pilot for the job, Tommy Hauptman. And perhaps most important of all, Darryl had a neighbor, Tom Hess, a successful building contractor who'd lately been begging to get into the game. Darryl thought Hess would eagerly kick in most of the cash.

There remained two related obstacles. To carry out their plan Darryl and Gary needed to operate out of Thule Air Base, and to get the Huey to Thule they needed a U.S. Air Force C-141 transport airplane. Both required official permission from the U.S. Govern-ment. Darryl turned to the Smithsonian National Air and Space Museum, which, if you ask, will tell you it doesn't sponsor expedi-tions. But the museum had Darryl's Bearcat in its collection and had dealt with him before. On July 14, 1993, Don Lopez, senior adviser to the director of the museum, wrote the Air Force, requesting the expedition be granted air transport of 10,000 to 15,000 pounds of equipment to Thule, billeting on base, and the authority to pur-chase aviation and jet fuel.

———

Now, at long last, they were at the *Kee Bird*, transported back in time in that stark Arctic desert. The four days there went quickly and easily, the perfect weather seducing them like a pool shark nurturing a mark's false sense of confidence. Under twenty-four hours of sunlight, with never a cloud to mar the scene, they jacked up the plane, raising its tail high into the air. When Darryl connected the *Kee Bird*'s electrical system to a battery, there was an unexpected whirr; the landing lights suddenly unfurled from the wing. Usually when a plane crashed and sat abandoned for decades, the complex electrical system went to hell, rusted or corroded, but this appeared to mean the electrical systems were working. The landing gear wouldn't operate, but they could fix that. They cranked the gear down by hand and found the tires were as full of air and firm as if they'd been filled yesterday.

As the jacks lifted the *Kee Bird* from the lake's shallow water, its nose stuck in the mud, leaving the plane at a cockeyed angle. "I got an idea," said Tommy, jumping in the Huey. "Rig up the cargo nets and get your shovels."

A few hours later they'd shoveled thousands of pounds of tundra into cargo nets, which Tommy deftly placed on the rear stabilizer. The nose lifted effortlessly. They cranked the front gear down and, lo and behold, the *Kee Bird* was sitting on its tires—for the first time in forty-six years.

Their luck continued, although tension was popping up like hives. Gary was digging and getting cold and wet, while Darryl kept directing everybody and poking around in the plane, especially the cockpit. But the next day they changed the spark plugs on the left outboard engine, filled it with oil and then ran a hose from the engine to a fifty-five-gallon barrel of fuel. At the flight engineer's station inside the *Kee Bird* Darryl primed the engine and hit the starter and ignition switches, while Tommy pumped fuel by hand into the carburetor. While Darryl primed and primed, fuel rained out onto Gary and Rick in the water below. *That little Napoleon,* thought Gary, standing in fuel as the engine coughed, *he's gonna ignite us like a torch!* Gary was finding it hard to contain himself. When he traveled with his usual team, whom he called the "Pirates," he was the boss and it was his stories everyone wanted to hear. Now here he was at *his* plane, getting bossed around, being treated like some hired hand, gasoline raining down on his head. *Either him or me,* he was starting to think, *one of us is going to have to go.*

The prop, bent in ninety-degree angles, spun slowly, jerked, and thick black smoke poured out of the exhaust. For ten minutes they fiddled with the engine and hoses, and then, suddenly, the engine caught, exploding into a hacking rumble. Forty-six years! Tensions evaporated for a few moments.

Gary and Rick Kriege, Darryl's mechanic, had never met before, but they liked each other instantly. Originally from South Dakota, Rick was a veteran roughneck from the oil fields of Wyoming. He was small but strong and wiry. Acne scars covered his cheeks, and although he walked with a bounce, he had a slight limp dating back to when a pipe had crushed his ankle on an oil rig. And he was missing the ring finger on his right hand, the mark of another oil-field accident, while the deep scar across his palm was the souvenir of a bar fight in Gillette, Wyoming.

In 1985 his wife, Irene, had bought Rick a gasoline-powered remote-controlled airplane. He got into the hobby, taking the plane apart, learning to fly it, racing it against the models of his friends, and building others. Airplanes are like that; they get hold of some people and won't let go. When the oil fields went bust in 1986, Rick figured he wanted to work on the real thing. He enrolled at the Spartan School of Aeronautics' airframe and power-plant course and he and Irene moved to Tulsa. One day, near the end of the two-year program, Darryl and Ascher Ward came calling. They were flying a C-123 recovered out of Texas as payment for an Air Force deal when engine problems forced them down in Tulsa. After having the engine repaired, Darryl and Ward taxied out to leave. But as the C-123 took wing, the plane rolled sharply to the left. Darryl screamed at Ward to hold the throttles at full power—he thought the left engine was failing (in fact, the prop on the left engine was reversing)—while he tried to keep the plane upright. But the runway was on a little mesa with high-tension power lines just off the end, and the plane plummeted at 110 knots into the wires. The left wing broke off and the plane smashed onto the highway below. Sparks from the wires ignited the spewing fuel and the whole left side went up in flames. By the time Ward and Darryl crawled out, Rick Kriege, a rough-looking mechanic, was at their side. He helped them clean up the mess, and turned out to be a good mechanic—with a clear head and a big heart, to boot.

Before Darryl left he offered Rick a job. It was a dream come true. One day Rick had been just another rookie airplane mechanic hoping to find work, and the next he was having a blast doing crazy stunts around the world for Darryl Greenamyer, even building Darryl's new racing airplane. When it was finished the custom-designed and -built Shockwave would be powered by the most powerful piston aircraft engine ever created, a 5,000-horsepower monster. Now here he was, flying around the North Pole in a Huey, tinkering on the *Kee Bird*, and walking places where, maybe, no people had even ever set foot before.

On the fourth day an Air Force Reserve C-130 came calling. Afraid that the *Kee Bird*'s tires might sink deeply in the underwater mud by the time they got back next year, Darryl and Gary had called Thule, angling for something they might brace the plane with. The 109th Air National Guard happened to be there and they were eager to help. The next day their C-130 swept in for a low pass, banked, and swept around again. As the plane slowed to 120 knots, the ramp at its rear opened like a mouth. Suddenly the plane's nose jerked upward and seven flat aluminum pallets hurtled out, spinning into the dirt in a cloud of dust. The pallet's cargo identification tags gave their destination as: "Somewhere in the

Arctic." After placing the pallets under the *Kee Bird*'s tires to keep them from sinking in the mud, the team packed up the Huey and headed back to Thule.

For all its desolation, Greenland can be magnificent and beautiful, a pure and haunting wilderness of sky and tundra, ice and cliffs. Free of supplies, the Huey was light this time around, and Darryl, Rick, and Tommy felt euphoric. They banked past high brown cliffs and skimmed over a green ocean dotted with mountains of floating ice as blue as bottles of Aqua Velva. Darryl's mind raced. He loved unbelievable challenges, challenges that other people considered impossible. After his Reno victories he'd spent a dozen years assembling the only home-built F-104 Starfighter in the world, and he'd gone faster in the thick air of near sea level in his tricked out 104 than anyone. After that, he had hoped to take the absolute altitude record from the Soviet Union, a feat even Chuck Yeager had backed away from. But then his Starfighter had malfunctioned and Darryl had to abandon it in flight. He punched out over the California desert and watched his beloved plane crash and burn while he floated to earth, strapped to his parachute. He'd almost given up on aviation after that. But here at last was another worthy challenge.

Darryl thought it through as Tommy thundered the Huey a hundred feet over a herd of reindeer. The *Kee Bird* was definitely worth going after. His neighbor Tom Hess had agreed to put up most of the cash. The weather wasn't really so bad up here—you could work in your shirtsleeves, for Christ's sake. The bowl in which the *Kee Bird* sat was at least a mile long; flat, dry tundra, with plenty of room to get even a pig like the *Kee Bird* up in the air if it had enough power. Four new props and four new engines would give it that power. New tires (rubber gets brittle with age and those old things on the *Kee Bird* might explode on the rough tundra or on landing at Thule); new flight controls and new flight-control cables; a bunch of fuel. With all that, he'd be taking wing over this magnificent ice and rock in a time machine.

Sitting just a few inches away, Gary was experiencing an entirely different sort of emotion—a rising sense of dread that he couldn't shake: Greenamyer was impossible to work with. *Somehow, Darryl was going to have to go,* he thought as Tommy set the Huey down at Thule. But, once again, elation washed over them as they were greeted if not quite like heroes by the skeptical Air Force, at least with a grudging respect. They had done what others had only talked about. The Air Force didn't charge them one cent for billeting or hangar space or getting the chopper to Thule, or even for flying the pallets out to them. That night at Thule's Top of the World Club they all got drunk, toasting their unqualified success.

SIX

—

THE LABORATORY IS OPEN

Midland, Texas

"You tired, or d'you have enough energy to spin by for some ghost hunting?" Thad Dulin said, swinging my luggage into the trunk of his white BMW. It was near midnight and the moment we pulled out of the fluorescent daylight of the Midland International Airport arrivals terminal, the black Texas night closed in. The filmy gauze of the Milky Way shone overhead, and every once in a while as Dulin slid the BMW around the streets behind the airport, I caught sight of desert and scraggly sagebrush in the flush of the headlights.

I'd hoped Dulin could put me in the air in the world's last flying B-29, a Superfort named *Fifi* owned by the CAF, the Confederate Air Force. At the top of the warbird food chain ranged a handful of rich collectors—new-money guys mostly—and the swashbuckling characters like Darryl Greenamyer and Gary Larkins, who fed their hunger for new old airplanes. At the bottom were the hundreds of thousands of people who worshiped the planes at museums and air shows every year. In the middle was the CAF, 9,500 "colonels" who supported its "Ghost Squadron" of 130 warbirds. Becoming a colonel was easy. You paid your annual dues of 160 bucks and, as Dulin put it, you were admitted into "the laboratory," becoming eligible for a mere fifty bucks extra a year to join an aircraft support team and even to fly in CAF airplanes. *Fifi* was the jewel in the CAF's crown, the plane most requested on the summer air show circuit. The guys who flew and maintained it out of Midland were the elite of the CAF, the keepers of the flame, the only people in the world who tinkered with and flew a B-29.

But Dulin dashed my hopes. *Fifi* was grounded. Fuel leaks had revealed not only corrosion in *Fifi*'s fifty-year-old fuel tanks but corrosion metastasizing throughout the airframe. The CAF was scrambling for money to restore the plane and promising in press releases that she'd be flying in a few months. "Bullshit," confided Dulin, when I phoned. "That old plane isn't going nowhere anytime soon—it's gonna cost a big bundle to get that old gal flying again. But the CAF's big air show is this weekend and I think I can get you up in a B-17."

We tracked along beside a high, gleaming chain-link fence topped with barbed wire and came to an electronically controlled gate. Thad swiped a plastic identification card through the magnetic reader and the gate whirred open. Ahead was an old-fashioned water tower, painted in big red and white squares and topped with a revolving searchlight. We wheeled past a hangar and up onto the concrete apron of the flight line. Flashing in the car's headlights were gleaming rows of Avengers, AT-6 Texans, Mustangs, Corsairs, Hellcats, and Bearcats. In the blackness and shadowy beams of the headlights they appeared dreamlike, late-night phantoms of my imagination. "Man," Dulin said softly, as if setting eyes upon them for the very first time, "I just love seeing 'em in the night!"

As we tooled through Midland to Dulin's house, he gave me the short history of the CAF, the creation of a former World War II Army Air Force flight instructor named Lloyd P. Nolen. In 1957, Nolen and three buddies bought a P-51 Mustang for $2,500. One Sunday morning they arrived at the airfield in Mercedes, Texas, where they kept the plane, and found "Confederate Air Force" scrawled in red across the fuselage. The name stuck. In 1958 they bought two Grumman F-8F Bearcats for $805 apiece. They had their own little air force.

But in searching for more airplanes they discovered what was simultaneously horrifying Walter Soplota: the planes of World War II were disappearing rapidly. What worried Nolen wasn't just that the planes would be gone soon, but that the skills to fly them and maintain them would vanish as well. In 1961 he chartered the CAF as a nonprofit corporation and started actively collecting airplanes. Over the years people donated money and airplanes and the ranks of colonels swelled, the planes maintained and flown by volunteers around the country in local "wings" and "squadrons." Every summer the planes, especially the big, high-profile bombers like *Fifi* and the CAF's two B-17s, *Sentimental Journey* and *Texas Raiders*, tour the country, flying from air show to air show, performing for the general public in the air and available on the ground for tours. A twenty-minute flight costs $350.

Crews of volunteers sign up for two-week "missions," during which they fly and maintain the planes, flopping onto sofas or the beds of cheap hotels at night, and hustling souvenir patches and key rings when they aren't flying. "It's twelve to fourteen hours a day," said Dulin, a massive, gentle man whose forearms were as big around as my thighs, as we slid past endless rows of fast-food joints and Circle K convenience stores, "but you get a lot of people who come up and say, 'I flew on that plane,' or women who bring their grandkids and say, 'I worked on that plane.' They get real emotional."

Like any organization, the CAF is rife with politics, especially surrounding its bombers. Competition to fly and work (and spend your own money) on the big planes is intense, and things can get pretty catty. But, as Dulin said, swinging into the perfect white concrete driveway leading up to his tidy brick rambler, "When you get past the bullshit, this is the only place in the world where if you're interested in the old planes and you're a regular guy, the laboratory is still open." A former oil-drilling engineer, Dulin had been flying as a flight engineer for Emery Worldwide ever since the market dropped out of the oil business in the 1980s. He lived comfortably, and even owned a couple of small airplanes, but he couldn't possibly afford to own, maintain, and fly a rare warbird. "I love the airplanes and this is the only way I can get my hands on 'em," he said, showing me into a living room filled with photos of B-29s and a desk piled high with aviation magazines.

It was still dark when Dulin woke me and led me to his car to head back for the airport. It was Friday, the day before the air show— spelled, for some inexplicable reason, "Airsho"—and he was now dressed in a gray, one-piece cotton jumpsuit festooned with patches identifying him as a member of the elite Ghost Squadron, the CAF wing that operates *Fifi*. Riding with us was Chuck Harley, a tow-headed aeronautical engineer at Boeing's Wichita factory and a CAF colonel who'd flown down the day before in a Fairchild PT-23. PT stood for primary trainer and hundreds of thousands of World War II pilots had earned their wings in the simple Fairchild, a fabric-covered, open-cockpit monoplane. Harley had recently finished restoring one. "It's kind of like leasing a car," Harley explained, munching on an Egg McMuffin as we zoomed through the desert to the Midland airport. "The CAF owns it but I supply the gas and oil, and since I restored it, I get to fly it most of the time." His face was as red as a ripe tomato from the seven-hour flight from Wichita in the open cockpit.

Some 35,000 spectators were expected for the weekend event, but today was a time for the colonels to hobnob with each other and get in some flying. We parked the car and headed out onto the flight ramp. It was September, but the Texas sun was coming up strong. Old Willys Jeeps raced by, driven by guys in gray flight suits and baseball caps. Most appeared to be in their seventies, with gray hair and beer bellies. Dulin and Harley, both in their forties, were relative youngsters. Crowds were already milling around more

World War II airplanes than I'd ever seen in one place. Among the vintage aircraft were *Diamond Lil'* (one of the world's only two flying B-24 Liberators), the only flying Heinkel He-111 German bomber in the world, and the two B-17s. At the end of the flight line stood a row of modern F-14 Tomcat jet fighters, capable of searing through the sky at twice the speed of sound. A threatening-looking B-1 bomber, like some huge gray shark, lurked behind. But for all their needle-nosed speed, the modern jets looked like toys compared to the Flying Fortresses. Bristling with machine guns and rotating turrets, broad wings, high tails, and long graceful propellers, they instantly took me back to those photos I'd stared at in my attic in Newport. These planes had history and pedigree; everyday men and women had built them and tens of thousands of men had died in them. They had changed the fate of the world.

Built by Douglas in 1945, *Sentimental Journey* was bare aluminum, a one-hundred-foot-long polished silver beauty resting on her little tail wheel. She had been converted to a fire tanker after the war and was picked up by the CAF in 1978. Scott Appal was making her shine even brighter. "These planes are a sickness, that's all there is to it," he said, fetching the *Journey*'s logbook. Appal was unusual out here on the tarmac: a young guy in his twenties with trendy wraparound shades. "I maintain four corporate jets and then on my vacations I come and work on this old thing," he said. He'd been out now on the air-show circuit for two weeks and this was the last before he returned *Sentimental Journey* to its winter base in Tucson.

Hanging around the plane put Appal in touch with the past, but it also made him think about the present. "There's such a difference between what we do and the real thing," he said. "Sometimes you're flying along to an air show and it's cloudy and rainy and cold in the plane, and water drips through the top turrets and suddenly you think of what it must have been like for real. Imagine it's winter and you're flying with no heat, no radar, sometimes at night, breathing bottled oxygen with guys shooting at you and your own machine guns going off. It must have been terrible. We fly this plane at 55,000 pounds, and it feels like a stack of lumber. But they flew at 65,000 pounds, wingtip to wingtip, all loaded with bombs and fuel. You wonder how they did it."

A crowd was gathering around a fellow peering through the rear hatch of the plane. He was thin and as straight as a two-by-six, dressed in pressed olive-green fatigues and spit-shined black boots. I wandered over, just as he pulled his head out of the plane. His hair was white, his face as wrinkled as an old leather sack. Bruce Wallace was seventy-six years old, with the body of a twenty-five-year-old. "Back then, a mission lasted ten to twelve hours," Wallace said, holding the crowd spellbound. He spoke in a hoarse, high-pitched whisper, the result of a recent throat operation. A native of Midland who'd come out to the show for the day, Wallace had survived forty-six missions as a B-17 tail gunner, the most dangerous position in the plane. "You didn't eat, didn't drink, didn't go to the bathroom. It was sixty-five degrees below zero and your hands froze if you touched the bare metal." We all took turns peering into the tail, a three-foot-high aluminum tube. Squeezed in a space barely big enough to squat was a primitive seat and a .50-caliber machine gun. "The life expectancy of a tail gunner in actual combat was thirteen seconds. I was shot down three times, the only man to survive in all three crews," Wallace rasped. "Twenty-nine men got killed and only I survived." A guy in a white polo shirt and creased blue shorts swept his video camera across the B-17 and settled on Wallace.

"Mickey, John, come listen to this," he said to his kids.

"The last time I was captured they put me in front of a fake firing squad," Wallace said. "Another POW was watching from a window. They tied me to a post and asked me if I wanted a last smoke. 'No,' I said and the son of a bitch ripped my shirt open and put out his cigarette on my chest. I've still got the scar. Then they fired blanks at me. But I escaped and five days later I was in England. If I'd have been in any other plane than a B-17 I'd have been dead. On my first mission we took forty-six holes and kept on flying. She was good to us. I tell you." Gazing back into the bomber and pointing at the seat cushions, he said, "These seats are better than the ones we had—they were rough canvas. I don't know how we did it. I think we grew up faster. I wonder if today's kids could do what we did and survive. I don't know."

"You ready?"

It was Floyd Houdashell, *Sentimental Journey*'s pilot. In real life he flew Boeing 747-400s from Los Angeles to Asia; like Appal he was on vacation, flying *Sentimental Journey* for this two-week sojourn. He was taking the plane up for a media "photo op," and, true to his word, Dulin had bagged me a ride. Wallace was going, too. We climbed a short ladder into the waist of the bomber. It was a bare tube of sheet metal riveted to ribs and cross members, about five feet high and five feet wide. There was no insulation and no armor; the sheet metal seemed thin enough to pierce with a screwdriver. It smelled as musty as an antique car. Two .50-caliber machine guns poked out of either side through three-foot-square Plexiglas windows; during the war there had been no Plexiglas; breathing bottled oxygen, the waist gunners were exposed to freezing temperatures and 200-knot winds. Houdashell wouldn't let Wallace into the tail gunner's seat—"Not a good idea," he said, eyeing the narrow crawl space back to the gunner's compartment. I moved forward, leaving Wallace to stare dreamily at his surroundings, suddenly speechless.

Stepping over the protruding top of the ball turret in the belly—it must have been a nightmare in there, the gunner suspended on his back, lying exposed to shell fire in the rotating ball— I passed through the radio operator's station and across a narrow bridge suspended in the bomb bay. Houdashell was strapping himself into the pilot's seat and Appal was serving as flight engineer. I squeezed by their legs and crawled on my hands and knees into the nose, as cramped as a telephone booth on its side. Edging past the navigator's small desk, I sat on the bombardier/nose gunner's stool at the very tip of the plane, surrounded by 180 degrees of glass. As a kid I'd spent hours dreaming about cutting through the clouds in this very place. Sweat dripped down my nose, it was about 150 degrees in the tin can, and suddenly I felt incredibly vulnerable. I imagined the cold and noise and fear I'd have experienced while flying over northern Germany in the dead of a nasty European winter with Messerschmitts trying to kill me and no insulation and no protection, the twin .50-cals screaming and spitting out shells. This was a bare bones killing machine.

"Contact three," came a disembodied voice through the headset. One by one the four 1,200 horsepower piston engines coughed and the propellers started churning. A jet whined like a high-powered Electrolux vacuum cleaner. A radial piston engine beat like eighteen frantic human hearts linked to a microphone, spitting black exhaust, making the whole plane vibrate. Crowds lined outside, a bank of video cameras staring up at us. Packed with newspaper and magazine photographers, a C-46 Commando, a big, twin-engined cargo- and troop-hauler named *China Doll*, lumbered out in front of us. We followed, lining up at the end of the runway. Behind us was *Texas Raiders*. The noise was overpowering. *China Doll* rolled out, and before she was even off the ground we surged forward. I was pressed into my seat. The power was overwhelming, surprising. If this had been 1943, dozens of planes would have been lined up with us, heavy with bombs and fuel and machine-gun shells, hurtling one after the other into the clouds and fog. Unaided by radar, some of us might have simply crashed into each other. Statistically, if it were early in the war, nearly 10 percent of us wouldn't live to finish the mission.

In moments we were airborne, a world of cloudless blue sky above and in front of me, the brown desert below, the view from the glass nose positively bird's-eye. Slightly behind and to our right, *Texas Raiders* pulled up in formation, *China Doll* ahead and to the left. Barely ten feet separated our wingtips, bobbing and jiggling in the wind. A dozen photographers clustered at *China Doll*'s open door, snapping away at two of the world's fourteen flying B-17s in tight formation.

After the plane had banked and circled for a while, I crawled back into the waist. The noise was deafening. Wallace was still crouching there with a misty look, his hands now resting on one of the empty guns, an old man wearing a half-century-old uniform that still fit him. I gripped the two handles of the other gun and scanned the sky for incoming fighters. We bounced in turbulence and I had to be careful not to grab on to the cables moving the overhead flight controls. In the claustrophobic tube I started to feel the nausea and light-headedness of motion sickness creeping up. Up here it was easy to see why Bruce Wallace couldn't forget his forty-six missions, why old guys got fixated on their war stories and why younger guys like Thad Dulin and Gary Larkins worshiped guys like Wallace and their airplanes.

The B-17 was horrible to fly in. That was part of its allure. In this cold, drafty, uncomfortable airplane, life had an essential purpose, an urgency, and nothing afterward could ever equal the experience. Today's world is a complex, gray-shaded place. Now planes fly by electronics—when Houdashell banks his 747 he does little more than activate a circuit that moves the ailerons—and fighters launch missiles from miles away without ever seeing their targets. Most of the gauges on Houdashell's 747 are television screens. But when he banked *Sentimental Journey* that day, his hands were literally *connected*, through the yoke and the flight-control cables, to the elevators pushing against the wind outside. This war was won by the air equivalents of hand-to-hand fighting, in airplanes regular people could understand and that had been built by the crew's wives and girlfriends and sisters and mothers. Watching Wallace bob up and down in the turbulence, I thought of something the legendary Bermudan treasure hunter Teddy Tucker had told me. After years of searching for gold and silver on sunken seventeenth- and eighteenth-century ships, it wasn't the precious metal that stuck in his mind but the odd, everyday artifacts, the tobacco pipes and unopened bottles of wine and unscratched porcelain. For Tucker, these objects reclaimed, even if only for a moment, an era of men and sailing ships that had changed the course of Western civilization but was now lost forever. Gary Larkins and Darryl Greenamyer's quest for winged treasure wasn't just a quest for riches, it was a similar quest to reclaim a lost time, to resurrect the Phoenix of another age.

When we landed, Appal handed out soft rags to me and Wallace and a flurry of waiting admirers on the flight line. Together we gently rubbed the oil off the heirloom wings.

"My daddy worked on one of these. I guess he was a mechanic because we've got pictures of him working on it," said a middle-aged woman in a bright sundress.

"Here's where the tail gunner had to crawl," said a guy in khakis and a red polo shirt to his video camera. "Everything about this airplane spells cold," he said, continuing his narration. "Look at the turret—that would be hard for *me* to get in."

It was Saturday morning and the flight line was open to the thousands of people streaming to the "airsho." Gusts of warm wind blasted across the tarmac and crowds surrounded the airplanes parked in neat rows, each of them with a sign welcoming "walk-throughs" for five dollars. A steady stream filed through *Sentimental Journey* and some bought pins and baseball caps and T-shirts.

"Is it possible to take a ride?" asked two elegant-looking men in pressed slacks.

"Three hundred fifty dollars each," said a heavy guy lounging in a lawn chair at the nose. "Sign up and if we've got enough people we'll go for a twenty-minute ride at the end of the show."

Stefan Schutz and Wink Versteegh nodded. They had come all the way from Holland to see the planes. "Three hundred and fifty is a lot of money," Versteegh said, "but looking at them is one thing. I think flying in this plane would be the ultimate experience."

Versteegh and Schutz didn't seem like most of the buffs on the tarmac. They wore no pins or baseball caps or patches. Schutz was an architect in Amsterdam. Midland, Texas, seemed a long, expensive journey just to see a bunch of old airplanes.

"It is very difficult to explain," Schutz said, gazing at the ground. "I was born in 1946, shortly after the war, and the war experience for my father—well, he was a sensitive age, and I've lived with that experience all of my life." Looking up at *Sentimental Journey* gleaming in the sun, he said quietly, "The Americans won the war but we Dutch were liberated. That's a different feeling." Nodding at Versteegh, he said, "Three hundred and fifty dollars? I think maybe that's a small price."

Just after noon, eager Boy Scouts cleared the flight lines and I settled under a tree with Thad Dulin. "Ladies and gentleman," echoed a voice through the loudspeakers, "join our giant chamber of imagination for the Confederate Air Force air-power demonstration. Ladies and gentleman, close your eyes. It's December of 1941. Germany and Europe are locked in total war. Imagine, if you will, it's a peaceful, serene Sunday morning in Honolulu . . ."

A biplane whined over the runway in a series of lazy loops. A high-pitched screaming pierced the air and white-and-green Japanese Zero fighters and Betty bombers dived low across the runway. Explosions of fire and black smoke rocked the field. The crowd went wild, yelling and cheering as if Mick Jagger were preening on the stage.

For an hour planes dived and swooped, creating a rough chronology of the war. The TBMs and Corsairs wheeled overhead, dropping bombs in a throaty, powerful rumble of thousands of horsepower. But their noise was like a child's voice compared to the two- and four-engine bombers that fired up late in the "war." The last flying Junkers in the world whizzed by, streaming black smoke. A Mustang ripped overhead, twirling in victory rolls. "Now the iron is coming out," Thad said, rising to the edge of his seat. "Hear that? The big boys are cranking up. Man, that sounds good." I could barely hear him over the whombling roar, the ground shaking, as four B-17s and a couple of B-25 Mitchells and A-26 Havocs took wing, one after another. Paratroopers rained out of *China Doll.* For twenty minutes the bombers attacked the airfield, cutting a couple of hundred feet over the field to open their bomb-bay doors, while ground-planted "bombs" exploded relentlessly. Thick black smoke wafted through the air as silence, at last, descended. The war was over.

"Time for a 4606," Thad said. A few minutes later we joined a cluster of other colonels lounging under the wings of the Heinkel bomber. There was a big bucket of ice and a cooler full of "4606s"—Bloody Marys—named for the red hydraulic fluid the cocktail resembled. Soon it was hard to hear again as the "Airpower Today" demonstration ripped overhead. F-14s and F-16s and an A-10 Warthog gymnastically shot straight up into the sky like rockets, then screamed slowly by at incredible angles of attack, performing maneuvers World War II pilots only dreamed of. None of the colonels paid much attention. But as the sun set the four B-17s briefly took wing again for a night show. The colonels paused and conversation quieted as the four high-tailed, straight-winged bombers came together in a tight formation in the cloudless sky and soft, golden light of dusk. "You know," Thad said, tracking the Flying Fortresses on the horizon, "not everyone gets what this is all about. There are only fourteen flying B-17s left in the whole world! Fourteen planes out of twelve thousand! Let me tell you, there aren't too many places in the world where you'll see four B-17s flying in formation anymore." In that moment, the memory of my dad's beloved old airplane room in Newport, gone for almost twenty years, flooded through me, come to life in the skies above.

SEVEN

—

LIVING THE FANTASY

Thule, Greenland; July 1994

It was a cold, clear afternoon in July 1994 when Vernon Rich and Tommy Hauptman kicked down the aluminum steps of a C-141 Starlifter onto the tarmac at Thule Air Base. Nearly a year had passed since Darryl and Gary's successful four-day reconnaissance trip the previous August to jack up the *Kee Bird* and start an engine. Vern, dressed in a garish short-sleeved black and white Hawaiian shirt, looked at the treeless hills of scree dappled with snow, the icebergs floating in the distance on North Star Bay, the blue hangars as big as city blocks, the white 10,000-foot runway, the guys in crisp blue Air Force uniforms and big parkas, and then back at Hauptman. "Fuck!" he said, and the two started laughing uncontrollably like two teenagers who'd just started something irreversible and crazy that they had no control over, like popping a hit of acid or stealing a car. They were in it now and who knew how it would all end?

Vern was forty years old, with a thick auburn beard and a receding hairline. He had alert eyes, a Louisiana accent, and a big, easy, rolling laugh. It was hard to say precisely what his trade was. Born in Texas, raised in Shreveport, Louisiana, he'd helped his father in a small business selling tools and drilling equipment to the booming oil and gas industry. And like everyone else coming together for the recovery of the *Kee Bird*, he was a dreamer, a romantic, an independent spirit, impatient when taking orders or locked in the nine-to-five grind. He'd spent two years in the mechanical engineering program at Louisiana State University, where he'd learned just enough engineering to be dangerous. After dropping out of LSU, he took a few business and economics courses at a junior college in West Texas, got married, got divorced, got married again, then worked as a technical representative in the oil tools business. He'd maintained a fleet of classic Ferrari and McClaren race cars for a rich family in Tennessee, then fielded a high-performance Camaro for a season on the stock endurance circuit. Vern was good with engines, even better with a set of calipers, an arc welder, and a machine shop. When you raced cars you couldn't just buy high-performance parts off the shelf; you designed them and you made them, and if they were going to endure the stress of all-out racing, they had to be perfect. If they weren't, at best the car broke down, at worst the driver died in a spectacular whirl of tumbling tires and flipping chassis. Vern had brains and a deep reservoir of patience and attention to detail. Given a few good machine tools and a welder, there wasn't much he couldn't make, and make well. Even more important, he didn't seem to need the security of a job, he wasn't bogged down with kids, and he was cool in a crisis—a perfect project man. He moved to sunny Scottsdale, Arizona, and started building race cars. One day a guy walked into his shop and asked him to weld a weird-looking piece of aluminum. The part was a cabin-pressurization manifold for a high-tech balloon capsule called the *Earthwinds*, in which Larry Newman, who'd been a member of the first team to cross the Pacific and Atlantic by balloon, was hoping to become the first person to circumnavigate the earth by the same method.

Vern quit his job and worked on the *Earthwinds* for two years, spent eight months in Hawaii building racing boats after Richard Branson pulled the financing plug on Newman's balloon quest, and finally set up a high-performance fabrication shop in Scottsdale. His customers were the oddball characters he'd met in his travels, and he made everything from racing dune buggies to machine-gun mounts for rich guys whose passion was to rip over the desert in their helicopters blasting the hell out of full-sized remote-controlled cars and ten-foot-long airplane models.

One of Vern's clients, a man who seemed to know the craziest and coolest guys, showed him a picture of Darryl Greenamyer streaking across the desert in his *Red Baron* Starfighter and told him that Darryl was putting together an expedition to get the *Kee Bird*. *Man, would that be cool,* Vern thought.

One afternoon in late November of 1993 he was shooting the breeze in the office of another client, Mike Dillon, when the phone rang. Dillon owned a company that manufactured ammunition-loading devices for the military, and he had a stable of helicopters and airplanes for which Vern was always making stuff. Vern had recently made a new set of exhaust headers for *Nemesis*, an undefeated Formula One class racing plane. The office, a bare, plush-carpeted room filled with stacks of aviation magazines, ammunition loaders, and a design computer, overlooked Dillon's private hangar. When the phone rang that afternoon, Dillon took the call on the speakerphone. It was his old friend Darryl Greenamyer.

They chatted a minute about airplanes and then Greenamyer said, "You know, I saw this set of headers on *Nemesis*, and I want the guy who made them to build a set for my race plane."

"Would you believe," Dillon said, "that guy is sitting right here?"

"You tell that son of a bitch I'm not going to build anything for him," Vern blurted out, not believing his luck.

"What?" Darryl said.

"Unless you take me to Greenland with you, I'm not going to build anything for you!"

———

February 20, 1947. Formal crew portrait of the original *Kee Bird* crew prior to their last flight. Left to right, back row: Lt. Vern Arnett, pilot; Lt. Russell Jordan, copilot; 2nd Lt. Robert "Lucky" Luedke, flight engineer; Lt. John Lesman, navigator; Lt. Burl Cowan, navigator; Lt. Talbert Gates, copilot. Front row: M.Sgt. Lawrence Yarborough, photo-gunner; S.Sgt. Ernie Stewart, photo-gunner; S.Sgt. Robert "Bucky" Leader, radio operator; S.Sgt. Paul McNamara, photo-gunner; Lt. Howard Adams, radar observer. (U.S. Government photo.)

February 22, 1947. The crashed *Kee Bird* lies on the frozen lake in north Greenland, amid pools of engine oil. Its crew waves to a B-29 Superfortress rescue airplane, the first plane to sight the downed *Kee Bird*. (U.S. Government photo.)

Darryl Greenamyer leans out the copilot window of the *Kee Bird*. (Tim Wright/timwrightphoto.com)

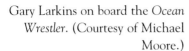

Gary Larkins on board the *Ocean Wrestler*. (Courtesy of Michael Moore.)

Air Pirates Rick Whitmire, George Carter, Rafid Tuma, and Wayne Lloyd (left to right) on the shore of a fjord in east Greenland; they're happy after finding a World War II vacuum tube at the campsite of the survivors of the B-17 Fortress *Later*. (Courtesy of Michael Moore.)

Vernon Rich pauses during *Kee Bird* recovery operations. (Tim Wright.)

Rick Kriege surveys the project ahead. (Tim Wright.)

John Cater in front of the *Kee Bird*. (Courtesy of author.)

Gary Larkins and the Pirates try to match their vintage photograph with the surrounding landscape. (Courtesy of Michael Moore.)

The *Ocean Wrestler* pulls up to the *Kissavik* outside of Narsaq, Greenland. (Courtesy of Michael Moore.)

The *Ocean Wrestler* sails among icebergs. (Courtesy of Michael Moore.)

The key fits. Gary Larkins matches the photo with the fjord; the *Later* (seen at the bottom of the photograph) lies somewhere beneath. (Courtesy of Michael Moore.)

World War II B-17 Fortress recovery near Ruby, Alaska: Gary Larkins connects the rigging to the Bell 212 rescue helicopter for the first lift attempt (top, left). The tail section is connected (top, right). As the tail section emerges, the well-preserved paint job is exposed (above). (© 1996 Photography by Scott Highton.)

Roger von Grote, Cecelio Grande, and Vernon Rich work on the *Kee Bird* on a rare beautiful day. (Courtesy of Albert Bailey.)

Cecelio Grande inspects his collapsed tent. (Tim Wright.)

Darryl Greenamyer waves from the pilot's seat of the *Kee Bird* before taxiing for take-off. (Courtesy of author.)

The *Kee Bird* comes to life. (Tim Wright.)

Six months later, in July of 1994, there he was in Thule with Tommy. On paper, the plan was simple, straightforward. Vern and Tommy were to get the Huey, which had been stored in a base hangar for the past year, ready to fly by the time Darryl, Rick Kriege, and three other team members arrived a week later in Darryl's 1962 de Havilland Caribou. Joining them would be a four-man crew filming a documentary for the PBS series *Nova*, a still photographer, and me, arriving several weeks later. When everyone was assembled in Thule, Rick and Tommy would fly to the site in the Huey and scout a landing strip for the Caribou. In six round-trips the Caribou would ferry all the people and supplies into and out of the site. The Huey would be a backup, and could do all sorts of heavy lifting. Putting a fresh set of engines on the *Kee Bird* was the biggest job. Though they'd gotten one of the original engines started back in August, Darryl didn't want to risk trying to lift a forty-five-ton bomber off a short, unpaved runway without rebuilt, perfectly tuned engines. Changing them would take two days per engine, a total of eight days. Then it was just a matter of wiring the props, replacing the flight controls and tires, grading the runway, and chasing down any remaining mechanical gremlins. Add a few days for unexpected events, and they ought to be in and out of the site in three weeks. Of all the plans to recover the *Kee Bird* that had been floated so far, Darryl's was the most cautious and thorough. Once Darryl got the *Kee Bird* to a hangar in Thule, they'd go over it in fine detail before its long flight back to California. (The Reno races were usually the second week in September, and Darryl was thinking it would be cool to lumber by the grandstands in the *Kee Bird*.) If the work took a few weeks longer than planned, still not a big deal. But any more time and there was a problem: winter. The *Kee Bird* was 1,145 miles north of the Arctic Circle. What passed for summer at the site lasted about thirty days. Practically speaking, there was no fall. The moment the sun set on August 22, the days would grow shorter by forty minutes every day. Winter, the Air Force at Thule warned, would roar in like some fanatical Khmer Rouge guerrilla band.

Vern and Tommy checked into a three-storey box called the North Star Inn, were issued a navy-blue Chevrolet Suburban, and drove over the base's gravel roads to the hangar where the Huey had been stored for the past year. The pug-nosed, olive-green helicopter squatted forlornly in a dark, dusty corner of the hangar, surrounded by wooden crates. Splattered with dry mud, strewn inside with candy wrappers, it hardly looked like the high-tech chariot of a dream expedition. Vern and Tommy had to get it flying on their own—and suddenly the reality of this whole deal flooded over Vern for the first time since he'd so boldly presented himself to Darryl a few months before in Mike Dillon's office. It was one thing to fantasize about going on a once-in-a-lifetime expedition worthy of *National Geographic* or a Hollywood action-thriller, quite another to do it. You could sit in the bar all night, planning a deal like this on a napkin or in your beer-strengthened brain and it was a cinch: fly up there to the *Kee Bird*, fiddle around on it, and fly it out. Such treasure hunts and record-breaking projects are hatched and nourished every night in countless smoky bars around the world. In the auto-racing world there was even a name for guys who did it: bench racers.

But Vernon Rich was living the fantasy, and this battered green Huey was an incredibly complex and fickle machine that could kill you in a nanosecond, and it would have to be put back together by his very own hands just to get to the starting line. "When I saw the Huey," he said later, "I suddenly realized that this was a no-bullshit deal; it was the first indication of what might come later."

A lot of things had changed over the past year, and the biggest of all concerned Gary Larkins. He was gone, excised from the picture as thoroughly as Trotsky had been eliminated from official biographies of Lenin. Vern hadn't even once heard his name uttered. Although they had managed to get the *Kee Bird* jacked up and the engine running the summer before, Darryl and Gary Larkins despised each other. Gary thought the project and the plane were his; it had been his perseverance, after all, that had gotten the permits, and they were issued in the name of his nonprofit company, the Institute for Aeronautical Archaeological Research. But Darryl had supplied the helicopter and the guy who'd advanced the money, and in his eyes Gary was working for him.

"When I get on these projects, I get mean and bossy," Darryl admitted later. "I put my foot down and go—there's got to be someone leading the pack, and all Gary was doing was puttering about."

"Darryl didn't *do* anything up there," Gary said. "Rick and I were working our asses off and Darryl would be messing around in the cockpit."

Underlying their disdain for each other were their fundamentally conflicting viewpoints; Gary Larkins and Darryl Greenamyer were coming at the mission from two completely different directions. Gary was a salvor. He schlepped to the ends of the earth, found airplanes, took them apart, and somehow dragged the pieces back to civilization. Darryl was a pilot. When he looked at an airplane, all he wanted to do was fly it, and he couldn't keep away from the *Kee Bird*'s cockpit. To Gary the *Kee Bird* was an exercise in salvage; how they got it back didn't really matter, as long as they got it back safe and sound. For Darryl the *Kee Bird* was an exercise in flight; everything else was secondary to the overarching challenge of flying an abandoned four-engine bomber that hadn't moved in nearly half a century. And, of course, both were used to being in charge.

By the time they got back to Thule from that four-day trip in 1993, Gary was convinced that Darryl had to go. "Gary looked like he'd eaten a shit sandwich," says Tommy Hauptman. The problem for him, though, was that Darryl, Tom Hess, and Ascher Ward had a majority stake in the project. For a while Gary tried to figure out a way to get rid of Darryl. Finally, seeing no other way, Gary reluctantly sold his share to Darryl and Hess, and immediately started making plans to find two B-17s in southern Greenland.

Then Ascher Ward bailed, too. "Once we had all the permits and owned the plane, I could have sold it for a million dollars—without even bringing it home," Ward says now. "I had a firm offer! We could have all made money! But Darryl, he just wanted to fly that plane."

So did Tom Hess. He and Darryl budgeted roughly $350,000 of their own money and Darryl suddenly found an energy and purpose he hadn't felt since he'd set out to break the low-altitude speed record. He spent a year scrounging for parts. He found four unused, half-century-old B-29 engines in an East Los Angeles scrap yard. He bought them for $10,000 each and Kriege overhauled them, managing to run two of them on a test stand. They ran perfectly and he hoped for the best on the other two.

Belly-landing the *Kee Bird* in 1947 had bent all sixteen of its propellers, and if there was anything Darryl felt strongly about it was props. Prior to World War II, propellers had usually been made of wood. They rotated in one direction and the angle of their blades relative to the air was fixed. Increasingly sophisticated engineers designed ways to rotate the blade at the propeller hub, thereby changing its angle of attack, or bite, allowing pilots to "feather" their props for more efficient flying at different engine RPMs and at different speeds and air densities. Some propellers swiveled so far they actually reversed; instead of pulling the plane forward, they pushed it back, slowing it down once it landed.

The *Kee Bird* crashed with Curtis Electric reversible propellers. When Darryl himself had crashed years earlier in the C-123 in Tulsa, the crash had occurred when one set of the propellers reversed on takeoff. Darryl hated Curtis Electric reversible props. There was no way he was going to take off in a half-century-old plane on tundra with Curtis Electric props. He wanted a different make, Hamilton Standard, and he needed sixteen of them. In a Burbank, California, prop shop he found fifteen. A friend of a friend knew an aviation nut in Pine Mountain, California, who, he told Darryl, had a Hamilton Standard B-29 prop hanging on his living room wall. Darryl found the guy and the house and bought the prop right off the wall.

He found three propeller hubs, the units that hold the four blades together and attach them to the engine, still wrapped in their original packing in a parts warehouse in Van Nuys. A fourth hub turned up in Texas.

As "modern" and high-tech as Superfortresses were in 1944, their flight-control surfaces—the rudder, ailerons, and elevators—were still covered in fabric, as were nearly all fighters and bombers in World War II. Fabric was lighter and easier to make and repair. The *Kee Bird*'s rudder had been torn off the plane by winds over the five decades on the lake and would have to be recovered. The elevators and ailerons were still intact, but their fabric was brittle and torn. Either those flight-control surfaces had to be replaced, or the fabric recovered. After searching unsuccessfully for B-29 ailerons, Darryl acquired a pair off a KC-97, a similar-sized airplane, out of the Air Force boneyard at Davis-Monthan Air Force Base in Tucson.

A pack rat himself, Darryl happened to have a set of the appropriate tires at his hangar in Ramona, California, the result of an old Air Force trade.

From watching old World War II films showing B-29 field maintenance, Rick Kriege built a portable, wheeled crane strong enough to lift and move the 3,500-pound engines.

Tom Hess supplied a 9,000-pound John Deere bulldozer and a crude iron road-grader to smooth out a runway.

There still remained two crucial pieces of the puzzle: an airplane that was big enough to fly the bulldozer and engines into the site and which could land and take off on a short runway of soft dirt. And enough fuel to supply the whole operation, from the generators to the bulldozer to the ferry airplane to the Huey to the *Kee Bird* it-self, which would gulp 400 gallons an hour on its two-and-a-half-hour flight to Thule, and again on its much longer flight from Thule to Darryl's base in southern California.

In Darryl's mind there was only one plane for the operation: the de Havilland DHC-4 Caribou, the rugged, short-takeoff-and-landing airplane designed to insert men and small arms into un-improved airstrips in the jungles of Vietnam. (Its slightly larger, turbine-powered sibling, the de Havilland Buffalo, was a favorite among United Nations relief pilots in Africa.) It carried three tons of payload, opened wide at the back, and could hold—barely—the bulldozer or one engine at a time. Plus, at about $200,000, Caribous were relatively cheap. Darryl found an aged veteran in the Davis-Monthan boneyard.

He had 9,000 gallons—weighing 63,000 pounds—of 1940s high-lead, 130-octane aviation fuel specially refined in New Jersey.

As for getting it all to Greenland, there weren't many choices. One ship, once a year, sailed in June from New Jersey to Thule, ar-riving in July during the one month when the harbor wasn't choked with ice. The *Green Ridge* was the only way, but when Darryl got his 9,000 gallons of fuel to the dock, the captain balked. The potential firebomb would have to be shipped in a Coast Guard–approved container, which Darryl didn't have. He begged and finally bor-rowed an acceptable fuel tank, on the condition that it be emptied of the fuel in Thule and returned immediately with the boat. At last, in June, the fuel, the tires, the engines, the crane, the bulldozer, the generators—all the heavy and bulky supplies—sailed for the Arctic.

On July 13, Darryl followed by air. The *Kee Bird II*, as the Cari-bou was dubbed, took wing over the windswept palm trees and scrubby hills of Ramona, California, east of San Diego. Rick's wife, Irene, their eleven-year-old daughter, Hallie, Darryl's wife and their three daughters, and a few of the local airport rats waved as it lumbered into the blue yonder.

The Caribou's interior looked like a school bus stripped of its seats, an oil- and grease-stained tube filled with six fifty-five-gallon drums of fuel, Rick's five-foot-high tool chest, camping gear, a propane gas grill, and a ragtag assortment of coolers and cardboard boxes. Rick, his assistant Cecelio Grande, and cook Bob Vanderveen sat strapped to a bench of red nylon webbing, dressed for southern California in their T-shirts. Twenty-seven years old, with a pregnant wife at home, Cecelio was a quiet, hardworking native of the Mexican state of Hidalgo, a minimum-wager who'd been helping Rick and Darryl around the hangar for five years. Bob was an unpaid volunteer, the owner of a hamburger joint in Ramona, California, where Darryl kept his hangar and shop. An airplane nut who had photos of the dashing young Reno racer Darryl Greenamyer on the walls of his Ramona Café, he'd been hanging around the airport and turning the occasional wrench for Rick—and then begged Darryl to take him on the big adventure. A free cook seemed an offer too good to refuse; Bob was on his way.

Piloting the Caribou was Roger von Grote. He was sixty-two, a tall, long-legged, recently retired Boeing MD-80 captain for American Airlines. He'd first met Darryl in the Air Force and, like Darryl, he'd been a Lockheed test pilot, running production tests on the F-104. Roger, Darryl, and Bill Dana, who went on to become the head test pilot for NASA and flew the X-15, had been roommates. Later, Roger headed the F-104 test program for the West German government. He, too, loved the Starfighter, especially the adrenaline-pumping, ground-hugging sorties at a hundred feet and 700 knots over the German countryside. Some of the flights were out of the pages of Buck Rogers. Worried about the Red Menace, the West Germans explored unconventional ways to launch and recover fighters dispersed from traditional airfields. Roger and his German pilots strapped rockets to their Starfighters and then launched from the backs of trucks, and they experimented with landing on the

Autobahn with the kind of arresting wires used to stop planes landing on aircraft carriers—sometimes at full takeoff weight and a
speed of 190 knots. Once Roger had come down so hard his overloaded Starfighter had simply hit the arresting wires and split in
half, the cockpit and nose careening forward even as the rear
stopped dead.

It was a hair-raising blast for a while, but Roger was smart
enough to get out while he could. Unlike Darryl, he settled down,
returning to the States and a stable, if unexciting, career with
American Airlines. But Roger had never completely beaten the ad-
diction to adrenaline that had enticed him to Germany and the 104
program in the first place. His flying skills and long friendship with
Darryl made him a perfect choice to pilot the Caribou, which would
repeatedly have to land and take off carrying heavy loads on a dirt
strip in the middle of nowhere.

En route to their first fuel stop, at Billings, Montana, the Caribou blew a cylinder. They made an emergency landing in Las Vegas,
worked on the plane for twenty-four hours straight, then flew on to
Billings, and then Regina, Saskatchewan, and Churchill, Manitoba.
Below them the land slowly changed from flat green fields to the
low, endless miles of northern pine trees. It was high summer, but in
the back of the unheated Caribou the temperature hovered near
freezing. Near Churchill an oil line blew and oil poured out of
the engine. They fixed it in Churchill and flew on, mile after mile
of droning props and shaking airframe. Five days after taking off
from California, they landed in Rankin Inlet, in the Canadian
Arctic, their last stop before the thousand-mile crossing over icy
Baffin Straight to Thule. While refueling in Rankin, the weather
closed in—a low, gray sky overhead and headwinds and icing reported between Rankin and Thule. They hunkered down and
waited.

———

With the Caribou delayed en route to Thule, Vern and Tommy faced their first logistical test after getting the Huey running. The freighter from New Jersey arrived and Vern had to figure out how to empty and store 9,000 gallons of fuel. The Air Force refused to help; Vern and Tommy already had been reprimanded for unauthorized use of a forklift and a car. The year before they hadn't been billed for anything; this year an eager captain named Thomas "Max" Dugan made sure every penny was accounted for; he even sent Darryl a heating bill for keeping the Huey in the hangar (which had to be heated anyway). The Thule Aero Club loaned them two 3,200-gallon tanks. For the rest, Vern and Tommy drove around the base, absconding with every empty fifty-five gallon drum they could find. When they had over a hundred piled at the far end of the base, almost a mile from the barracks and hangars, they cleaned every one, then laboriously transferred each and every gallon. The only pump available, other than a hand-cranked one, was a gasoline powered "trash" pump like those used to pump water out of construction sites. It was a dangerous undertaking—a gasoline powered, air-cooled engine pumping 9,000 gallons of explosive fuel in the static electricity of the super-dry Arctic air—and the process took hours. Vern and Tommy were drenched in fuel from the sloshing drums and hoses; one spark and they would have been cremated in a flash. Still, they loved it. Their beds were warm, the views from the sprawling base fantastic, and the Top of the World Club stayed open until three A.M. every night. They could be photographing at the 1849 gravestone of William Sharp, an early polar explorer, overlooking timeless North Star Bay, or watching Inuits come off the ice with their sleds and dogs one minute, and the next they could be cutting steaks or dancing to some live country band flown up from New Jersey in a C-141 in the TOW club.

―――

At 3:30 A.M. on July 19, the weather cleared between Rankin Inlet and Thule and the Caribou took off for the journey's final leg. To complete the thousand-mile flight over water and ice, Rick had to refuel and re-oil the engines in mid-flight from fuel drums in the plane, using a battery-powered pump. At one point the pump was smoking and sparking; it was a miracle they didn't just blow up. Finally, a week after taking off from San Diego, Darryl touched down at Thule.

It was showtime at last.

EIGHT

—

A BEAR BY THE TAIL

Daugaard Jensen Land, Greenland; August 1994

Two days after Darryl arrived at Thule, Rick Kriege, Tommy Hauptman, and *Nova* cameraman Noel Smart rattled off in the Huey,
overloaded with a belly of fuel drums, to lay the first fuel cache between Thule and the *Kee Bird. BOOM!* Twenty minutes out, on the
far side of North Star Bay, a horrible vibrating and grinding rattled
the helicopter. It sounded like something important was about to
rip apart. Suddenly the high-temperature lights on the rotor shaft
went on. "She's gonna quit," yelled Tommy. "We've got a choice,
guys," he said. "It's forty miles around the fjord over the ice or seven
miles across it. I don't think she's gonna make it around, but she
might make it back across the bay. And if she goes when we're over
the water we might be able to land on one of those big bergs."
If they didn't make a berg and survived a water landing, though,
they'd die in minutes in the near-freezing water.

But the Huey was still flying. "Water," they yelled in chorus.
Tommy swung the Huey around and dropped swiftly and safely back
to the base. The Huey's transmission had blown a bearing. They
didn't have the parts to fix it. The Huey was dead.

Oh well. Although Darryl had wanted the helicopter as backup
transportation, an extra lifeline to Thule in case something happened
with the Caribou, the clock was ticking, and the window between

when the snows left and came again was short. They'd continue without it. Two days later, Darryl and Roger von Grote filled the Caribou with sleeping bags, tent, a generator, microwave oven, coolers of frozen ham and steak, a propane grill, Rick's tool box, a couple of barrels of fuel—a light load—and blasted off with Bob Vanderveen, Rick Kriege, Noel Smart, and Cecelio Grande. High over the ice cap, the back of the Caribou was below freezing and so noisy you couldn't hear someone shouting right next to you. The boys, as they had started calling themselves, huddled in their parkas. From here on it was a trip into the unknown. Once he got to the site, Roger had no way of knowing which way the wind was blowing for landing, no way of knowing if the ground was hard or soft. The permafrost tundra always looked hard, but was often a few inches of spongy dirt and moss floating on a sea of water. With the Cold War over, Thule had become a shell of empty barracks and hangars—just 150 Air Force personnel and about 700 Danish civilians manned it as a satellite tracking station and Ballistic Missile Early Warning radar station. Save the Aero Club's single-engine Cessna 172, there wasn't one airplane permanently hangared at the base. If Roger screwed up the landing, if the plane were damaged, there'd be no way out. The closest possible rescue airplane was a thousand miles away in Resolute, Canada. A rescue flight would take hours, if not days, and would cost $15,000—that is, if the Caribou's radios still worked and whoever was alive was in good enough shape to use them.

After two and a half hours, Roger swept low over the lake. Even now, in high summer, only its edges were free of ice. The brown hills, the blue water, a couple of barrels of fuel, it all looked the same as the day Darryl and the boys had left a year ago. With no trees or shrubs to mark it, time stood still up here, the *Kee Bird* poised on its landing gear in the southwestern corner of the lake, just as they'd left it, and still barely changed from the time of its landing in 1947. Roger planned a "touch and go"—he'd hit the ground, roll across it, and take wing again—just to test the surface.

He tried to gauge which direction the wind was blowing by the ripples on the lake. Darryl lowered the flaps and the landing gear, and the Caribou touched the ground lightly, bumped along a few hundred feet, and swept into the air again. Rick had been watching the tires. The ground seemed fine.

"Okay, this is it," Roger said.

"Go for it," Darryl said.

"Make it good," Bob muttered to himself.

Roger swept around, touched down, and the Caribou bumped to a lurching stop.

"Goddamn!" Rick yelled.

"*Fantastico!*" screamed Cecelio, who usually spoke in Spanish.

They tumbled out into the silence, shaking hands, laughing, on top of the world at last. The temperature was forty degrees Fahrenheit, the ground surprisingly damp and soft.

"I'm not going to be happy until we get the Caribou turned around for takeoff," Roger said.

They unloaded the plane and started setting up the tents. Darryl fired up the Caribou. The quicker they could get it back to Thule and start flying the heavy stuff in, the better. But the ground, while hard enough to land on at ninety miles an hour, was like trying to drive on sand. As the Caribou groaned and strained, the tires sank deeper. When Darryl tried to swivel the plane around, the two parallel nose-wheel tires popped off their rims.

Bad news. Even if they had an air pump, which they didn't, it would have been useless. The air we breathe expands at high altitudes, which means you can't fill airplane tires with it: if you filled them with enough air to taxi and take off, they'd blow up as soon as plane reached cruising altitude. You have to use an inert gas; nitrogen is the usual choice. But the boys didn't have any of that.

"You've got to innovate, goddamnit!" exhorted Rick, shaking his head and plunging into the pile of cargo. "You guys dig out the dirt under *one* of those wheels." Of all things, he dragged the rickety gas grill over to the Caribou. Wedging the tire back on, he fitted a hose onto the grill's propane gas tank. Psssst . . . In seconds, the tire was plump again, filled with highly explosive propane. The propane held out, and soon the second tire was also in good repair. As long as nothing sparked on takeoff, or on landing at Thule, the tires were perfect. So Roger fired up the plane and, with the Caribou's engines and props screaming, he slowly spun it around, as Rick and the boys placed box tops and the pallets dropped by the Air National Guard a year ago under the wheels to keep them from sinking as the plane swiveled.

Leaving Bob, Rick, and Cecelio behind to set up the camp, Roger and Darryl returned to Thule the next morning. The 9,000-pound bulldozer fit inside the plane with an inch to spare, although it made the Caribou 4,000 pounds overweight. Roger got off the ground all right, but the weather closed in quickly. He couldn't see a thing, and the Caribou's indicators were consistently reading ten degrees off—when the Caribou was level the instruments said he was in a ten-degree bank. Plus, the Caribou had no deicers. "We can't fly through this weather," Roger said. "Let's head back to Thule."

"No," Darryl said, "let's go on for fifteen minutes and climb out."

Roger was nervous; there were two small mountain ranges ahead. "Any ice on the wings?"

"No," Darryl said. "They're clean." Roger didn't bother to respond as a big sheet of ice broke off the plane and slid down the windshield. A few minutes later they broke free, climbing above the clouds. When they reached the *Kee Bird* site, it, too, was socked in by thick clouds. They flew thirty miles to the coast, found a hole, descended, and flew back to the airplane underneath the overcast, just a few hundred feet above the ground. By this time, they'd burned most of their fuel.

"Gear down," Roger called as they buzzed over the *Kee Bird*. The gear dropped. "Flaps down." The flaps didn't extend. As Roger flew in circles, Darryl tried pumping more hydraulic fluid into the flap system, but to no avail. No matter how hard he pumped, the flaps wouldn't go down.

"We can't land," Darryl said. "Go back."

"No, it's too late, Darryl," Roger said. "I'm taking her in."

As he came in to land, the stick started shaking—the Caribou was stalling. He was about to try inserting a grossly overweight airplane on a 1,400-foot dirt strip with no flaps, going thirty miles an hour faster than he was supposed to. Just before he hit, he applied power, trying to bring the nose up to flare the airplane. The yoke rattled like mad, the plane stalling. *Wham!* Roger hit the tundra and slammed the props into reverse. The Caribou hurtled forward. In a hail of spewing dirt the plane pitched forward and jerked to a violent stop.

The wheels were buried eighteen inches in the soft dirt, the propeller tips a half-inch from destruction.

"This," said Roger dryly, looking at the props and tires, "is a little higher risk than I thought."

"This is the first time I've ever seen Darryl shook up!" Rick said, laughing.

A week passed and they hadn't yet flown a single engine in. Although it was light twenty-four hours a day, the Air Force and Max Dugan would open Thule's runway only between nine A.M. and five P.M. Monday through Saturday. And getting synchronized weather between the *Kee Bird* and Thule, 240 miles to the south, was difficult. For two days the sun shined at the *Kee Bird* while forty knot winds, gusting to sixty, and thick, low clouds socked in the runway at Thule. While they waited, Rick, Darryl, and the boys drove a long iron spike into the permafrost, rigged it with block and tackle, and ran a cable from the *Kee Bird* around the post to the bulldozer. Inch by inch, over two long days, they dragged the *Kee Bird* out of the lake until it rested on firm tundra, thirty feet from shore.

On July 28, weather permitted the Caribou to fly back to Thule. It flew out again the next day, returning with Vern and financier

Tom Hess, who had just arrived in Thule by C-141. The days were ticking by. Vern climbed into the Caribou. *Well, if Darryl and Roger will fly this, I guess I can, too,* he thought. This time, coming in to land at the *Kee Bird*, the nose gear wouldn't go down. As Roger frantically pumped it down by hand, Vern got his first sight of the *Kee Bird*. It changed his mood instantly and sent a bolt of adrenaline through his body, as it had for every person who'd ever seen it. *It's brand-new!* he thought.

But up close, Vern was struck, as he had been when he'd seen the Huey, by the reality of the task at hand. The flaps, which had been extended when the *Kee Bird* landed, were partly mangled. The control cables were frayed, the flight controls missing. The panorama of glass in the nose of the cockpit was yellowed and split with hairline cracks. The plane was incredibly cool, Vern thought, and in relatively perfect condition. But airplanes, much less four-engine bombers, weren't cars, and "relatively" was a scary term in the world of flight. Suddenly Vern looked at the plane and saw not how perfect it was but how much crucial work there was to do, the countless small steps that had to be taken to get it airworthy. He shook off his doubt. Rick and Darryl knew this stuff backwards and forwards. And wasn't this exactly what he'd wanted, after all?

As for Tom Hess, he arrived at the site in pressed blue jeans, furry après-ski boots, and a fleece-lined bomber jacket, and proceeded to set up a tent filled with pillows. He left on the Caribou flight out the next day. "It's so desolate it's scary," he told me a few days later from his home in sunny Rancho Santa Fe.

Seven small tents and a big floorless green canvas Army mess tent clustered at the edge of the mile-long lake next to the bomber. Inside the tent it was cold and dank, a dirt-floored room of blue-and-white lawn chairs surrounding Formica-topped folding tables and a kitchen consisting of a microwave oven and two twin-burner propane gas stoves. The smell of oil and exhaust fumes permeated the camp. Generators and air compressors roared eighteen hours a day. Darryl and Roger slept on foam pads in the back of the Caribou. Cecelio slept curled around engine parts in a Coleman umbrella tent hardly suitable for the Florida Keys, much less the high Arctic. Rick alternated between sleeping in the mess tent and the back of the bomber, where the *Kee Bird*'s original radar operator Howard Adams and photographer Ernie Stewart had toiled so many years before. Reminders of the plane's past were everywhere. Tucked in an engine cowling Vern found a wrench scratched with the initials "W.B." Near the navigator's station they found a scrap of paper on which celestial fixes were scribbled, dated February 22, 1947. On late-night strolls around the lake, Roger and Vern found life rafts and snowshoes and canisters of K rations and flares, mosquito netting, sleeping bags, and machetes, all of which had been kicked out by overflying airplanes while Adams and Stewart waited for rescue. "It's like King Tut's tomb!" said Vern.

Over the next week a routine developed. Rick and Cecelio attacked the engines. Each had to be disconnected from its tangle of fuel and oil hoses, and the various electrical wires and cables controlling it. Carburetors, fuel pumps, two generators, the starter, the oil cooler, and the motor mount itself were stripped. The exhaust system—a five-foot-diameter ring with eighteen individual cylinder ports—had to be removed. Then all of those components had to be reattached to the new engines. If you've ever tried to change the puny, primitive exhaust system of your car on a nasty winter's day, you know how mean the job is. (And your car has, at most, eight cylinders.) The nuts were stubborn and frozen. The angles were impossible. The ratchets and wrenches slipped and the sharp metal corners sliced fingertips and bit the skin off knuckles. As the temperature dropped to thirty degrees, a cold wind began howling at thirty miles an hour across the valley, whipping the tents like flags on a pole and numbing fingers. The work was too delicate to allow for gloves. It's a crummy job in a warm, clean hangar. On the windswept tundra, it was brutal.

Vern attacked the four fuel pumps—they, too, had to be disassembled, cleaned, repaired, and reassembled—and the cowl-flap motors, a series of tiny, complex electrical motors that opened aluminum flaps surrounding the engines to regulate their temperature. There were four main drive motors, eight six-station junction boxes, and twenty-four screw jack drives, plus forty flex cable assemblies, all of which had to be removed, disassembled, cleaned, repaired, reassembled, and reinstalled. Tommy Hauptman, without a helicopter to fly, went home. Darryl "proceeded in all directions simultaneously," as he liked to say. Bob cooked and helped wherever needed, as did the *Nova* crew, as the normal distinction between journalists and their subjects dissolved in the all-consuming fight to stay alive and get the job done. The task was so overwhelming, the life so hard, there was no place for anyone who failed to contribute. And, in addition to survival, they had a shared interest. Without an airplane to fly, there wouldn't be much of a film or a story, and without six more useful bodies turning wrenches or cleaning or lifting, the airplane would never fly.

On August 3, in thirty-mile-an-hour winds, they hung the first engine. What would take minutes in a heated hangar took hours in the wind and near-freezing temperatures.

On the fourth and fifth it rained and snowed and blew. Darryl and Rick replaced the flight-control cables anyway.

On the sixth they hung the second engine and Vern replaced two of the four booster pumps.

On the seventh a blizzard hit the site. The wind was so strong that the snow blew sideways and everyone huddled in their tents, unable to work. After a while the team took refuge in the Caribou, which creaked and groaned in the wind. The realization sunk in that the four days of beautiful blue skies and calm winds Darryl and Tommy and Gary Larkins worked in the year before had been an aberration.

In Thule, on August 12, Darryl readied for his sixth flight back to the *Kee Bird*. I had flown up to Thule the day before. A bitter wind cut across the white concrete apron, the high swirling clouds a welcome change from the previous day's leaden overcast. The Caribou looked like a war-torn, bedraggled beast, a homeless family's station wagon. The undersides of its camouflage-painted belly and wings were covered in mud. Globs of oil dripped steadily from its two piston engines, and a thick viscous sheen covered the engine nacelles. Dents covered the leading edges of the wings and the strips of rubber on the edges that deiced the wings were shredded. A rickety ramp led up into the rear of the belly, a long, narrow tube of exposed ribs, wires, and cables, reeking of oil and grease. Pringles potato chips cans and an orange were wedged between wires and ribs, the floor was littered with pieces of Styrofoam packing and scraps of oily shag carpeting.

Darryl, Roger von Grote, Cecelio Grande, and I muscled the last eighteen-cylinder radial engine—weighing nearly two tons and bolted to a wheeled stand—up the ramp and into the plane. An inch at a time, using six-foot iron bars as levers, we wrenched the engine forward, and Cecelio chained it down. Behind it Darryl and Cecelio stacked three 250-pound tires, each four feet across; four 250-pound propeller hubs; two twenty-foot-long fabric-covered ailerons; a bottle of nitrogen gas; a wooden crate the size of a freezer; two fifty-five-gallon drums of fuel; a case of beer; and several cases of popcorn and Pringles. Cecelio tied it all down with nylon cargo straps.

By the rule book, maximum takeoff weight wasn't supposed to exceed 31,300 pounds. "Looks like we're real heavy again today," said Roger, peering into the belly and squinting into the sky, ticking the numbers off out loud. "The engine is thirty-five hundred pounds, the hubs two hundred and fifty pounds each, the crate is two-fifty. We've got forty-six hundred pounds of fuel, five people and their gear—that'll be about thirty-three thousand pounds."

"We all ready?" said Darryl, dressed in brown corduroy pants, a blue parka, tennis shoes, and a blue baseball cap. He and Roger were freshly showered and shaved, but their hands were already covered in black grime.

"Yeah," said Roger, with a worried grin. "As usual, we're so heavy it'll be difficult to fly if one engine quits. If that happens I'll just try and keep us out of the water. The ice is okay; we'll just set her down on her belly. But I worry about climbing out of here over that bay—that's twenty miles of water."

"Let's go," Darryl said, climbing into the copilot's right seat.

"Where's the takeoff checklist?" Roger said.

"Forget the checklist," said Darryl, "we've got to get out of here. I've got a bear by the tail and I can't let go."

Cecelio latched the rear door and we buckled into the red nylon seats. If Roger crashed, the engine, a corncob of giant cylinders, and the tires and ailerons—10,500 pounds of cargo—would come hurtling forward like a giant pestle. No one would stand a chance. In minutes, though, the Caribou was up, groaning north over a vast sea of dirty ice. The temperature in the unheated, unpressurized cargo hold plunged.

Two and a half hours later we droned over the lake, the silver bomber below looking like a toy airplane surrounded by dots of blue and green tents in a brown desert. The landing was soft and Roger rolled to a stop in about 500 feet. Rick, Bob, Vern, and the *Nova* crew looked wild: sunburned, unshaven, and covered with grease and mud. But there wasn't a cloud in the big blue sky and the wind was gentle as Rick towed the Caribou, leaking oil, to a dirt loading ramp plowed out of the tundra. He used the bulldozer to drag the engine out of the Caribou with a chain, then lifted it out of the belly by the bulldozer's shovel. "That's four!" he yelled above the diesel roar. At last, nearly everything was there: the four engines, the prop hubs, the elevators and ailerons. One more round-trip to get the props and one more to fly in the fuel and the *Kee Bird* might be ready to fly.

The next day was Darryl's fifty-eighth birthday, and late that night Bob swept out the "clean room"—a roofless but floored three-sided shelter of aluminum cargo pallets—placed the lawn chairs in a circle, and we had a party. There was a six-pack of Bud, a case of Tuborg, and fifths of Glenlivet and Seagram's. For heat, the

400,000-BTU Herman-Nelson aircraft engine heater, a giant blow-dryer, poured dry, hot air on us. As the sun circled slowly around the horizon and the Herman-Nelson roared, the tales spun.

"So what was it like flying the Blackbird?" Vern asked. The Lockheed SR-71 Blackbird and its CIA predecessor, the A-12, were supersonic spy planes designed to fly so fast and high they were impervious to Soviet surface-to-air missiles. Though officially retired from the Air Force in 1989, no airplane has yet equaled the Blackbird's 90,000-foot altitude and Mach 3.2 speed.

"It's hauling ass," said Darryl, cupping a brushed-aluminum mug of Glenlivet, his blue eyes twinkling. "You just pull the stick slightly—there's this periscope in the cockpit so you can see behind you—and you can see the body ripple right down the length of the titanium airplane. I'd leave Edwards and an hour later I'd be flying over Eglin Air Force Base in Florida."

"How about the 104?"

"A big fucking thrill!" he said, breaking into a smile and sipping his drink.

"How'd you actually break the speed record?" I asked.

Darryl leaned back in his creaking chair, crossed his legs and explained. High-performance jet fighters routinely break 1,000 miles per hour, but they do it at high altitudes, where the air is thin and the drag low. And going that fast requires afterburners, which gulp vast quantities of fuel; an F-16 can fly at Mach 2 for only about two minutes. Breaking the speed record required flying through a one-kilometer timed course twice in each direction without landing in between, and from a distance of five kilometers on each pass through you had to be below an altitude of 300 feet. That prevented hitting the trap in an accelerating dive. At no point, even turning around after a pass, could you fly higher than 1,500 feet. "So it's really more of an endurance test because lots of planes can go that fast but they can't do it four times," Darryl said, sipping his drink.

It was, however, much more than just an endurance test. Above an airplane's "redline" airspeed, an airframe can begin oscillating or its flight control surfaces fluttering, and it can happen so fast and so powerfully that one instant the plane is straight and level and the next it disintegrates. A lucky pilot might catch his airplane beginning to oscillate (when a control surface flutters it happens so fast a pilot is helpless; ejection or death is the result); but as often as not in an effort to correct the problem he makes it worse by overcompensating. In the thick air of the low-altitude record, airplanes reach their redlines at lower speeds, and a hundred feet off the ground there's no room for error.

Rick shivered, then jumped up and adjusted the blower on the Herman-Nelson. The hot wind swept over us.

Darryl said he wanted to use a 104 because he thought it was "a great but maligned airplane," his attitude being "I'm going to show those bastards." But first he had to get one, and in the late 1960s they hadn't yet been released to civilians. "It started out low-key, and for the first four or five years I was just collecting parts, but then I got to where I said, 'By golly, I can do this,' and I got more serious," he said.

Cecelio passed around a can of Pringles.

"I got the front end from a Lockheed mock-up," continued Darryl, munching a handful of chips. "I got the tail from a junkyard in California and the horizontal stabilizers from a scrap yard in Tucson." When a scrap pile came up for sale at Eglin Air Force Base, Darryl drove his father's Pontiac LeMans with 109,000 miles on it across country from Van Nuys. Amid the 25,000 pounds of scrap were a 104 fuselage and a set of wings. Darryl bought the pile, sold the remainder to the next highest bidder, and drove the wings and fuselage home on the back of a U-Haul trailer. They weighed 10,000 pounds and stuck out thirty-eight feet behind the car. "At first I couldn't drive over twenty because the thing would start to wiggle violently, but after screwing around a while, I could maintain about fifty miles an hour," he said, holding his hands up in front of his chest, like a kid pretending to drive a car. "But we'd driven all the way from Van Nuys to Florida nonstop, so I'd hardly slept, and I couldn't stay awake. Finally I said to the guy who was with me, 'You drive.' Well, it's pitch dark, we're heading down the freeway in Louisiana and I fall asleep. Suddenly I jolt awake and I can feel the car dancing and thrashing back and forth and then we jackknife off the freeway. We slide down this grassy slope, a wing flips off the trailer and the fuselage smashes into the trunk of the car.

"We get this tow truck to come and he pulled the plane out of the car and pulled the car up and towed us to this little village. I started looking at the car, and the axle is bent, but I said, 'Hell, let's see if this thing goes.' So we loaded it all back up and headed down the road at ten miles an hour.

"Two weeks later a Lockheed tech rep called and said, 'Darryl, there's a fuselage in Puerto Rico that maybe you can get.' The Puerto Rican National Guard flew 104s. So I flew to Puerto Rico and there's this complete 104 sitting on a cradle because the landing gear and the tail had been damaged. These pilots took me to the officer's club and everybody started getting wildly drunk. They ran me in shifts for three days, partying. They said I could have the plane as long as I partied with them. 'Don't worry,' they kept saying, 'we'll crate it up and ship it to you.' Finally I made it out of there, and a few weeks later I got a call and one of the guys said, 'We're so sorry. You can have the plane, but we accidentally burned it up. But don't worry,' the guy said, 'I'll crash another one for you.'"

It was near midnight but the sun was just as bright as it was at noon, a cold yellow ball glinting off the silver B-29. The Herman-Nelson roared and Darryl poured another round. Suddenly Mike Rossiter, the *Nova* producer, jumped up and grabbed a flare Roger had found that afternoon. It was dated 1944. Rossiter pulled the cap. POP! Smoke shot out of the flare and then two brilliant orange balls arced high in the sky. "Happy Birthday, Darryl!" shouted Vern.

Assembling the 104, Darryl said, was the ultimate backyard project. The mock-up had round-headed rivets, every one of which he had to drill out and replace with flat-heads to reduce drag. He traded sponsorship of the Bearcat for 1,000 hours of electrical work.

On many nights he slept in the hangar beside the plane. Twelve years after starting his quest, he had a complete, hand-built F-104 Starfighter. It was 2,000 pounds lighter than a stock 104, carried 200 extra gallons of fuel, and carried the name *Red Baron*. His wife upholstered the instrument panel with red velvet.

On October 24, 1977, at Mud Lake, California, Darryl climbed into the *Red Baron*, flew twenty-five miles out, turned around, lit the afterburner, and accelerated toward the measured kilometer. When he hit the trap not quite ninety seconds later he was barely thirty feet off the ground, traveling a hair under 1,460 feet per second, 87,648 feet a minute, 988 miles per hour. He was 100 knots over redline, his airspeed gauge indicating 850 knots. (By comparison, at his fastest in the A-12, about Mach 3.2, or nearly 2,500 mph, his indicated airspeed in the rarified air of 90,000 feet was only 190 knots.) "The plane is very sensitive but stable," Darryl remembered, scrunched forward on the edge of his rickety aluminum lawn chair, "and you're hauling ass!"

To those below, the *Red Baron* was dead silent; he was traveling nearly one and a half times the speed of sound. The silence didn't last long. The sonic boom blew out a woman's contact lenses. The headlights of cars parked below exploded. Darryl flew so low the shock waves kicked up waves of dust from the desert floor. Lockheed, he says, measured the highest "overpressure"—the technical term for the shockwaves hitting the ground from Darryl's airplane— ever recorded.

Leaving the trap, Darryl killed the afterburners, flew out twenty-five miles, turned around and seared through again. Sixteen minutes after taking off he'd done it four times, burned 1,000 gallons of fuel and buried the absolute low-altitude speed record of 902 mph set in 1961 by a U.S. Navy F-4 Phantom II.

But that had been just a warm-up, a teaser to what Darryl Greenamyer was capable of. "I wanted to break the altitude record held by the Russians," he said, "but I thought if I could get notoriety by breaking the speed record maybe I could get some sponsorship money." What Darryl wanted, in fact, was to do as a civilian what the U.S. Air Force had consistently failed to do for years. In the early 1960s, a Soviet pilot flew a MiG-166 to 113,890 feet. Immediately, the Air Force decided to win back the record. A Lockheed test pilot had unofficially flown a rocket-powered Lockheed NF-104, their fastest airplane, to 120,000 feet on December 6, 1963; but as a matter of national pride the Air Force wanted to best the Russians officially. To do it the Air Force rolled out the NF-104 and called on an American icon, the man with the right stuff. But on December 10, 1963, Col. Chuck Yeager, commandant of the Aerospace Research Pilots School, found himself in an uncontrollable spin at 104,000 feet. After plummeting helplessly for seventeen and a half miles he punched out at 11,000 feet. The plane crashed, Yeager lived, and the Air Force promptly killed the program. That story actually inspired Darryl Greenamyer! "Yeager hated civilian test pilots," said Darryl, grinning, raising his drink, and you could still see the I'm-gonna-show-you coals burning in his gut.

For the speed record Darryl needed fuel economy. For the altitude record, Russia having raised the bar to 123,000 feet in 1977, he needed thrust and control at the edge of space. At 45,000 feet Darryl intended to go as fast as he could, then pull up into a "zoom climb," riding the plane to the top of an arc like a bullet shot skyward. Engineers at Lockheed had calculated the optimum angle at which he should shoot. The plane's airframe was rated for Mach 2 and cleared to withstand Mach 2.2. But to shoot above 120,000 feet Darryl figured he needed to hit Mach 2.5 prior to his pull-up, a speed at which the aluminum airframe would heat up and begin to weaken. "I calculated I could do it ten times before the airframe would fail," Darryl said, shifting in his chair.

Darryl was preparing to land after a test flight over Mojave on February 27, 1978, when his left landing-gear light blinked, telling him the gear wasn't down. He flew by the control tower for visual confirmation. Your gear is down, the tower reported. Low on fuel, he flew thirty miles over to Edwards Air Force Base. Again, their tower reported his gear down. But the light was still on. Touching down lightly to test the gear, Darryl felt it rattling. It was down, but not locked in place. It was an awful moment. There was nothing he could do. The 104's fuel system ran underneath the fuselage, and with its wingtips mere inches from the ground and a strong cross-wind that day, a belly landing would risk rollover or fire. The manual recommended one thing: ejecting. Darryl flew out over the desert, climbed to 10,000 feet, and pulled the ejection handle. "When that thing fired, I thought the plane had blown up. They say you black out, but I was counting the rivets and looking for my chute as I flew up. It was cold. I was freezing my ass off. I missed a couple of saguaro cactuses and did a face plant you wouldn't believe. Finally I walked up to an ambulance and said, 'I think you guys are looking for me.' " His hand-built, one-of-a-kind 104 with the velvet-covered instrument panel, "Darryl Greenamyer" artfully inscribed in shiny red paint below the cockpit, crashed in a fiery ball.

But that's what people loved—and hated—about Darryl Green-amyer. He could be careless and reckless, he could be mean and wily, and he could be stingy and stubborn. He stepped on people's toes. After his last disqualification from Reno he'd been banned from racing for a year and the FAA had even suspended his flying li-cense. Gary Larkins couldn't stand the man, and that same feeling was growing among the Air Force personnel at Thule. He was al-ways trying to bend their rules, flying around in that unsafe Cari-bou, wanting to land or take off when the airport was closed, "borrowing" the forklift when Air Force regulations required an OSHA-certified driver for the damn thing. But you didn't win Reno more times than anyone else, didn't break speed records, didn't fly World War II bombers off of the North Pole if you played by everyone else's rules. Darryl dared to dream bigger than most people ever dreamed, and he wasn't afraid to fail. And the boys sitting around Darryl Greenamyer on that cold and bright Arctic night would have followed him anywhere—they had, in fact, followed him to the frozen wastelands of what the ancients called Ultima Thule, the farthest north—because he wasn't slowed by the possibility of failure but was inspired by the dream of achieving the impossible.

"We must be getting close to departure. Darryl is starting to read the manual!" Roger said, laughing and stamping into the mess tent. It was breakfast the next morning and Darryl sat in a lawn chair, clutching a mug of coffee, a thick, dog-eared B-29 manual in his lap, his silver-rimmed half-glasses perched low on his nose. Two weeks had already turned into four, but the *Kee Bird* was starting to come together. The ailerons still needed to go on, the rudder needed to be covered in new fabric, the props had to be assembled, the last engine was waiting to be hung, all the fittings and hoses and wires and cables on the engines had to be connected, and the landing gear tested. It was easy to get overwhelmed by the task at hand and to forget that repairing the *Kee Bird* was merely the beginning. The real challenge was yet to come: flying the thing out. Just as it was one thing to read a guidebook on, say, Paris in your home in New York, and another to read it when you actually were in Paris, so it was one thing to read the flight specs of a B-29 at home and quite another to read them in that valley, your feet squishing in the soft ground, your eyes firmly taking note of the wall of mountains 3,500 feet ahead that you'd hurtle into if you didn't get off the ground. Darryl was taking note.

"This manual says that in a war emergency the plane can take off at twenty-six hundred RPM in two thousand feet. That's encouraging! And that's with eleven men and all their stuff and all the guns and a full load of fuel. Hell, we'll only have four men and six thousand pounds of fuel. I'd like to report," he said, slipping his glasses into his breast pocket and standing up, "that I think we'll probably make it! I'll give it a forty-percent chance! Anyway," he said, striding off to the *Kee Bird*, "that manual is nothing but estimates."

It was sunny that day, and we hung the right aileron. Darryl fired up the bulldozer, raised the fourth and last engine, dangling on a chain high on its shovel, and we bolted it on. Dark, leaden clouds descended over the valley, the temperature dropped to near freezing, and a frigid rain started falling. The trash-strewn campsite quickly turned to mud, an Arctic trash dump of tea bags, spilled oil, airplane parts, cracked hoses, and roaring generators. But near midnight we muscled a jack under the nose and Darryl swung the nose gear up and down for the first time. "First-class!" he said.

The days passed in an endless stream of work, the Herman-Nelson heater, the air compressors, the generators roaring ceaselessly. Except when they stopped working, that is. They were the heart of the operation, supplying the air pressure for the air-powered drills and saws and ratchets, the electricity for the radios and batteries that started the dozer and the Caribou. When the generators broke down the batteries couldn't be recharged, the radios wouldn't work to call for help, and the Caribou couldn't be started. To keep them all beating steadily, Rick danced from the *Kee Bird* to the Caribou to the little engines, repairing one before moving to the next. "Innovate, you've got to innovate," he'd admonish, lying under a leaking engine or perched atop a ladder. Simply put, our survival depended on his ability to keep the generators running.

For three days Darryl and Roger were stuck at the site. At noon on August 15, the weather cleared enough for takeoff, and in a mad rush—clouds and fog and rain could descend at any moment—Rick dragged the Caribou onto the makeshift runway, now soggier than ever. Armed with shovels and the lids from oil drums, we turned it slowly around, throwing the lids under the turning tires, diving to dig them out as soon as they started sinking. The tundra, inundated by the rain and floating on a crust of permafrost, rose and fell as the wheels passed over it like a carpet floating on a layer of water. Poised at the end of the runway, Darryl and Roger climbed in, throttled up in a roar, and the Caribou heaved slowly off the ground, banking toward Thule.

It rained the rest of the day and all the next, low, steel-gray clouds covering the hills, darkening our moods. The temperature was dropping. Winter was coming. You could feel it. Rick was exhausted, a scraggly-haired, nine-fingered goblin drenched in oil and grease. Sure, he was getting a lot of work done, but the more he did the more he had to do, it seemed. Everybody was always telling him he ought to accompany Roger and Darryl on a Caribou flight, just to get a break, take a hot shower, eat a good meal, have a good long talk on the telephone with Irene and Hallie. But there was just too much to do at the plane; if he went in, he kept saying, work might grind to a halt.

Dinner that night was instant mashed potatoes and fried steak, without a hint of seasonings. But engine number one, Norma, was hung, rewired, gassed, and plumbed. The rudder was repaired and the first coating of fabric covering had been applied.

We were starting to hate Bob's cooking, an endless parade of those mashed potatoes and pan-fried steaks or microwaved slabs of baked ham. It wasn't so bad when the sun was shining or we'd made a big leap in progress, but to come into that dim mess tent, starving, after hours of rain and cold to be confronted with another dollop of unadorned mashed potatoes or microwaved boiled ham seemed a cruel disappointment. He had even nicknamed the mess tent the Ramona Café, after his restaurant in California, but mysteriously he showed virtually no interest in cooking tasty food. Unappreciated, Bob looked glum, plodding about camp, zealously guarding his pet project—replacing the rudder's fabric—from us reporters and cameramen, who were becoming increasingly important workers. The perpetual daylight didn't help. It was hard to get a good night's sleep, even harder to know when to put the tools down and go to bed without the enforced pause of darkness. Sometimes, I'd wake up in the night and the tent would be so bright it seemed aglow. Sun! I'd think, squeezing out of my sleeping bag and popping my head out to revel in the glory; instead there would be that perpetual gray drizzle, the glow a cruel trick. As the days passed, the relationship between our routine and the clock became more and more askew. We often didn't wake until ten A.M., eat dinner until ten P.M., or stop work for the day until well after midnight.

It rained and snowed all night, a cold, wet, viscous slime covering the mud and dirt of camp. The damp was corrosive, permeating everything, from sleeping bags to the mess tent. It was hard to get warm when it was thirty-three degrees and raining. Once again, the Caribou couldn't get in. We were running out of fuel to power the generators that powered the batteries that powered the radios. Food was starting to get scarce, too. "Man, maybe we could get a C-130 just to blast in here and drop us some lobsters and caviar!" giggled Vern, sipping hot lemonade in the mess tent that night. It wasn't much of a joke. What if the Caribou couldn't get in for a week? Or two weeks? As a nonessential, basically unskilled worker, a reporter (and one of the few, it seemed, who hadn't brought a firearm), I found myself wondering what would happen if the food really ran out. Suddenly Rick piped up: "Who we gonna eat first?" No one answered and no one laughed.

By morning the clouds had dissipated like a puff of smoke. Glorious sun poured down, drying the ground, warming our spirits. Why were we so glum? Darryl and Roger sputtered in at noon. "I think we're wearing out our welcome at Thule," Darryl said, shaking his head, climbing out of the Caribou.

"The base is getting impatient," echoed Roger. "We tried to borrow a compressor to fill the tires and Erik Thomsen"—the Danish liaison officer, the highest-ranking Danish military official at the base—"said we didn't have authorization. Jesus! And Erik said the first frost came a couple of days ago at Thule, right on time, and that from now on the temps will be dropping and the sun will be rarer."

As usual, something had gone wrong on the Caribou. "Coming out here the fire warning light on the right engine came on," said Roger, "and old Darryl just disconnected the fuse. I finally got him to put it back in, but of course now it doesn't work."

"You know," said Rick, with a laugh, "we could fix everything on the Caribou by just taking out all the gauges and warning lights. Or better yet, we could just paint lines on the gauges where they're supposed to be registering!"

Showered and shaved, in clean clothes, Roger and Darryl looked like a couple of golden retrievers in a dog-food commercial touting the "High Pro Glow." The plane was full of treats. Unloading it felt heroic, wondrous. Four cases of Tuborg beer. A bottle of champagne. Cashews and peanuts. A handful of vegetables. The last of the propellers. And new things to do: the elevators and the rusty iron grader, the key to building Darryl's runway, and aluminum piping to drain the delta of rivers now fanning across it, beginning just fifteen hundred feet from the plane. That was starting to be worrisome. The whole valley had been as dry as the Empty Quarter during Darryl and Gary's four-day jaunt the year before. Now it was wet, soggy, a giant bog with new ditches and trickles inching down from the surrounding hills every day.

We worked like Noah, struggling to get the animals loaded on the Ark before the coming flood. Vern installed all the cowl-flap motors and cables, and the oil lines on engines Norma and Ida. We changed the two left main landing-gear tires. Each tire and hub weighed nearly 500 pounds, and five of us wrestled with them for hours. Late that night Darryl fired up the bulldozer and puttered and bumped out onto the future runway, dragging the grader. Everyone else was thinking about fixing the *Kee Bird*. Darryl was thinking about flying it. As we stumbled off to our tents and sleeping bags, the record-shattering test pilot lumbered back and forth at two miles per hour, plowing his own runway. Was the silver-haired elf building his path to glory or digging his own grave?

On Friday, August 19, the clouds descended and it started to rain again. We missed two radio checks with Thule because the batteries were low and the battery charger was broken. But near midnight, after finishing the right main tire change, Darryl climbed into the flight engineer's station, pressed a button, and the *Kee Bird* emitted a loud whine. The landing gear wasn't working, and Rick had been messing with it off and on for days. Rain fell, dripping off the wings, sliding over the fuselage, and collecting in broad puddles. The APU, the *Kee Bird*'s little auxillary power generator that supplied power to the plane, screamed. Rick stood by the gear and everyone else gathered round. The landing gear slowly moved up. "Stop!" yelled Rick. He fiddled for a moment. "Okay, try again." The gear slid into its compartment and the doors folded neatly behind.

Rick raised a fist in the air. It was intoxicating, after so much work on the big chunk of aluminum, to see it move, to hear it whine, and over and over again Darryl cycled the gear like a kid with a new toy.

"We're almost at the end," Rick said. He was pale, filthy, rain dripping off his formerly red parka. "We've swung the gear and now it's just the stabilizers, the rudder and the prop governors, and a bit of plumbing on the engines. And then we'll be home free."

It poured all day, Saturday, August 20, the seventh straight day of rain. "The rain is relentless," noted Vern in his journal, "but it doesn't matter so much, you just press on." Dinner was like a scene from Sartre's play *No Exit*. It was forty-one degrees in the mess tent. Dank. Dark. Piles of dirty plates and unwashed pots. Bob was so depressed and withdrawn, he'd stopped cooking. Albert, the *Nova* sound engineer, was cranking out spicy meals in his place. Bob crawled into his tent and wouldn't speak or come out. That night the sun was supposed to set for the first time. Over the radio Thule warned that the weather would soon be getting ugly. Already the tops of the surrounding peaks were covered with snow. Rick looked like an overworked caveman. He was splayed out on a lawn chair, his head back, his eyes closed.

"Seems like everything we touch turns to shit," Darryl said.

"No," Rick said, "I think we've got done some pretty good stuff."

The end was drawing near, but no one knew when that would be or how it would turn out. There was so little to do and yet so much. All four engines were installed, but none of them had been started. Who knew if they'd spring to life? All the fuel still had to be flown in. The props had to be wired. A suitable runway graded—and that was impossible to do until the rain let up.

"The biggest worry is the runway," Darryl said.

"How far is the shore from here?" asked Rick, suddenly.

"Roger says it's thirty miles, but I think it's more," Darryl said. "Why?"

"Maybe we could come up here with a barge and . . ." Rick trailed off, shrugging his shoulders.

"We've got another week, and then I think it will get dangerous," Roger said. "We won't be able to get the Caribou out."

The sun exploded through the clouds on Sunday and we charged ahead with desperate energy. We hung the last prop, the elevators, and the rudder. By eleven that night it was a glorious evening. The sun was bright, but low on the horizon. To the south, the moon glowed. We watched as the sun set behind wispy clouds, dipping below the mountains, a glimpse of twilight that ended with a sunrise ten minutes later. Ducks honked across the lake—larger flocks of them were now pausing at the lake on their way south. When the weather was like this, the still lake and the silent valley seemed friendly, and you almost wanted to stay. "Wow," said Darryl, lingering over dinner. "We've got a lot of little stuff to do, but I'd say two days until we can fire the engines."

At breakfast on the twenty-second, Darryl, Rick, and Roger pored over the manuals. We had more blue sky but it was raining in Thule, so the Caribou couldn't fly out for the last load. We noticed a thin layer of ice over the lake; winter was marching in.

"It says don't try to lift the nose under ninety or ninety-five miles an hour or else 'latitudinal instability' will result," said Rick.

"I think those charts for takeoff are confusing," said Darryl. "It says one thousand, seven hundred and fifty feet for a hard runway and nineteen-fifty for sod."

"I'd say this is definitely a soft surface," Roger said.

"No shit!" Darryl said, laughing and grabbing a fresh cup of coffee. "You know, nowadays the charts are different. They don't give you estimates but the exact stats. But these are estimates. Look, it'll take two thousand feet to get that turd in the air."

"You'll have to jerk that sucker off!" Rick said.

"How about fuel?" Roger said. "How much do you want in each wing?"

"I want four hundred gallons in each tank, that's sixteen hundred gallons. And we've already got six hundred here."

"Twenty barrels is one thousand gallons," said Roger, "so we need to bring in two hundred and fifty a tank, which is seven thousand pounds, which with any other shit brings the Caribou flight up to a full load. And it would be really nice to be able to fly on one engine in case we have to go down, especially carrying all that fuel."

All afternoon Rick and Cecelio readied Ida, the number-one engine. It took Cecelio a couple of hours perched on the top of the ladder to fill Ida with gallons of oil. Cecelio worked like a machine, tirelessly and without complaining. In the flight engineer's seat Darryl primed Ida and hit the starter. The starter whined in an electric hum, then a *punk! punk, punk,* as the props swiveled, followed by muffled, throaty thumps. Suddenly the spark caught and the pistons exploded in a thunderous cough. The *Kee Bird* shook violently, black smoke and oil pouring out of the exhaust stacks, the propeller spinning faster and faster, the ground shaking. "I told you that thing would run," Rick shouted, his exhausted and smudged face breaking into an electrifying smile just as the sun was rising over the mountains, a clear, crisp day. Somehow, Rick reminded me of my wife after she'd given birth to our first daughter—beyond tired, spent, jubilant.

"That's only one!" Vern bellowed. "When all four are going, that'll be awesome—eight thousand fucking horsepower sitting there going, roar, roar, roar!"

Cecelio danced in circles, his greasy hands held high in the Arctic sunrise.

"Yeee-haww!" hooted Vern.

Dust and debris flew behind the bomber, a rocking, shaking airplane, finally, a living piece of history.

"It's smooth," Darryl said, with a quiet satisfaction.

"And this is one that we didn't run in the shop!" Rick said.

Suddenly the B-29's awesome power was unleashed.

On days like that everything seemed possible. Pity all those poor suckers cruising through another day at the office back home. What could be better than freezing and starving in northern Greenland while tinkering on one of the world's great flying machines! Bills, taxes, pushy salesmen, painting your house, what to wear—all the mundane tasks and cares of everyday life were gone, subsumed by this airplane. Except for Bob, we were working purposefully and as a unit, dedicated with all our being to a single physical task. You could look at that airplane, look at all the barren landscape surrounding it, feel the smooth, cold ratchet in your hand, and know where you stood and what you had to do. It was scary and awesome and uplifting, all at the same time.

Before bed, Darryl tromped down to the edge of the lake, tiptoeing out on a two-by-six to where the water was a few inches deep and he could brush his teeth. If he held perfectly still, he could see himself perfectly in the dark water. It was starting to freeze.

The rain held off, but apocalyptic clouds, dense billows the color of greenish pewter, hovered over the brown hills to the northeast the next day. Now it was truly cold. A thin layer of ice covered most of the lake. The puddles and ditches around camp were frozen, as was the top layer of wet tundra under our feet. No snow or rain was predicted for four days. Rick's list was down to twenty-five items, mostly minor things. Four more days seemed realistic. If, that is, they could get the last load of fuel, food, and engine fittings into the site. But Thule was still socked in. "It's really getting critical," Roger said, as Darryl slogged from the lake carrying a jug full of water. "I'd hate to be ready to fly and have no fuel. We've got to get that fuel in here!"

"I know it," Darryl said, working on lunch for us. Bob still refused to come out of his tent.

The twenty-fourth dawned in a hail of sleet; zillions of tiny white ice crystals covered the ground. But the sky was clear enough for flight, and Bob emerged from his tent looking like he'd cast a huge weight from his shoulders. He had decided to call it quits and go home. (With another assignment scheduled, and not knowing when I might get another chance to leave, I had to do the same.) With that announced, he even started to work. Rick was always trying to make sure anything no longer needed at the site was flown back to Thule. Vern, Rick, Bob, and Cecelio lugged a jack to the plane. It was so awkward and heavy that even the four of them could barely lift it into the belly. Suddenly Bob slipped, dropping his end. The jack struck the ground and the shock rocked Rick's body like a heavyweight body blow.

"Damn!" he shouted, staggering and clutching his back.

"Get your shit together, Bob!" Vern yelled, as Rick winced.

But Bob was going home. "Here," he said, thrusting a green backpack toward Vern—it was a parachute—as he walked out to the Caribou.

"I don't want it," Vern said, shaking his head. "If something goes wrong we'll die and that's not going to do anything. It'll just prolong the inevitable."

"Hey, Darryl," Bob said, "I've got something for you."

"I don't want it," he said, shoving Bob in the door.

With the runway now hard and frozen, the Caribou leapt into the air. Four more days. "We can be ready to fly on Saturday," wrote Vern in his journal. "That seems realistic."

NINE

—

CRY UNCLE

Daugaard Jensen Land, Greenland; August 1994

Were it occurring at an Air Force base in southern California, the sheer mechanics of trying to make the *Kee Bird* fly would have been daunting. But Daugaard Jensen Land, the map's name for the *Kee Bird* site, was so far away, so remote, so barren, it was like being at the end of a frighteningly long, thin hydraulic line, where small inputs at the beginning had powerful consequences. In the closing years of the twentieth century it was easy enough for a few individuals, unassisted by governments or huge corporations, to get to the *Kee Bird*. Bob Ellis of the Kalamazoo Aviation Museum had proven that. But to stay there for weeks and weeks, to keep all those people fed and warm and dry and healthy, to keep a thirty-two-year-old, twin-engine airplane and a slew of generators and compressors running and fueled, all while rebuilding a second, even more complex, airplane—this required a mechanical, logistical, meteorological, and human web that was coming under incredible strain. As long as only one strand broke at a time, the web could be fixed. But suddenly they all started breaking simultaneously.

The day the Caribou left for Thule to pick up the last load of fuel, Rick Kriege and Vern Rich and Cecelio Grande started engine number four. Rick was clearly hurt, wincing in pain, his face a ghostly white, his brown canvas Carhartt work pants black with grime. He had been working seven days a week, eighteen hours a day since the Caribou left Ramona. He'd been at the site, slaving in the cold and damp, without a shower or a change of clothes, for thirty-four days. He'd looked exhausted for days and had moved from the mess tent into the back of the Caribou. He had complained of back pains and looked increasingly ill. "I gotta lie down and straighten my back," he said, slumping toward his mattress and sleeping bag in the back of the *Kee Bird*. "And I feel like I'm getting the flu."

He wasn't at breakfast the next morning.

In Thule, Roger and Darryl loaded the Caribou with eighteen drums of fuel and picked up Tom Hess, who had just arrived at the base from California in anticipation of the *Kee Bird* taking wing. Darryl's eighty-three-year-old father, George, who had been hanging out in Thule for weeks, came along, too. The Caribou was an overloaded, flying firebomb. Forty-five minutes from the site the next morning the low oil pressure warning light blinked on. Darryl crawled back into the belly of the Caribou to look at the engine and saw oil pouring out of it. As usual, they landed safely—but one of the cylinders on the Caribou's left engine was blown. Darryl had a spare to replace it, but it was back in Thule. The Caribou was grounded with no way to fix it. The temperature hovered below freezing. Ominous gray clouds curdled around the hills. A cold, steely wind was slicing across the valley like razor wire. They were living on borrowed time, for sure, and everyone knew it. But the *Kee Bird* was nearly done: perched on fresh tires and her landing gear, sporting four new engines and propellers, new flight controls, a real airplane after a mind-numbing and body-breaking effort in a frozen, wet void.

Just after lunch on August 26, Rick crawled out of his sleeping bag—*Man, he looks like shit,* thought Vern, seeing Rick's ashen face—and they got all four engines started for the first time. Dirty rags and abandoned hoses took flight behind the bomber, blown by the propeller wash as all the engines screamed for the first time since Vern Arnett had pulled off his gutsy landing in 1947. Four engines, sixteen propeller blades, and seventy-two pistons drummed in a gut-thumping chorus, beautiful music to the men who had wrenched every part back to life with their very hands. The engines leaked like crazy, oil dripped from hoses and fittings, making grimy puddles on the tundra. They were flying the Phoenix, by god, and after all those dreams and tales, from Gary Larkins to Darryl to Bob Ellis to William Schnase, the *Kee Bird* was nearly ready to take wing again. A few days of good weather to fix the leaks, iron out the squawks, wire the propeller controls and get Rick back in shape, and Darryl would be bound for Thule in one of the world's last B-29s.

There was even further cause for celebration: Niels Jensen, a Danish fireman stationed at Thule and a member of the Thule Aero Club whom Vern had befriended, had located Darryl's spare cylinder. And he was going to fly the thing up in the club's little single-engine Cessna 172 that night.

The clouds dropped, the wind picked up, the rain fell, and still Jensen came on, buzzing under the low cloud ceiling, a few hundred feet off the deck, using nothing but dead reckoning to find them. He finally bumped onto the rutted tundra at one in the morning. They fueled him up.

"How's Rick?" Darryl asked Vern. "Do we need to get him out of here?"

Vern climbed into Rick's hovel in the back of the bomber. His face, sticking out of the red down sleeping bag, looked awful. It was paler than white. *But we all look awful,* Vern thought. "How do you feel?" he asked.

"My back is killing me!" Rick said.

"Niels is going back now. Do you want to go back with him?" Vern asked.

"No!" Rick said, emphatically.

"Are you sure? He's got plenty of room for you."

"No!" he said again. "I'm gonna be fine."

"I asked him ten times," Vern remembers, "and he said, 'No. No. No.' "

Jensen lifted off, and Vern, with fresh cylinder in hand, attacked the Caribou. Darryl was focusing on the *Kee Bird*, still 100-percent determined to get it off the ground. Caribou pilot Roger von Grote and *Nova* producer Mike Rossiter weren't so sure. "Look," said Rossiter to Roger, standing in the mess tent, "it's time to go. The *Kee Bird* isn't coming out. The weather is worsening. And Rick is sick."

Just then Darryl walked in and poured himself a cup of coffee.

"Darryl, we need to think about getting out of here," said Roger. He repeated Rossiter's summation of the situation. "I think it's time to go."

"I don't believe I'm hearing this!" said Darryl, a strained, almost plastic smile on his face. Then he stormed out of the tent, walked to the edge of the lake, and stood there, gazing at the still water.

Vern had never changed the cylinder on a radial aircraft engine before. Rick had at first been vague about exactly what to do—it was *his* job, after all. But then Rick staggered out of his tent. "Just don't mix up the push rods," he said, "because they all look the same. And don't lose any of those bolts and nuts. I'm gonna go lie down," he said. He looked ghostly. *To pass the baton like that,* thought Vern, *he must really be feeling bad.* Vern assembled some aluminum scaffolding under the Caribou's engine and, when the wind picked up, wrapped a tarp around it to shield him from the wind. The wind built and the rain drummed down. The cylinder nuts and bolts—twenty-five of each—and push rods and gaskets lay in neat piles on a piece of plywood. At midnight, exhausted, Vern and the boys turned in for the night.

By morning the wind was howling up the valley at fifty mph. The rain turned to blinding snow, hurtling sideways. The mess tent collapsed. Cecelio's tent ripped into shreds, the aluminum posts snapping like balsa wood. Vern's tent collapsed. The scaffolding blew over, the precious nuts and bolts and push rods scattering in the sand and snow. Vern, Rick, Cecelio, Roger, everyone crowded into the Caribou for shelter. It bounced and shook and echoed in the raging blizzard. Rick was lethargic, as if he were drugged.

Suddenly, flying the *Kee Bird* seemed truly impossible, but no one besides Rossiter and Roger wanted to admit it. More work had to be done, but Rick was down and he wasn't getting any better. And he was supposed to fly as flight engineer when Darryl took wing. The weather was worse than ever; the Caribou, their only way in or out, was broken. Darryl wanted to stay, to fly. Vern and Mike Rossiter fought the wind and had crawled into the mess tent to inventory the food. Nothing but MREs now. At two meals a day per person, they had four days left. And they were nearly out of diesel fuel for the Herman-Nelson, necessary to warm the Caribou's engines—if they could get them working.

"I want to get my people out," Mike Rossiter confided to Vern. "Someone's got to be an asshole and get Darryl to pull the plug. He'll never give up." Rossiter knew from a late-night conversation with Darryl that he had failed to buy the expedition insurance required by his permits. Darryl had asked him to keep it quiet, but Rossiter figured he had no choice, that sowing the seeds of dissent within the group might pressure Darryl to call it quits. And even if they did call for a rescue plane it would take forty-eight hours—if the weather was good—for it to arrive from Canada. Rossiter figured that by the time they called for a Twin Otter it might be too late. He wanted one on alert and stationed in Thule.

"Yeah," Vern said, "but without insurance, think what that will cost!"

"It doesn't matter how much it costs if we're dying!" Rossiter shouted. "At least I can save my crew and we can get Rick out. If you and Darryl want to stay, you can."

Near midnight, after they huddled in the Caribou for fourteen hours, the wind began to die. Vern, Tim Wright (our still photographer), and Cecelio returned to their scaffolding. Like hungry prisoners scrounging food, they desperately pawed the snow and frozen ground on their hands and knees. Somehow, they managed to find every piece. Then they went to work. For sixteen hours Vern worked gloveless in the snow, his hands above his head, sixty-weight oil dripping in his face. He strained to reach nooks and crannies. The cylinder intake cover wouldn't fit; getting it attached took fourteen hours. On a car, the spark-plug wires simply snap onto the plugs. On an airplane they screw on; were they to vibrate off, the engine would die. But the new cylinder wire wouldn't fit onto the plug. Vern had to make it work, he didn't have a choice. He attached it like the wire basket holding a champagne cork into its bottle.

Then the wind hit again, worse than before, forcing him to retreat to the Caribou. Darryl's father, George, was shivering in his sleeping bag. Rick was barely conscious. Darryl looked disconsolate, brooding, as the Caribou bucked, its wind-speed indicator registering sixty-five-mile-an-hour winds.

"Darryl," said Roger, over the banging and howling of the wind, "what are we going to do?"

It was the question everyone was now wondering and no one wanted to ask. The *Kee Bird* was so close, mere days, from being ready to fly. To give up now after so much work seemed inconceivable. Darryl had everything on the line. He'd lost the *Red Baron* back in '77, he'd been kicked out of Reno, he'd endured the wrath of the Air Force and a host of naysayers who wanted nothing more than to see Darryl Greenamyer fail. He couldn't just give up and run away.

And think of the money. With every extra week and extra Caribou flight, Darryl and Tom Hess had watched the dollar signs multiply; the project was hemorrhaging money. If he fled home now he might as well have just dumped $350,000 on a bonfire in his backyard. Of course, maybe he could return in another year. But that would cost even more. And who knew if the plane would make it through another winter? True, the *Kee Bird* had survived forty-seven of them with relatively little damage. But she'd been resting on her belly, not perched five feet up on her landing gear. Winds up here had been clocked well above a hundred miles an hour. What if a gust roared across the plain and literally swept her airborne for an instant, dumping her in an awful heap of aluminum? If just one landing gear collapsed, the props might be ruined. And what about the new, delicate fabric flight controls? No. The weather might clear in a few days and the nourishing sun might make everything right in a flash. Rick might perk up, shake off that backache, or the flu, or whatever it was that was eating him up. It was amazing what a little sunshine could do to your mood. Nope, Darryl couldn't cry uncle any more than he could commit suicide.

The snow and sleet echoed on the Caribou; it was like being inside a tin can with someone drumming on the sides. Every gust of wind rocked the airplane. It was coated with ice. Icicles hung from the props and wings. What if Rick wasn't okay? Darryl had gotten through to the doctor at Thule on the radio and he'd said to bring Rick in as soon as possible. Even if he could evacuate Rick, he wouldn't have a full crew on the *Kee Bird*. Tom Hess was scheduled to fly copilot, but he would be useless; he was the glory passenger, and Darryl didn't want Tom touching a thing. Roger had to fly the Caribou to get everyone else out. What if the weather stayed shitty for two weeks straight? What if it got worse? There were already six inches of snow out there, blowing and drifting wildly. Could he get the *Kee Bird* off on snow? Could they fix the Caribou? Could he or Roger get *that* piece of junk off the ground in the snow? And, damnit, they were out of food and almost out of diesel. And there was his dad, stuffed in two sleeping bags and shivering like a bowl of Jell-O.

Darryl looked at Vern. "What do you think we should do?"

"Call Thule weather," Vern said. "Let's see what the weather is supposed to do."

"Look," Darryl said, gazing at the cluster of plaintive faces huddled in the Caribou. They all looked terrible, as black and dirty as a bunch of coal miners. They were scared. "Even if I call an emergency right now, what good is it? There's no magic plane that can swoop in here and pick us up in this wind and snow and rain."

But, somehow, he knew, he'd made the decision. "Well," Darryl said, "I guess that's it. I don't see any other solution. If we can't get the Caribou fixed by tomorrow at noon, you can call in the Otter." At three A.M. he called Thule. In nine to twelve hours, the meteorological office said, the weather should improve. And he decided to order a Twin Otter up from Canada to stand by at Thule in case they couldn't get the Caribou working.

An hour later Rossiter heard footsteps scrunching through the ice and snow outside his tent. "Michael. Hey, Michael!" It was Darryl.

"Yeah?" said Rossiter, peering out into the wind and snow.

"I've contacted Bradley's," Darryl said, "and they're gonna get an Otter ready. Just thought I'd let you know."

Four hours later, by seven, the wind was dying, the clouds lifting, and the goal of the mission had changed: a race to fly themselves out had begun. Darryl adjusted the Caribou's valves. Cecelio attached the last exhaust section. Vern fixed the right-front nose tire and then the Herman-Nelson heater, using it to thaw out the engines. Roger and Tim climbed on the wings, beating the ice off with sticks and brooms. Darryl shimmied up a cargo strap onto the ice-coated tail and horizontal stabilizer, fifteen feet above the ground. It was slippery as hell and Darryl found ice blocking the elevator mechanism. He chipped away, and by two P.M. the motor was finished. Roger fired it up and it seemed to work, but there were oil leaks.

By three the weather started to close again.

Vern reopened the motor, chasing down the leaks. They tried the motor again. No leaks, this time. *A miracle!* Vern thought. He towed the Caribou out to the runway with the bulldozer. The boys gathered up the mess tent and tied it under the *Kee Bird*'s wings, while Roger warmed up the Caribou. Everyone was scurrying like mad, packing tents, piling parts under the mess tent, breaking down the scaffolding.

To keep the *Kee Bird* from being carried away by the winds, Darryl and Vern chained the bulldozer to the nose-wheel landing gear. "You'd better drain the radiator," Darryl said. The Caribou was running, burning precious fuel. Everybody else was inside. Storm clouds threatened. Time was up.

Vern slashed the hose with his Buck knife and ran for the Caribou. He leapt onto the rear ramp and Roger hit the throttles. The Caribou roared and jerked across the frozen dirt as the ramp doors whined shut. Rick was lying in his sleeping bag in the middle of the plane, Cecelio at his side. The rest of the boys were clustered on the floor and on the red nylon bench behind the cockpit. The Caribou usually leaped off the runway in 800 feet. But after 1,000 feet the nose still hadn't come off the ground. "I can't get it up! I can't get it up!" Roger shouted. "It's not flying right!" He was pulling back on the yoke as hard as he could but the elevators were frozen—the plane wouldn't rise.

"Get everyone in the back of the plane!" yelled Darryl.

The boys stumbled to the back, just like the original crew of the *Kee Bird* in Bobbie Joe Cavnar's *Red Raider* forty-seven years before. The nose lifted and the Caribou took wing—right for the hills. Roger wrapped both arms around the yoke and tugged with all his might. Darryl joined him. The plane wouldn't rise above 200 feet. Roger banked left, turning the yoke with his arms. They were about to slam into the mountains. Darryl grabbed the trim wheel and tugged as hard as he could. There was a pop and the elevators came loose. They cleared the hills by fifty feet. "Goddamn, that was close!" said Roger.

Half an hour later they were cruising at 8,500 feet, just 1,000 feet over the glacier, sweeping along with a tail wind at nearly 170 miles per hour, pantomiming the cutting of steaks and grinning like men who'd just escaped death. It was seven below zero in the airplane and they could hardly hear themselves think, but they were alive and headed to Thule. Hot showers! Steaks! Whiskey! The sun was low on the horizon, the sky a pinkish hue over the glistening white of the Humboldt glacier. Man, the Arctic could be beautiful!

Then the right engine blew. It all happened in a second. Vern saw wisps of smoke through the window; Darryl and Roger noticed the oil pressure dropping and the oil temperature rising. "You noticed the oil pressure?" Roger said to Darryl.

"Yup," said Darryl. He thought the engine was leaking oil. He climbed out of his seat, heading back to see if he could put more oil into the engine. Suddenly the low oil pressure caution light flashed on. Then there was a shudder and the engine stopped dead.

The Caribou dropped toward the ice.

Darryl jumped back into his seat. "Prepare to jettison the whole load, if we have to," he yelled to Vern.

Vern herded everyone again into the back to keep the nose pointed up, running back and forth with his knife in the air, ready to start cutting cargo loose. Rick couldn't move. Cecelio prayed on his knees at Rick's side.

Darryl cut the fuel feeds to the stricken engine and feathered the propeller, reducing its drag on the plane. Roger hung on, just trying to keep the Caribou level as the plane's airspeed and altitude dropped. When the Caribou approached its minimum airspeed of ninety-one knots, Darryl went to maximum takeoff power on the left engine, the "bad" motor that Vern had just repaired (its spark plug tied on by wire). The descent slowed, but the engine couldn't operate long at maximum power.

"Vern," Rick managed to yell, waving him over. "Watch the left engine for smoke. Don't take your eyes off it." At the first sign they'd have to land on the ice with what power and control they had or risk crashing.

Abetted by a seventy-mile-an-hour tailwind, the Caribou held altitude, and Roger turned toward the Inuit village of Qaanaaq. Darryl wished he was flying the plane—at least that way he'd be in control. Still, the plane seemed to be holding altitude, and Rick needed to get to a hospital. Roger and Darryl looked at each other, nodded, and turned toward Thule instead of Qaanaaq. Eight miles from the Thule runway, they left land and flew out over water. A wave of turbulence hit the plane, tossing Vern completely into the air. Seventeen minutes later, Roger greased the single-engine landing on Thule's 10,000-foot runway, amidst a crowd of fire trucks and ambulances. The engines were covered in oil. The fire department carried Rick out, still in his sleeping bag, onto an ambulance gurney. Cecelio was sobbing.

A few hours later Cecelio had his first shower in forty days, Vern his first in thirty-three. The boys felt ecstatic, even Darryl. Christ, they were all alive and doctors were taking care of Rick. The ordeal was over. For now.

Within days, as August rolled into September, Darryl and the boys were back home, basking in the heat of late summer. But Rick Kriege wasn't so lucky. A few days before they fled the *Kee Bird*, Tom Hess's wife had called Irene. "Rick's sick," she'd said, "and they don't know what's wrong. He's hurt his back." Rick phoned Irene from the hospital in Thule. "I feel terrible," he told her, "and my back is hurting." But don't worry, he said, he'd be on a plane home with everyone else in a few days.

He wasn't. The boys flew home, but Rick, instead of being taken to a hospital in the United States, was flown to the closest hospital, at Pond Inlet on Canada's Baffin Island. Pond Inlet is a small Inuit community, and the doctor there recognized that it clearly wasn't the place for Rick, who was getting worse every day. Again he was put on a plane and this time taken to the Royal Victoria Hospital in Montreal. Irene left their daughter Hallie with her mother and flew to see him. When she got there, Rick was barely conscious. "He was real bad and hallucinating about being up there with the airplane," recalled Irene. "He was babbling, and finally I got him to recognize me and then he'd drift off."

Rick hadn't hurt his back, it seemed, nor did he have the flu. He had polycythemia vera, a rare but treatable disease in which the body churns out an overabundance of red blood cells, so many cells that the blood turns gloopy and thick. It was one of those mysteries of life. No one knows how or why people get it, but normally polycythemia vera isn't a big deal. Just bleeding off a pint of blood is one of the recommended treatments. Rick, however, had been sick a long time. No one really knew how long; he'd reported bloody stools well before he'd collapsed. He'd probably been in pain for weeks. Like water freezing in a pipe, his blood was bursting from small capillaries and veins in places like his esophagus even as it stopped flowing to his vital organs. His liver and bowel were almost bloodless, his spleen was nearly exploding.

Irene could do nothing but watch helplessly. "It was so frustrating to me," she remembered. "It was a fight to get the doctors and nurses to do anything. I talked to Darryl every day and I pleaded with him to help us move Rick to a hospital in New York. 'Rick will be fine,' he said. 'He's a strong young man.'"

Finally, surgeons removed part of his small intestine. Rick seemed better. He regained consciousness and told Irene about all the hard work and how much he had loved it and how close they'd come to getting the *Kee Bird* out.

Then something happened. Suddenly he didn't look good. Irene called the doctors and nurses. "'You gotta get out of here,' they said. "I didn't want to leave, I didn't want them to say there was nothing they could do, but that's what happened." On September 12, 1994, eight days after arriving in Montreal, Rick Kriege was dead.

TEN

—

FIRE AND ICE

Daugaard Jensen Land, Greenland; May 1995

It was the ninth of May, 1995, and it was hard to believe that nine months had already passed since the expedition had fallen apart and Rick had died. The departure lounge at McGuire Air Force Base in New Jersey had an air of neglect. Nicotine-stained plastic chairs lined the room. Anemic fluorescent lights flickered dimly overhead. Surly eighteen-year-olds wearing Air Force camouflage fatigues and spit-shined black boots staffed the check-in counter. Twice weekly an Air Mobility Command C-141 Starlifter flew from McGuire to Thule, and slowly the boys drifted in to catch the flight. Outside, fresh leaves hung in the balmy spring air and the grass around the base was deep, emerald green. It seemed odd that in a few hours we'd be in Greenland again, where there were neither spring showers nor May flowers. Greenland in May was as cold as Vermont in January.

Safe at home, my arms bare in the warm air, never far from my house or car when the clouds opened up, the pathos of those weeks at the *Kee Bird* had been hard to connect with. I could tell people about it, but they just didn't understand, not really. The intensity of focus, the forbidding weather, the desolation and utter remoteness of a place that made me feel one step away from death's door all the time was not just hard to convey to people who weren't there, it was hard to remember. No, I could remember it, but the sharp anxiety and discomfort were dulled. They seemed exaggerated, somehow, far enough removed that I couldn't wait to get back, couldn't wait to throw myself back into the maelstrom. But there was no question about it this time; as the boys trickled in, I noticed they were a little bit more sober, a little bit more reserved about what they were getting into.

They'd last gathered at Rick's memorial service—Darryl and Roger and Vern and Cecelio and Tom Hess and thirty or so others meeting with Irene in Darryl's hangar in Ramona. He'd pushed a Corsair to the back and his rare Grumman F7 Tigercat outside, so there was plenty of room for everyone. It was a casual service. There was a table with photos of Rick working on the *Kee Bird* before he got too dirty and beaten-looking, and a photo of Rick standing by his Harley. Darryl walked in front of everyone and started to read a letter I'd written to him about how I'd recently fixed my lawn mower—and how it was Rick who had taught me to do it. He got about halfway through before he broke down sobbing; he just couldn't go on, and everyone stood there awkwardly until Tim Wright stepped in with his own words of appreciation.

Today, here at McGuire, Darryl looked smaller, older somehow, carrying a battered plastic Samsonite briefcase in one hand and rolls of stainless-steel cable—controls for the *Kee Bird*'s aileron trim tabs—in the other. But he still had that Cheshire cat smile and those disarming blue eyes. Rick wasn't the only person missing from the original group. With nothing big to carry in or out of the *Kee Bird* site, Darryl had chartered a de Havilland Twin Otter on skis, so Roger wasn't needed to fly the Caribou. Tom Hess had finally conceded the obvious: he was plenty happy in good old Rancho Santa Fe, thank you very much. And, anyway, why freeze your ass off and risk dying when he'd have plenty of chances to play in the bomber when it got home?

The Air Force wasn't exactly looking forward to Darryl's return. Indeed, Air Force Capt. Max Dugan, the head of Thule's airfield, had done everything he could to put Darryl out of business. Darryl made his blood boil. The Air Force did everything by the book. Darryl did nothing by the book, and Dugan viewed him as a cancer on the base. One fiery crash on Dugan's watch and his Air Force days would be numbered. After a little digging, Dugan discovered that Darryl was still using the original permits—issued not to Darryl Greenamyer but to Gary Larkins and his Institute of Aeronautical Archaeological Research. And suddenly in April, just weeks before round three of the *Kee Bird* saga was to start, the Air Force was saying Darryl's permits weren't in order and he didn't have a U.S. government sponsor. Without that he couldn't use Air Force planes to get to Thule and couldn't use it as a base of operations. Not only that, but Darryl couldn't even go and get his Caribou out of Thule. "How can they do that?" stormed Darryl. "I need to be figuring out the expedition and instead all I'm doing is paperwork and bullshit red tape!" But after all his years flying for Lockheed and trading planes with the Smithsonian and the Air Force, Darryl had a few friends around in high places. Finally, once again, the Smithsonian National Air and Space Museum stepped in and Darryl got his permits with days to spare.

After the eight-week ordeal last July and August he figured he needed to do two things differently. He needed a beefed-up crew: more mechanics skilled in radial engines (round, air-cooled piston engines in which the pistons are arrayed in a circle around the crankshaft, creating a balanced engine easily cooled by air hitting the cylinder heads); and a real flight engineer to help him get the bomber off the ground; and someone he could depend on in the copilot's seat. And he couldn't count on enough fair weather in the summer to make the valley dry enough to give him the 3,000 feet of smooth runway he wanted for liftoff. The valley had been so cut with little rivers and ditches last August from the incessant rain that even if they'd finished the *Kee Bird* then, he might never have been able to take off. He and Rick had started talking about it before Rick collapsed. The thing to do was to come back just before the snow started to melt. If Darryl could time it right, the Arctic spring would be hurtling along, the sun would be up longer and the temperatures rising every day, but the lake would still be frozen solid and the valley filled with snow. He could plow a rock-hard runway over a mile long. The weather might be cold as hell, sure, but anything was better than that rain.

Now here we were, heading across the McGuire flight line to the cavernous Starlifter just as the May flowers were blasting out. Vernon Rich and Cecelio Grande and even Bob Vanderveen were back, along with Mike Rossiter and his *Nova* crew and photographer Tim Wright and me, the two of us now on assignment for *Smithsonian* magazine. But taking their places in rows in the cavernous, exposed belly of the Starlifter was an unusual collection of people perfectly suited to the task.

"I'm from right down yonder by the Mexican border," said John Cater, in a high-pitched south Texas accent as he slid into his seat and stowed his carry-on luggage—a battered gray toolbox. He was dressed in a short-sleeved powder-blue cotton jumpsuit and slip-on leather work boots. He had a scraggly gray beard and a deeply lined, forty-nine-year-old face. When he opened his mouth you saw a lot of spaces where teeth used to be. Cater's specialty was working on radial piston engines in less than ideal circumstances. He'd started in Vietnam in the Navy in 1964, and moved on to places like Detroit and Dayton. "We'd deice the planes with a rubber hose 'bout that long," he said, holding his arms wide, as the Starlifter took wing for Greenland. He then spent the last fifteen years as a "freelancer," working for everyone from the Nicaraguan contras to smugglers moving the opium of the late twentieth century—televisions—into Mexico. "Oh yeah!" he yelped, of the smuggling. "That was fun! You got armed guards around you and planes circling overhead and you start thinking about Mexican jail and you'd be surprised how quick you can work on an airplane!" He wrenched old twin-engine DC-3s and four-engine Constellations, and the crews were paid a buck a pound—8,000 pounds in a DC-3 and 24,000 pounds in a Connie. "We'd file a flight plan and as soon as we crossed the border we'd shut off the lights and the radios and just head south." Those days were history, John claimed—he now had a contract with the state of Texas to maintain a few miles of interstate highway median— and he'd never heard of Darryl Greenamyer until the telephone rang recently. "I don't know how people hear about me. I sure don't advertise," he said, cracking a knowing smile. "I was heading down the highway, doing about seventy, when my car phone rang. It was Ascher Ward."

Matt Jackson had met Darryl in 1965, when he was seven years old. His father raced Formula One airplanes at Reno, and back then Darryl had been at the top of his game, in the faster unlimited division. "Darryl was my hero," he said, "and I've always vowed to whip his ass someday. Could be this year." Matt had thick brown hair, a boyish face, and a wild laugh. He was boisterous and loud. He owned an aviation shop at the Van Nuys airport, and he was an aggressive racer who consistently finished among the top ten in the Reno unlimited class. He'd built and raced some of the fastest planes at Reno, and, like Darryl, he was building a custom-designed race plane. His dream was to go head-to-head with Darryl.

Al and Cathy Hanson, too, were old friends of Darryl's. Al was fifty-four, a tall, red-faced building contractor from Mojave, California, whose personal collection of airplanes included an F-104 Star-fighter, a Hawker Hunter, an F-86 Saber, and a Russian MiG-21, all high-performance jet fighters. Al and Cathy, who was planning to stay at Thule when we went up to the *Kee Bird*, had met Darryl in 1969, when there had been some air races in Mojave and they'd volunteered on his Bearcat. The Hansons had been at Darryl's side for years. "That was spectacular," Al said of Darryl's speed record in 1977. "I've never seen anything like it. It was totally still and wind-less and you just saw him coming over the sagebrush and suddenly when he went by it just seemed to suppress all sound. I thought it would be noisy. But it streaked past totally silent and it was almost out of sight when *BOOM!* this incredible noise hit me and all you could see was the afterburner."

In Al and Matt, Darryl had two loyal friends who were as good at fixing airplanes as they were at flying them, and he could trust either one of them up there with him in the cockpit of the *Kee Bird*.

Of all the new gang, Thad Dulin was the most ambivalent. You'd think the first people to cheer the return of the *Kee Bird* would be the Confederate Air Force. But the CAF's B-29 was the only one on earth still flying—most of the time, that is—and its uniqueness and popularity at air shows, as well as the occasional Hollywood role, accounted for a good deal of the CAF's income and notoriety. When you looked at a flying B-29 you thought of the CAF. It was hard to imagine your average small air show shelling out the big bucks for two B-29s. The *Kee Bird* would be a competitor, and around the hangars at Midland the colonels weren't exactly rushing forward to help. In their eyes Thad was a traitor. Not only that, but Thad was no Darryl Greenamyer or Vernon Rich or Gary Larkins. He was quiet and easygoing and a bit overweight. "Daring" wasn't a word he ordinarily used to describe himself. He had a comfortable house and a comfortable life and he had no particular urge to jeopardize it. "I got a yellow streak a mile wide," he once said to me.

But then again, Thad Dulin knew a once-in-a-lifetime opportunity when he saw it. He loved four-engine bombers, especially the B-29, more than any other airplane. He had photos and drawings of the things all over his house. Like a lot of warbird fanatics, he sometimes wondered if he'd been born in the wrong time. Flying the *Kee Bird* off the snow would be awesome and, sour grapes aplenty though there'd be, he'd be legend when he got back home after the flight. And though he was entirely happy ensconced in his living room easy chair, Thad had been to some pretty weird places thanks to the oil industry. He was a second-generation oilman, and had lived in Libya as a kid. As an adult his job had taken him to Moldova, South America, and even Siberia. He didn't much like the odd nooks and crannies of the world, but he wasn't afraid of them. He probably wouldn't have admitted it, but deep inside he was just as romantic and restless as the rest of them. When Tom Hess called him it really wasn't such a hard choice. Still, there was no question about it—as he stepped off the Starlifter into a world of frozen whiteness at Thule, it was twenty-five degrees and he was wondering if he ought not to have just stayed put in Midland.

That was Monday. Within hours, as the Starlifter was unloaded at Thule, it became clear that the crate with the tents and sleeping bags and insulated foam pads hadn't made it onto the plane. The next flight wouldn't arrive until Friday. But Matt, John, and Thad got right to work on the Caribou, sitting forlornly on a frozen patch of snow-encrusted concrete, changing the blown engine.

By Wednesday night, Darryl was getting antsy. Nine months ago he'd been worried about it getting too cold to work; now he was worried about it getting too warm and the lake and snow at the site melting. It was near midnight and we gathered in the spartan quarters of our barracks at the air base. The heat was cranking in our "living room," which, with its utilitarian sofas and chairs, looked like the lounge in a college dorm. Darryl was shirtless, leaning back on a sofa. Thad had his B-29 flight manuals spread across his knees.

"Is it cost effective to go in? Is there something we can do?" Darryl asked rhetorically, clearly annoyed by the delay. "I think there is and we should go in Friday morning," he continued. The boys looked doubtful. They'd almost died last August—and it had only been August. This time the temperature might be zero at the *Kee Bird*. And think about those winds! Vern shifted in his seat. Here we go again, he thought. But to Darryl, time was the enemy. There really wasn't too much left to do on the *Kee Bird*: wire the aileron trim controls; wire the prop controls; replace an oil cooler on engine number two; install the oil-cooling-duct flaps; examine and possibly replace a lot of the fuel and oil lines that had been so leaky last year. A couple of good days was all they needed. But with every passing day, the weather might warm. And who knew when those damn storms might rip through, halting everything for days at a time? If the supplies came in Friday afternoon, they still might not be able to leave until Saturday. The Air Force wouldn't let them fly on Sunday, so if the weather was bad on Saturday, that meant Monday at the earliest. It was already the second week in May. If they dicked around and just two weeks went by, it would be June. And then it might be too rainy and wet to take off again for months, maybe years. No, if Darryl had learned anything about the Arctic and the Air Force, it was that both would do everything in their power to get in his way. And once you got everything out to the site, it was like being up in the rarified air and killer winds near the top of Everest. You only had so long before men and equipment started to break. Speed was his friend; it always had been.

"I'm not suggesting that we go in without adequate bags, but we need to get everything in as fast and furious as we can. I want to get in and out of there. Al has his sleeping bag and I've got two shitty ones that together can make one good one. Tim has a tent that we can squeeze four in, I've got a tent for two, and there's the mess tent that we left under the wing. I'm sure we can scrounge some mats from somewhere. We can get the batteries in, the camp set up, and get the heater and bulldozer going. If five of us go in tomorrow, the next flight can come in Tuesday with the rest of the equipment. I think it's worthwhile to go."

"What if the flight can't make it out of here on Tuesday?" Matt asked.

"We'll survive."

That was Darryl's attitude. To prepare for temperatures far colder than last year's, Darryl had bought insulated Carhartt coveralls for his crew, a propane heater, and two kerosene heaters. And a new tent: a floorless, green canvas model that was nearly as old as the plane he was trying to salvage. These days, you can hardly turn around without stumbling on an L.L. Bean or REI adventure outfit-

ter, or an *Outside* or *National Geographic Adventure* magazine hawk-
ing the latest technical tent or extreme sleeping bag or climbing
boot. Hardly anybody even rides their bike without a thousand
bucks' worth of helmets and special shoes and shorts and tight
Technicolor jerseys. But that's all part of a certain high-end, afflu-
ent fantasy world. Darryl, John Cater, Matt Jackson, even Gary
Larkins—they were from a different world. Darryl had never read
Outside magazine in his life and he sure as hell wasn't going to pay
$500 for some flaming yellow Gore-Tex jacket. People had been
merrily riding their bikes and successfully returning from the Arctic
long before Gore-Tex and titanium. So now his newest old canvas
tent and some of the sleeping bags were stuck in New Jersey. Big
deal; Darryl would survive.

The matter decided, Darryl was just going to bed when Niels
Jensen, the Danish fireman who'd flown the cylinder in back in August, trooped in with a six-pack of Carlsberg. He was a hero. It had
been his bold, selfless flight that had allowed the Caribou to fly out
in August. Yeah, it was risky, he admitted, recalling the tale, "but I'd
do it again in a second. It was great, a once-in-a-lifetime thing!" he
said, raising his beer in a toast, his eyes sparkling.

"You got it!" John Cater shouted, his gray beard jiggling up and
down. "Why do you think I'm here?"

Early the next morning Al Hanson, Matt Jackson, Darryl, Tim
Wright, and Bob Vanderveen stuffed their ad hoc assortment of
camping gear, shovels, a few hoses, a couple of oil coolers and airplane batteries, a barrel of fuel, and a light collection of wrenches
and ratchets and parts into the back of the chartered Twin Otter
and took off for the *Kee Bird*. Dressed in insulated brown canvas
coveralls, they looked like overstuffed teddy bears. The plane was
small—it carried only 2,500 pounds—but compared to the Caribou,
the Otter was like taking the shuttle between New York and Washington. Powered by reliable twin turboprops, it had radar, deicers,

plenty of heat, wide skis attached to the landing gear, and two pilots who made their living flying in the Arctic. Nobody had seen the *Kee Bird* in nine months and, as Darryl gazed at the frozen wasteland of ice and snow and rock a few thousand feet below, he hoped to God it was still as they'd left it, and that they'd be able to get the heater and the bulldozer working.

Two hours later, the Otter swept into the valley. It was stark white, as white and featureless as a bedsheet. In the summer, with the bomber sitting by the lake, there was a sense of scale to the site. Now Darryl couldn't see the lake at all, but there was the *Kee Bird*, all right, surrounded by snow and gleaming silver just as it had been during every one of the forty-eight winters since Vern Arnett had set her down in 1947.

The Otter pilot knew what he was doing. He came in low, dragged the skis across the snow, and swept skyward again. The snow seemed stable and relatively smooth. He flew around again, landed softly, and taxied up to the plane. No one screamed in triumph this time. They piled out onto crusty snow two feet deep and stood there for a moment, no one saying a thing. There wasn't a sound or a piece of lichen or a stick or even a gnat, nothing but dry, freezing air and whiteness in all directions. Matt was overwhelmed. *Oh my God!* he thought. *What am I doing here?* Darryl walked around the *Kee Bird*, and Matt and the boys followed him, their boots crunching and squeaking in the dry snow. If anyone was a balls-out flyer like Darryl it was Matt. He'd fly anything, and screaming around a pylon a few feet over the desert floor at 450 miles per hour at Reno didn't bother him. But walking around the *Kee Bird* encircled by five-foot-high drifts of snow that reached the engine nacelles, and seeing the lonely valley that was the runway, almost sent him into a panic. His mind whirled. *This is crazy,* he thought. Once they charged down the snow for takeoff there would be no room to abort. *Either we're going to launch or we're going to be rolled up in a ball.*

Al had his doubts, too. He climbed up inside the airplane, sat in the pilot's seat, took in the old controls and the dangling insulation, and imagined the takeoff. *This could bite you,* he thought.

But then, as with Vern before them, there was no time for second thoughts. They were here. The *Kee Bird* had survived the winter unscathed—the fabric-covered flight controls looked perfect. Matt and Al plunged in. It was cold, but the sky was a spectacular deep blue. The bulldozer, the Herman-Nelson heater, the mess tent and generator were all covered with snow. They dug the heater out and attached it to a battery, and, miraculously, it fired up. They tunneled to the bulldozer, ran a hose from the heater to the dozer, and thawed it out. Darryl and Al replaced the radiator hose Vern had slashed, filled it with antifreeze, and got it started. The clutch was broken—it wouldn't back up. They took the casing off, plunged in and fixed it. Then Al started pushing snow from around the plane. Matt took the engine cowlings off and started checking oil and fuel hoses and the oil coolers. Two were cracked. Bob dragged the mess tent out and set it up. With the sun beating on their backs and no wind, as soon as they began working, it wasn't too bad.

Within four days, by Tuesday, everyone but Thad, Vern, and the *Nova* crew was in, including me and most of the gear. Vern was calm, organized, discreet, a master "appropriator," as the boys called the rounding up of empty fuel barrels, spools of wire, and God knows what from the workshops and hangars of the base. Darryl wanted Vern to stay behind to manage the movement of people and equipment on the Otter flights from Thule. Thad and the *Nova* crew would come in last. The site had its old familiar look: cowl flaps lay on the ground, black oil and grease puddled on the white snow, boxes of tools and hoses and fuel barrels littered the revetments of snow. Cathy Hanson had sent in mounds of fresh food that she'd cooked in Thule, and we were lunching on steaming beef stew in the mess tent. The air temperature was twenty-two degrees. The floor was hard-packed snow. About half the flimsy lawn chairs had survived. The wind was picking up, a haze sliding over the big blue sky visible through the tent's rips and tears. Darryl was talking about the flight—it was about all he could talk about. "Once I get going and get some speed up," he said, creaking in his chair, a floppy paper plate on his lap, "by the time I leave the lake and hit the snow I ought to have some rudder control."

A gust slapped the tent and the poles, and guy ropes groaned. Matt shivered. "On a hard surface this plane needs three thousand feet," he said, pulling his hat down over his ears, "and we've got maybe five thousand feet of snow. We'll need every fucking inch. But at least this thing will be light!"

By the end of lunch the sun was gone and the winds were howling as if someone had aimed a giant fan at the site. Snow flew sideways, stinging our faces like needles. An hour later there was a total whiteout—you couldn't see a thing, the winds screaming at nearly seventy miles an hour. To be outside was suicidal. A few false steps and you might never find your way to shelter, and the winds and extreme windchill could freeze you to the bone in minutes. There was nothing to do but huddle in our sleeping bags and wait. I shared a tent with Matt and Tim. Hour after hour the winds howled, the tent shaking as violently as if King Kong were trying to rip it apart. Though the doors were tightly zippered and shut with Velcro, fine grains of snow jetted into the tent. "This is the first time in my life I'm not sure I'm coming back from something," said Matt, his face poking out of his bag. "I hate camping. Either we're going to die of exposure or we're going to die of something else. Maybe I'll just kill Darryl first!" He gave a wild, high-pitched laugh.

I crawled out of my sleeping bag and, kneeling over it, peed in a plastic water jar.

But Darryl was having his own problems. In a chaos of nylon and cracking aluminum, his tent collapsed. Dragging his sleeping bag through the blinding snow, he found the *Kee Bird* and crawled up inside. *How long would this last?* he wondered, not for the first time sheltered in a quivering airplane. Hours? Days? *This is the worst hellhole on earth!* he thought. *We've got to get out of here.*

Twelve hours later the wind fell to twenty miles an hour. Two tents were destroyed. The mess tent had collapsed once more, a heavy green pile of torn canvas cut with long tears. Bob propped it up again, suturing the worst rips with dental floss, wire, and string. Inside, snow covered everything, mounding over the food and tables as if they'd been sprayed with a snowblower.

"Why?" Darryl pleaded, surveying the snowy havoc. It was a big, pregnant why. Why was he there? Why was he putting himself through so much?

"Where's the lemonade?" asked Matt, stomping his feet. The air was so dry my leather watch strap had snapped. Throats were parched, lips were cracking.

"I don't know," Bob answered, shuffling through the wreckage.

"Well, where was it?" Matt said. "We've got to get those props working and go for broke," he said to Darryl, "just blast on out of here. We've got to get out!"

Wednesday dawned as lovely as an April morning in Aspen. Twenty degrees, not a breath of wind, a blue sky and a sun powerful enough to make you want to sit back and catch a few rays. Work surged ahead. Darryl and John Cater wired the props. Matt double-checked the landing-gear motors. Cecelio tightened fuel and oil hoses. At dinner, talk turned to blasting off again.

"We'll just pull out and turn with macho power and I'll just make a big sweeping turn right here and head out to the lake," Darryl said.

"If we lose an engine we're going to run right into that mountain," Matt said.

"No, I don't intend to die," Darryl said. "I think we can go with one engine out. If an engine fails we may have to crank up the gear by hand, though. But I do want to get this son of a bitch out of here."

"Hey, wake up, it's a beautiful day," Darryl said, shaking our tent the next morning. I crawled out. "I lied," Darryl said, grinning. It was gray and overcast, miserable-looking. But Thursday *was* a beautiful day. Not sunny, but warm and totally still, the icicles on the wings melting in steady drips. "Tomorrow is Friday, no?" said Cecelio, taking me by the arm.

"Yes," I said.

"Saturday it will fly."

Back in August the mantra had been "two more weeks." No matter how many weeks passed, the *Kee Bird* was always two weeks way from takeoff. Now it was two days. Two days more. If the weather held. But to look at the *Kee Bird* standing in the vast whiteness, the very idea of that chunk of aluminum flying seemed absurd. We hadn't even started an engine yet. Thick bundles of wires remained exposed in the cockpit and the flight engineer's station. That afternoon, however, there were signs of life, a slow awakening at last. When Darryl plugged the batteries into the cockpit, the instrument lights flickered on. The flaps extended and retreated with a grinding whirr. Flipping the landing-gear toggle sent a sharp bump and click through the system. I imagined Dr. Frankenstein and his quest to bring his creation back from the dead. Flying the *Kee Bird* was an act of creation, a work of mechanical and technological art. Darryl and Matt and Vern and John and Al and Cecelio weren't just replacing parts, they were using their heads and hands and tools to re-create a dead machine that would defy gravity and take wing. It was a quest as old as man, as elemental an urge as drawing on a cave wall. And suddenly, two days seemed as reasonable as any other guess.

By Friday, the excitement was palpable. "Okay, what are we going to do today?" asked Darryl over breakfast. It was the first time I'd ever heard him say that, the first time that the list of what had yet to be done was short enough in his mind to focus on. The sun was shining again. The Otter brought in the *Nova* team and Thad Dulin. Darryl hopped on the bulldozer and started plowing snow away from the front of the bomber. Thad climbed into the flight engineer's seat. *Am I crazy?* he thought, looking at the bank of gauges and toggle switches and levers in quadruplicate. *Do I need to have my head examined?* There was no comparison between *Kee Bird* and the CAF's *Fifi*. *Fifi* had all her armor plating and turrets removed. *Fifi* was for playing in. This was the goddamn real thing. But then, like everyone else before him, he shook off his doubt. The only way home was in the *Kee Bird*, he told himself. Then he started fastening tiny strips of red and green and yellow tape to the gauges. When things got going, he wanted to be able to capture the plane's performance at a glance.

Late that afternoon, after blowing hot air from the Herman-Nelson onto engine number one for two hours, John, Cecelio, and Al started oiling Ida. "She's got all the things she needs to fly," said Al. "I'm not too worried about life and limb. These are awfully powerful bastards and they ought to pull us right off. We'll have a pretty good idea how she'll feel by the time we taxi out of here. If something happens, if there's a fire or something, we'll just put down on the next lake."

Darryl climbed into the cockpit. "Run number one for five seconds," Matt yelled, "and then you can hammer it." Ida whined and stopped. "Again," Matt yelled.

John Cater and Matt pushed the prop slowly around, checking for liquid lock. A piston engine worked by igniting a carefully measured mixture of compressed fuel and air in the cylinder, driving a piston and crankshaft. An eighteen-cylinder radial engine leaked oil constantly, but oil leaking *into* a cylinder can be catastrophic, because you can't compress a liquid; when a rapidly compressing cylinder hits oil, something has to go, and usually it's the cylinder. So Cater and Matt had to push the prop through one slow revolution; if no oil was in a cylinder, the prop would turn; if there was oil in a cylinder it would lock. And indeed, the prop locked. John climbed the rickety ladder and fiddled, removing the spark plug from each of the eighteen cylinders. When he found the oil-filled cylinder, black, viscous oil poured from the spark-plug hole onto his hands and arms. "Black blood!" he shouted, chuckling insanely. The process took hours.

Again Darryl hit the starter. The prop spun slowly and deliberately. Cough. Cough. Thick black smoke exploded from the exhaust, like a half-drowned man coughing water as he came back to life. After ten minutes of belching and spitting it stopped. John ran up the ladder, fiddled around, and jumped down. Again Darryl hit the starter. Again the massive coughs of black smoke and then the engine caught. With a thunderous roar the prop raced around and around, a few big gobs of black goo shooting from the exhaust, the engine running as smooth as a marching band in a parade.

No one whooped or danced, as they had a year ago. "If we get one, we get all," said Cecelio.

Suddenly oil started pouring from the engine, a viscous black pool on the white snow. "Shut it off! Shut it off!" screamed Matt. "She's puking her guts out!"

An oil line was blown.

"Goddammit," he shouted, "we sure are asking a lot!"

Two hours later, after Matt and John replaced the line, they started the engine up again. It was now nearly midnight and they had been tinkering in the cold for hours. The sun was low, a golden ball in an opalescent sky over a sea of white nothingness. But the engine thrummed steadily, the oil and fuel lines holding. Inside the *Kee Bird*, the plane shook and quivered, humming with life. Thad's flight-engineer panel glowed with dozens of red and orange lights. The oil pressure was climbing to normal. "She's been waiting to fly for forty-eight years," said Thad quietly.

"We're going to have to do that to every one of 'em, I bet," Matt said wearily, wiping the oil off his hands and face before crawling into his sleeping bag.

It was fifteen degrees the next morning, with a light breeze that cut like steel. John Cater walked slowly into the mess tent for breakfast. "I feel stiff all over," he announced. Today wasn't going to be the day. The three other engines had yet to be started. And tomorrow

"You help build the B-29." A B-29 Superfortress and its parts. (U.S. Government Printing.)

The veteran B-29 Superfortress beside the brash XB-36 Peacemaker superbomber. (Photograph by U.S. Army Air Forces.)

Eighth Air Force B-17 Fortresses lined up in preparation for an air raid on Berlin. (Photograph by U.S. Army Air Forces.)

Workers install fixtures and assemblies in the tail fuselage of a B-17 Fortress bomber at the Douglas Aircraft Company, Long Beach, California. (Photograph by Alfred T. Palmer.)

B-25 Mitchells approaching a rail target in northern Italy. (Photograph by Dan A. Sheetinger.)

Waves of B-24 Liberators of the 15th AAF amid bursting flak over the Concordia Vega oil refinery, Ploesti, Romania, May 31, 1944. (Official U.S. Air Force photograph.)

A North American P-51 Mustang nicknamed *My Girl* takes off from Iwo Jima, in the Bonin Islands. (Official U.S. Air Force photograph.)

Aerial view of three U.S. Navy SBD Dauntless dive bombers in flight. (Official U.S. Navy photograph.)

An aviation ordnance mate prepares to install a .30-caliber machine gun in a Navy PBY Catalina in Corpus Christi, Texas. (Photograph by Howard R. Hollem.)

Aerial view of four U.S. Navy F4U Corsairs in flight over the South Pacific. (Official U.S. Navy photograph.)

A F6F Hellcat fighting plane aboard an aircraft carrier stands ready for the takeoff signal. (Official U.S. Navy photograph.)

A cadet boards an AT-6 Texan at the Naval Air Base, Corpus Christi, Texas. (Photograph by Howard R. Hollem.)

Aerial view of 12th Air Force P-47 Thunderbolts flying in formation over the Apennines in northern Italy. (Photograph by Arthur F. Schramm.)

An A-20 Havoc bomber being serviced at Langley Field, Virginia. (Photograph by Alfred T. Palmer.)

Formation of B-29 Superfortresses releasing incendiary bombs over Japan in June 1945. (Acme photo.)

was Sunday; Thule was closed. No matter. "I want to get out of here," Darryl said, warming his hands over the single little propane heater (the two kerosene heaters weren't working). "If we're ready tomorrow, we're going." If there was any rule he was eager to break, it was that one.

"You watch," Matt said, a steaming mug of tea in his soiled hands. "We'll either go off really early or really late. If there's a good wind we'll be blasting off in no time. If there's no wind we're going to take every goddamned inch of runway there is. When we're blasting off toward the end at one hundred knots, that'll get your adrenaline going, eh? Hoo, wah!"

"It'll be exciting," agreed Darryl with a grin, his eyes twinkling. "I'm ready." Then he turned serious. "It's tough what they did during the war," he said. Gary Larkins was always talking about World War II, but Darryl seldom mentioned it. "We're taking off in an old plane on snow, sure, but they were taking off at a hundred and forty thousand pounds gross weight and they lost a plane for every three they launched." We fell silent. What Darryl was about to do was crazy, but guys had faced death every time they took off during the war. They never knew if they'd return. Darryl was flying the *Kee Bird* because he wanted to. Back then they didn't have a choice. That sobered everyone up in a flash. "Let's get to work," Darryl said, breaking the silence and heading out to the bomber.

After an hour and a half of heat, engine number four, Polly, flew to life as effortlessly as Ida had been difficult. She cranked right up. Nothing spewed from the exhaust system, no oil or fuel poured from the lines. Number three, Pat, was cranky and developed an oil lock. But by evening all four engines, Ida, Norma, Pat, and Polly, were thumping, Thad's gauges registering satisfactory cylinder-head temperatures and oil pressures. He pushed the throttles forward and the *Kee Bird* throbbed, the props blowing great white billows of snow behind the plane.

———

"Hey! Wake up! Today's the day." I opened my eyes and heard the sound of Darryl crunching across the snow. It was Sunday and the *Kee Bird* and Darryl were ready. Today was the Wright Brothers all over again. Darryl had never before flown a B-29. He still didn't quite know what it weighed, how many feet it would take to reach takeoff speed, how much power his newly installed engines would produce, whether all the new hoses would hold. All four engines had run, and run well—that alone seemed a miracle to me—but save for its fifty-foot journey by bulldozer from the lake, it hadn't moved since Vern Arnett had greased that landing in February 1947. One way or another Darryl Greenamyer was about to make history.

A strange sense of calm pervaded the camp. We moved slowly, deliberately, the waiting, two more weeks, two more days, finally over. It was a gorgeous day. The sun was bright and warm, the sky blue, a soft breeze blew up the valley. In the months and years to come, people would often criticize Darryl for being in a rush. It was a beautiful day. Why not wait a couple more and go over the plane in exacting detail? But if Darryl had learned anything, it was that the weather changed instantly. You had to seize the day. In an hour, in a day, the wind and snow might howl and hold us prisoner for weeks. We could all die in a blizzard tomorrow.

The plane was finished. The weather was good. It was time to fly.

The boys heated Ida and Norma, dragged the heater to Pat and Polly, and started firing up the first two. There was another liquid lock on Norma. John Cater fixed it. Cecelio, perched atop a ladder, topped off the oil in every engine. Darryl and Al swung into the cockpit. Darryl was in his seat, his intercom and radio headset on his head, sunglasses over his eyes, a small face behind a dirty window. By two, Ida, Norma, and Polly were throbbing, the bomber a real, living airplane at last. We scurried to pull the last drums of fuel and batteries and odds and ends away from the plane. The APU came on to start the last engine, Pat.

"Clear!" shouted Darryl.

Bob's head was poking out of the hatch in the rear of the plane.

As soon as Pat fired up, he was to shut off the APU, then watch for fires. Darryl and Al were in the cockpit. Thad was at the flight engineer's station. Darryl planned to taxi the plane out to the far end of the lake, get a feel for the plane, run up the engines a bit, then shut everything down for one last check and the final fueling. He still wanted to adjust the idle mixtures. Nothing that was too big a deal. Then Matt would get in for takeoff, perched between Thad and the cockpit to help pilot or engineer.

At two P.M. Pat kicked to life.

Ten minutes later Darryl throttled up. Suddenly, he noticed a wrench lying on the floor. He unhooked his seat belt, tucked the wrench away, and slammed his belt shut again. The plane screamed, shaking and quivering on the snow. The power and noise seemed enormous, sublimely frightening and exhilarating at the same time. Darryl was surprised at how much power he was giving the plane without it moving. Near maximum power the *Kee Bird* jerked out of its snowbound hole, paused, turned to the right and picked up speed. *Lovely!* thought Al.

"Go, Darryl, go!" screamed Matt, leaping up and down, as the *Kee Bird* bounded across the snow, long white rooster tails flying twenty-five feet behind the plane. "Forty-eight years, guys!"

Darryl had plowed a bit of runway, but first he had to get to it, and the snow was rough, windblown, and crusty. The rudder pedals controlled the rudder, but that was useless until the plane reached sixty-five miles an hour. Using the engines, his hands on the throttles, he struggled to control the plane. It was bouncing and shaking violently. A half-century of dust and dirt came loose, filling the cockpit with a gritty haze. In the cramped tail compartment, Bob didn't even have a seat belt. He was being thrown wildly back and forth and up and down. As the *Kee Bird* headed out on the lake, Darryl throttled up. He wanted to feel the speed, to feel the plane push against the air, to feel the lift. That was what flying was all about. He was cranking now and as he pulled back the yoke he could feel the *Kee Bird* lift. He got the nose off the ground. And the rudder was coming on—he was getting aerodynamic control. The plane was light. It wanted to fly! Al, too, could feel the nose coming up. But Darryl was speeding across the lake. The main wheels hit chunks of ice every twenty feet or so, violently bouncing the *Kee Bird*. The chunks jerked the *Kee Bird* left and right. "Jesus Christ, Darryl!" yelled Al. It was a wild ride. Just as Darryl turned the plane, Pat quit. At the far end of the lake the *Kee Bird* paused. Thad restarted the engine.

Back in the tail, Bob was choking in a thick cloud of dust and dirt kicked loose by the jarring airplane. Fighting the jerking, he crawled forward into the next compartment to retrieve a dust mask. He put it on, turned around and saw orange. The tail compartment was an inferno. "Fire! Fire! Fire!" he yelled through the intercom. He inhaled a breath of thick, yellow smoke, and dropped through the bomb bay onto the snow, rolling back and forth like he'd been told a thousand times as a kid.

An engine! thought Darryl. He yanked the throttles to idle. "Shut 'em down!" he yelled to Thad. He looked out the window. No smoke. The engines sure weren't on fire. "Where's the fire? Where's the fire?" he shouted.

Al popped his seat belt and shot down through the hatch onto the ground to look. There wasn't a sign of fire or smoke. Thad undid his belt and saw smoke coming toward them through the plane, curling around the front turret. Darryl reached down and yanked his seat belt clip. Nothing. It was jammed. He pulled and pulled, and couldn't get it released. He grabbed the wrench he'd seen on the floor and tried to pry his belt off. Thad was about to jump down the hatch.

"Thad!" yelled Darryl. "Help me! I'm stuck."

Thick gray-green smoke poured around the turret into the cockpit. It was a choking, noxious mixture of burning plastic and magnesium and aluminum. Thad reached into the cockpit and yanked hard on Darryl's belt. It wouldn't give. By then there was so much smoke Thad couldn't see the belt. Darryl handed him the wrench. He bent down with his head in Darryl's crotch and pried as hard as he could. The seatbelt broke free. Smoke was everywhere. Thad was big and round and there was no ladder. As he struggled through the hole, Darryl started gagging on the smoke. Finally Thad dropped through the hatch and Darryl vaulted after him.

Thirty seconds had passed. Smoke was pouring from the open cockpit windows. Big orange flames exploded from the tail. Darryl ripped off his jacket and beat the flames. He had a small fire extinguisher; it squirted the flames for fifteen seconds before giving out. I rushed across the snow with a second extinguisher. The flames were big and hot, almost white, a roiling ball roaring out of the hatch. Darryl sprayed the fire with the extinguisher but it was too hot now. The extinguisher did nothing but push the flames around. There was a loud CRACK! Then a terrible crunching and tearing sound. The Kee Bird's tail fell off. The Kee Bird was in two pieces. There were no more fire extinguishers. The magnesium welds and aluminum skin were burning white-hot, a roaring bonfire of metal and plastic.

The bomber was ruined.

Darryl was as pale as the snow around him. Suddenly he looked small. Old. The Nova camera whirred. Tim snapped photos. I furiously jotted notes. For so long we journalists and filmmakers had been a part of the team; now, suddenly, we had our own work to do. "I'm pissed off!" said Darryl quietly. "It would have flown! It would have! It would have done it! I had elevator control. I got the nose up. It would have done it!" He paced back and forth, his hands in his pockets. Filled with fuel, the Kee Bird was a bomb waiting to blow. Darryl and the boys stepped fifty feet back. But like family members around a hospital bed, nobody wanted to leave the body. Total silence, but for the sounds of fire, of metal cracking and glass popping. A long, slow breath, the sound of sucking air, came from the fire. Bob stood by himself. Al and Matt stood next to each other. The flames crackled, viscous smoke streaming from the cockpit windows. Darryl squatted in the snow, alone, a hunched figure in a vast field of snow and ice.

After fifteen minutes, there was nothing to do but watch, lined up in the frail lawn chairs by the mess tent, the *Kee Bird* a couple of hundred yards away. The sun was warm. The fire's cause, apparently, was fuel spilling from the APU's little five-gallon fuel tank onto the hot APU. Its fuel pump hadn't been working, and Al and Bob had strung the tank of gasoline from the ceiling using bailing wire so that gravity would feed the engine with fuel.

"These things happen," said Darryl. His voice was flat, soft, void of emotion. "I couldn't get the seat belt off."

There was a muffled explosion and two perfect black smoke rings shot high into the sky from the cockpit windows, slowly, beautifully, lingering in the still air 150 feet over the silver fuselage. But for its severed tail, the *Kee Bird* still looked intact. CRUNCH! The center of the fuselage, just behind the wings, broke, the two pieces collapsing onto the frozen lake. Roaring flames shot from the cockpit windows.

"Well, no problem warming it up now," said Darryl. No one laughed. "Did it look like it was jumping on the snow? It would have been better to slowly get on the ice and then just take off. Because she would have flown. She would have! It would have been airborne one-third of the way across the lake. It wouldn't have mattered which way we took off. . . . What a horrible waste."

"It wasn't because you didn't try," said Matt.

"We should have taken that tank out as soon as we got it started. How do you think of everything?"

Four hours later the *Kee Bird* was still smoldering, a pile of molten wreckage on the lake. The plane looked so fragile and the crater where she'd sat for the last three years so vacant, a mess of black oil stains. The sky was pearly white. The sun was low on the horizon and surrounded by a perfect round halo of rainbow. Cecelio gathered cardboard and trash and lit a fire—curiously, I realized, the first fire we'd ever had in camp. Darryl and the boys milled about somberly, staring at the wreckage, staring at the hole, like looking at the last footprints of a child who'd just been hit by a car. "It's so frustrating," muttered Darryl, motionless in his chair, staring blankly, replaying the events over and over as if, by reliving those last few moments, the moments when everything changed, he could somehow erase what had happened. "You know, this whole thing was improvisations and one of our improvisations failed. The fuel pump on the APU failed and so we hung the tank so it would gravity-feed. And we forgot to disconnect it. . . . Was she really jumping? She almost flew. . . . I couldn't get out of my seat belt. . . ."

Being at the *Kee Bird* was suddenly like picking an open wound. It was awful. The cold, the isolation, the quiet, the bad food—we could tolerate it and even get a rush off it with the silver bomber and its magical flight before us, egging us on, driving us forward, warming our bodies and filling our head with fantasies of glory and taking wing. But now that the *Kee Bird* was nothing but a smoldering wreck of burnt aluminum, there was nothing to do but stare at our failure. Darryl was nearly despondent. It almost would have been better if he'd wailed and screamed. But he sat there silently. Sitting with the boys over so many days, cupping a steaming hot mug of tea or a cold beer when they were available, had been glorious. The idea of seeing that old plane finally take wing was the one thing that had nurtured everyone through the cold and dirt, the despair and fatigue. We'd joked about who we were going to eat when the food ran out. And Rick Kriege hadn't even made it home to see his eleven-year-old Hallie. But watching Darryl throttle that thing across the lake had been the stuff of myth. In a world where it often seemed that technology was replacing God, Darryl and his team of tool users—plopped down there in the middle of nowhere—had been wrenching themselves out of the existential void. For a moment, with the *Kee Bird* poised to take wing, it had seemed there

157

was nothing we couldn't do, nothing we couldn't fix with a bit of wire or a piece of duct tape. With ingenuity and elbow grease the past had been about to come alive. An instant later it was gone.

All that remained of the *Kee Bird* was its big, beautiful tail and the midsection of the fuselage attached to the wings, engines, and propellers. They were untouched by the fire, which had burned the tail, then traveled through the little tunnel connecting the rear compartments to the nose and cockpit. It was weird: the fuel tanks in the wings never ignited. We dragged the Herman-Nelson, the bulldozer, the mess tent, the leftover supplies, and a few barrels of fuel under the wings. When summer came, the ice would melt and Darryl hoped the whole thing would disappear into the deepest portion of the lake, gone forever. Now, all anybody wanted to do was leave, get out, escape.

The next day, the chartered Twin Otter took us to Thule. "We've got to get the Caribou," Darryl said. "I've got to salvage something out of this deal."

Two days later most of the boys jumped on the Starlifter and were gone. All except Darryl, John Cater, and Vern. The Air Force was incredulous, as was Erik Thomsen, the senior Danish military officer at the base. In their eyes Darryl had ruined a priceless airplane, the sort of thing they'd been sure was going to happen all along. Even worse, as part of the permitting process, Darryl had promised to clean up the site and leave nothing behind. Not only had he left a burning airplane, a bulldozer, and who knew what on a pristine lake, he'd left an Air Force heater, too. Thomsen wanted to sit down with Darryl and hear the story and make sure he had a plan to tidy up what had been left behind. He was looking forward to a good, long talk.

Darryl, however, wasn't about to wait around and get tied into bureaucratic knots over all that. He, John Cater, and Vern finished patching together the Caribou and took off. They flew across Baffin Bay, Vern pumping fuel and oil into the engines throughout, to Iqaluit, Baffin Island, then on to Churchill, where they refueled and took wing again. Over Montana they blew another cylinder, taking out a landing light during an emergency touchdown at Billings. No matter. At every stop crowds streamed out to greet them, jazzed to meet Darryl Greenamyer and to hear the tale, the outlines of which they'd picked up on the radio fenceposts. "I was afraid people would want to stone us," Vern told me a week later, "but instead I think they understood the challenge. For Darryl to reach and grab that tiger by the tail—well, there's a lot to be said for that. I think they were so excited by what we were trying to do that they felt the same sense of loss we felt. People almost feel a personal loss. It was like we'd all gone in for the lottery, and if we'd won, everyone would have won." Still, he said a few months later, "I think about the *Kee Bird* every day. I've got a picture on my wall of me and Rick Kriege in front of her and I'm never going to take it down. I'm proud that I was there. And I keep waiting for the telephone to ring and it's Darryl calling to say, 'Hey, let's go strip the wings and get the motors.' I still have this feeling of unfinished business up there."

A few days later, Darryl was home, trying not to think about the fact that soon, whatever was left of the *Kee Bird* would disappear in the cold waters of the lake. Darryl had no idea what he'd do next. He hadn't ever considered losing the *Kee Bird*. There were other warbirds still out there, but he sure wasn't going after any of those. He had some mean bills to pay—selling the Caribou would help a bit—and Tom Hess to deal with. And the memory of a failure he couldn't quite accept. "It's still a nightmare," he said one day a few months after the fire, "and I still can't believe it really happened. I've tried a lot of things in my life and a lot have been failures, but occasionally I hit a home run and the home runs console. I lost Rick. I lost the B-29. I got in over my head financially. But that's life.

"I have this feeling that I'm going to wake up someday and realize that there's still something else that needs to be done up there—and that we'll go back and do it."

ELEVEN

—

SMOKE

Daugaard Jensen Land, Greenland; May 1995

Darryl was right. There was something else that needed to be done
up there, but it wasn't Darryl who was going to do it. It was the
thirty-first of May, nine days after the burning of the *Kee Bird*, and
Gary Larkins was back in the presence of the plane. Despite Darryl's
fear about the coming summer, the ice covering the lake hadn't yet
melted. To the west, the sky was a deep, unblemished blue. To the
east, wisps of high, thin, cirrus clouds stretched over the glowing ice
cap. It was cold, but as Larkins walked around the ruined plane the
sun felt warm on his back. The once perfect nose lay crumpled, a
single pane of glass left intact. The tail lay on the ice, the empen-
nage section between tail and wings melted away. Deep in the
wreckage the old rubber fuel bladder in the bomb bay was still smoldering, the occasional tendril of smoke wafting into the clear air.
Gary rifled through the canvas mess tent folded underneath the tail.
There were unopened cans of chili. Two blue and white aluminum
lawn chairs. Jars of Taster's Choice instant coffee. Paper plates
drifted across the snow. The yellow bulldozer, the rusty grader, and
seven barrels of fuel lay under the left wing, the Herman-Nelson under the right. The scene of destruction and carelessness made Gary
feel literally sick.

There were a handful of salvors and veteran's groups who'd

found and recovered warbirds over the last decade, but only Gary Larkins had made a career out of it. Besides stints at his dad's glass shop in high school, and a summer logging in Alaska, it was all he'd ever done. But the *Kee Bird* had been an anomaly. Despite the challenges of securing the permits and financing and getting to it, the ultimate challenge, as Darryl reminded everyone, had been flying it out. In the end, it had been a flyer's project. Gary Larkins was a licensed pilot, but most winged treasure wasn't flyable, and his specialty was wrestling it out by sheer elbow grease or, preferably, by helicopter.

Withdrawing from the *Kee Bird* project had been a crushing blow for Gary, but he hadn't sat around moping. He knew the whereabouts of more salvageable warbirds than anyone, having acquired and combed through the official U.S. accident reports for nearly every Navy, Marine, and Air Force plane that crashed since the services took wing—well over 100,000 airplanes.

Even as Darryl was trying to fly the *Kee Bird*, Gary had been home packing his bags for a new expedition to Greenland, this time to recover a B-17 Flying Fortress named *My Gal Sal*. He was just about to leave when a fax had rolled in. The Danish government was holding Gary's Institute for Aeronautical Archaeological Research responsible for failing to clean up the *Kee Bird* site. His permits for *Sal* and another B-17 named the *Sooner* were in jeopardy. Huh? Clean up the site? Holding the fax, he felt utterly confused. He'd had nothing to do with the *Kee Bird* since late 1993. He wasn't a big fan of Darryl, but he wanted that plane to come out just as much as anybody else.

He called Erik Thomsen in Thule and, for the first time, heard about the fire. The Danish government was furious; after Darryl left, a flyover of the site revealed the wreckage on the lake, along with the bulldozer, heater, and barrels of fuel. Darryl's permit from the Danish Polar Center had required him to leave the site in its natural state, as if *Kee Bird* and the expedition to recover it had never existed. Gary faxed Max Dugan and Thomsen copies of his legal agreement signing over the project to Darryl. He felt frantic. His equipment was packed and ready to be loaded on a C-130 at McGuire Air Force Base in New Jersey for the flight to Sondre Stromfjord, Greenland. He had a boat already chartered in southwest Greenland, a helicopter standing by there, a team in New Jersey waiting for him. If his permits were canceled he'd lose a summer's worth of work and maybe $150,000.

Dugan suggested he call Gen. Ronald Gray, commander of the 21st Space Wing at Peterson Air Force Base, Colorado. Hearing the story, Gray agreed Larkins was not responsible, but warned that satisfactorily proving it to everyone could take months. Something needed to be done right away to please the Danish government. I'll tell you what I'll do, Gray said. If you go up there to take care of the *Kee Bird*, I'll get you up to Thule for free.

Gary Larkins sent half his team to Sondre Stromfjord and flew in a second C-130 to Thule. Three days later, a Twin Otter ferried Gary, two teammates, and Erik Thomsen to the site. They stepped out of the Otter. It was silent, save for the clink, clink, clink of a cable banging in the wind on the *Kee Bird's* melted carcass. It was one thing to hear about the fire, another to witness its raw aftermath. Gary was overwhelmed. He'd spent so long assembling the permits, staring at the photos of the *Kee Bird* the whole time. Just yesterday, it seemed, he'd been hooting and hollering, watching the old bent prop spin on that one engine they had started, dreaming big dreams. *Goddamn! The destruction was total! What a complete waste!* He was there, inside that old Kodak print again, but now the *Kee Bird* was just a piece of junk.

Max Dugan had asked Gary to bring back the altimeter for the Thule officers' club. But not one gauge or instrument survived.

Gary couldn't believe the paper plates blowing in the wind, the batteries lying on the snow, the puddles of oil and abandoned equipment. It looked like everyone had just fled, run away on the spur of the moment. On days when the sun was shining and the air was still—as it had been during Gary's four days at the *Kee Bird* in

1993—and when you didn't have an enormous project in front of you, the place seemed so benign. What had been the hurry? How could they have just left everything? Gary couldn't understand it. But then, he hadn't been there during the winds and snow and freezing rain, hadn't felt the strain of a place that just seemed to want to beat you down. He couldn't do much with the site, but he could make things look better, at least, and that would save his permits.

The yellow bulldozer was mired on the frozen surface of the lake. The fire had melted the snow covering the lake around the bulldozer, and the ice was as clear as a windowpane. Gary could see through it into the dark water below. Afraid the fire might have weakened the ice and that freeing the bulldozer might break it, Gary tied a sixty-foot long piece of rope to his buddy and held on as he started the machine. It fired right up, and Gary pushed the oil where the *Kee Bird* had been repaired into a big pile, and made a little coffer dam so it wouldn't flow into the lake. He loaded the fuel and batteries and piles of trash into the Otter. It looked like a garbage truck. Here he was, picking up Darryl's trash, and to do it he was wasting precious time and spending thousands of dollars—the Air Force had flown him to Thule gratis, but he'd had to fork out the money for the Otter himself. And all his guys were just sitting around in southern Greenland, waiting for him, drinking and eating. And nothing was cheap in Greenland. He couldn't believe the indignity!

The Air Force wanted the Herman-Nelson, but the heater wouldn't fit into the Otter. He tried to drag the *Kee Bird* off the lake, but it wouldn't budge. He tied the Herman-Nelson to the bulldozer, slashed the radiator hose just as Vern had done a year earlier, in case someone ever wanted to get it, and fifteen hours after arriving, hopped onto the Otter and headed south. To hell with Darryl Greenamyer. At least the Danes and the Air Force were placated for the time being. The *Kee Bird* had been a once-in-a-lifetime find; Gary could search every jungle and ocean and glacier in the world and there would never be another warbird as good as that one, poised to take wing.

But it was gone and all the sour grapes he could muster wouldn't make it whole again. Still, there were a lot of hungry collectors around and the demand for warbirds far outstripped their supply. Some people just had to have rare things. If you wanted a B-17 or a B-29 or any other warbird, you had but two choices: either convince someone to sell you his treasure for millions, or salvage one from the wild. The easy ones were gone, but the world was still a big place, and if you looked hard enough it was full of rare airplanes, or at least pieces of them. And no one knew where they were or how to bring them home like Gary Larkins did. As the Twin Otter droned over the rock and ice, Gary ticked them off: My Gal Sal, ripe for plucking off the ice cap; he'd have her in a matter of months, he thought. The Sooner, hidden and preserved under icy water in a southern fjord; no one had ever recovered a B-17 from underwater before. And that unnamed B-17 in the Alaskan bush that he'd been thinking about? She'd be a piece of cake, if he could find the right customer. Now, with the Kee Bird a smoking ruin, he was more determined than ever to show Darryl Greenamyer how it was done.

TWELVE

—

PRECIOUS METAL

Ruby, Alaska; August 1997

The Dodge Caravan edged slowly along a gravel road bordering the outer reaches of the Fairbanks International Airport. It had been two years since the burning of the *Kee Bird*. A light drizzle fell and patches of fog dotted the ground. Although it was August, the temperature was a chilly fifty-five degrees. Don Carroll, a buddy of Gary Larkins since high school and an occasional accomplice in the wild, was driving. Gary rode shotgun beside him. Six feet tall, with thick jet-black hair and eyebrows, he was wearing faded Levis and a green nylon flight jacket. A baseball cap perched high on his head. Both cap and jacket sported an oval patch depicting a helicopter dangling a P-39 Aircobra—the logo of Larkins's nonprofit Institute for Aeronautical Archaeological Research.

As he'd planned, after cleaning up the *Kee Bird* site in 1995, Gary had recovered the B-17 *My Gal Sal* for Oregon collector Jack Erickson in just seven weeks. Working from a tent on the ice cap, Gary had dismantled *Sal* into dozens of pieces and flown them out by helicopter to a barge positioned at the head of a fjord thirty miles away. Erickson wanted to make *Sal* a flyer but her all-important center bomb-bay section had been destroyed. Restoration shops could do amazing things—a restored airplane routinely required all new aluminum skin, and even a bunch of ribs or stringers wasn't a big deal—

165

but the fundamental frame and trusses were prohibitively expensive to fabricate from scratch, especially if there was an alternative.

Gary, naturally enough, knew of one: the unnamed B-17 wreck in Alaska that he'd been thinking about ever since the *Kee Bird*. It had been cruising to battle the Japanese in the Aleutian Islands in 1942 when one of its four engines caught fire. The crew didn't waste time and energy trying to save their plane. They bailed out. But the plane was trimmed out nicely and flew on by itself until it slid onto a frozen lake and broke in half. The section from the wings forward careened into the bush; the tail sank into the lake when the ice melted. On an earlier trip Gary had scoped it out it from the air by helicopter. A single stabilizer, weathered to raw silver-colored aluminum, stuck out of the lake; how much remained beneath the dark water Gary couldn't tell. The wings containing the fuel tanks were burned and ruined. The nose had been crushed by its impact with the trees. This unnamed Fortress was no *Kee Bird*. But the center section to which the wings attached was perfect. If recovered and mated with *Sal*, Erickson could have the only flying E model B-17 in the world. And although that center section was the most important part, you couldn't just order the thousands of little pieces making up a B-17, from switches to engine cylinders to hydraulic hoses to gun turrets, from some catalogue. A ball turret alone was now worth around $40,000.

Erickson gave Gary $50,000 to bring back as much as he could.

Now here we were, waiting for the weather to clear before flying into the bush. Gary seldom rested, however, and over breakfast he'd suddenly announced a plan: "Let's go to the airport and survey the junk." Surveying the airport was one of the things he did when he was killing time in some distant outpost, part of his systematic and relentless search for airplanes. He never knew what he might see or find or hear about. Winged treasure was often in the most unlikely places.

"Hold it, hold it," Gary said as we came upon a World War II–era

C-47 cargo hauler under repair on the other side of a chain-link fence enclosing airport property. Leaning back on its tail wheel, with a rounded nose and two big engines and props, it had a 1930s art deco look. This one, announced its dented fuselage and exhaust blackened engine nacelles, was still a cargo workhorse. One of its propellers was spinning. "They're running her up a bit," Gary said. Carroll stopped the van. Down rolled the windows. The unmistakable low-pitched drumming of a powerful radial piston engine washed over us. "Hear that? That's why I like to see 'em flying," Gary said. "She looks like a big old rocket from the front. Pretty bitchin'!" Up rolled the windows and the van bumped on. "Let's go drop some of our gear off at the helicopter hangar," Gary said, checking his watch and grinning, "and then maybe it's time we found a bar, eh?"

At five A.M. the next morning, despite having spent twelve consecutive hours at the bar after unloading gear, we headed out. Gary ate no breakfast and drank no coffee. The helicopter cost $2,500 an hour, forty-two dollars a minute, and to make his budget he had to work fast. "I don't want to get caught in any sort of adverse reaction, if you know what I mean!" he said. But if everything went according to plan, he would recover a B-17 by the time the day was done. The weather had cleared. We dragged out to the helicopter two big yellow cases filled with steel and nylon rigging and shotgun shells, a couple of scuba-diving tanks, duffels of scuba gear, and a bright yellow nylon cargo net. The inside of the helicopter, a big, shiny blue twin-engine Bell 212, looked minuscule next to the pile of gear. "It'll be tight," Gary said, "and we'll be on the edge of the envelope but that's where we Pirates like to operate. We probably don't need half this shit if nothing goes wrong."

"Ever find out how much that center section weighs?" asked Jeff Reed, the helicopter pilot, looking over the equipment. He was built like a bear, wearing a blue one-piece flight suit.

"Don't know for sure," Gary said. "I've got the manual and I know what it's supposed to weigh, but there's no telling what she'll weigh now. I'd say about twenty-four, twenty-five hundred pounds. But who knows? You can have all the manuals in the world but there's no way to estimate the components after a crash."

"What are we doing for fuel?" asked Reed.

"I got ten barrels sitting on the dock in Ruby." Ruby was a village perched on the edge of the Yukon River, about two hundred miles west of Fairbanks and fifteen miles from the B-17. There were no roads to Ruby; you either arrived by air or by boat up the Yukon. Gary had sent the fuel up by barge the week before.

Reed nodded, hoisting one of the yellow cases into the helo. "What if we can't land?"

"We'll just have to get as close as we can. I'm thinking we'll get to Ruby, throw the gear out, and wrap it in the sling," Gary said, "then sling it right to the airplane, punch the line off, and while you're putting in the divers we'll knock down a few trees and clear you a place to land. But we'll have to play it by ear and just let it happen."

"I need the weights of everything," Reed said. He scribbled the numbers on a small yellow pad. "We're way over," he said.

"Damn!" Gary said. "Okay, shitcan anything that you absolutely don't need to do the job," he said to Rafid Tuma and Bill Roche, his two divers. The weather looked good, but it was late August and the trees were already turning yellow. Still, we jettisoned the tent, the cook stove, and all the spare clothes. Food would be cold, military-style MREs. Here we go again, I thought.

By nine we were up, belted, and scrunched onto a nylon jump seat in the back of the helo, Gary's long legs wedged over eight hundred pounds of rigging cables, power tools, two pistols, and a shotgun—the bush was grizzly-bear country. "Thirty years ago there was a B-25 at every airport," Gary shouted, as we raced 2,500 feet above a carpet of green bogs and small pine trees dotted with silvery lakes. "But those days were like the last buffalo hunts. Now you've got to go farther and farther to find planes in worse and worse shape."

After flying for two hours we floated over the Yukon, a massive ribbon of beige bordered by gravel and sandbanks. Wooden fish traps dotted the river. The helo banked low over the Yukon and the dusty log cabins of Ruby. Trash and sticks flew in the rotor wash, and excited children, like schools of fish, swarmed as we settled on Ruby's muddy beach. Gary bounded out like a quarterback who'd just taken the snap. The 200-mile flight had already cost him $5,000, and the meter was ticking.

"What are you guys doing? What are you doing?" shouted a pack of dark-haired kids.

"Let's just drop the stuff and then drop the divers from the get-go," Gary said to Reed.

On top of the bluff twenty feet away waited the ten fifty-five-gallon drums of fuel. We rolled five of them down to the helicopter, and Reed took out a hand-cranked pump and refueled. Gary spread the cargo net on the mud in front of the helo, piled all the cases and cables and packs onto the net, and attached it by nylon cable to a hook on the helo's underbody. Kids crowded around. "Who are you guys?" A dog yapped. Rafid Tuma and Bill Roche undressed in front of the throng, and slipped into their wet suits.

In minutes we were over the wilderness again, the inside of the helo empty of everything but us and the divers' scuba gear. The rest of the equipment dangled in the net twenty-five feet below. Five minutes later, Reed dropped over the lake, where a silver-colored rudder and stabilizer rose, ghostlike, from its green waters. One hundred yards away lay the rest of the airplane entangled in thick brush. As Reed hovered low over the twisted wreckage, Gary slipped open the door and leaned out, two of us clutching his belt. Brush flew and the slender pine trees swayed violently. "Tell him to back up," Gary yelled. "Okay. Perfect!" Reed hit a button, opening the hook and dropping the cargo net with its gear a few feet away from the airplane. We then swung out over the lake, which was boiling with whitecaps from the helo's rotor wash. Tuma opened the door on the other side of the helo. The noise was deafening, a hurricane of wind pouring in. He and Roche shouldered their air tanks and edged out onto the skids. Reed descended. Twenty feet. Ten feet. Five feet. The helicopter was shaking violently. Gary nodded and Tuma and Roche jumped feet first into the lake, bobbed up in the boiling water, and tapped their heads in an "okay" signal.

Reed slid away and started looking for a place to land. Twice, he aborted his descent; the trees and bushes were too thick. Finally, three-quarters of a mile from the B-17, he set down on a boggy clearing. We jumped onto wet, spongy ground. Reed lifted off and hovered over the wreck to guide us in. "He's wasting fuel! Let's go!" Gary shouted, charging through brush so thick I couldn't see five feet ahead. Fifteen minutes later, scratched and mosquito-bitten, our feet sopping wet, we stumbled onto the plane. It was burned and charred and twisted, a wreck worth every penny of the $15,000 it took to get here.

Reed immediately flew off to Ruby, to await our call on the radio. An engine lay half buried in the peat. Oxygen bottles were strewn across the ground. A rare ball turret lay on its side—that alone would probably come close to paying for the trip. The wings were blackened, the nose crushed. But the center, the bomb-bay section, was intact, entwined within a thicket of trees. Clouds of mosquitoes buzzed our heads. Gary lit a Swisher Sweet cigar, slipped a clip of bullets into his .45 pistol and eight rounds of lead slugs into the shotgun, picked up a machete, and attacked. Abetted by Don Carroll wielding a chain saw, we cut down every tree and bush within a sixty-foot-wide circle, clearing a landing zone for Reed. A heady mix of sweet pine, gasoline, and chain saw exhaust permeated the warm air. You could barely walk; every step in the boggy underbrush was like walking through three feet of snow and thick spiderwebs. We stumbled over and through brush that grabbed us and launched ever-thicker clouds of bugs. "This is a nasty place," Gary said, hacking at a tree.

Half an hour later Tuma and Roche appeared, squelching in their wetsuits through the bushes from the lake thirty yards away.

"There's a whole bunch of tail there," Tuma said, "but it's all stuck in the mud, and the water is really murky."

"Hopefully, the chopper will pull it out," Gary said, wiping sweat off his face and waving the mosquitoes and gnats away with his cigar. "Rig it up."

Tuma and Roche grabbed twenty-five-foot-long nylon straps from the pile of gear and disappeared into the dark waters of the lake again.

Two hours later the landing zone was clear and Gary called Reed in from Ruby on the VHF radio. A gasoline-powered circular saw screamed as Don Carroll sliced the wings off the fuselage along lines Gary spray-painted just outside the points at which they attached to the fuselage. Working around the plane was difficult, a Gordian knot of razor sharp aluminum, twisted hydraulic lines and a tangle of two-inch-thick, ten-foot-high trees. Looking it over, Gary discovered that the aileron controls had been removed from the wings. "Interesting," he said, peering into the wings. "Who do you suppose came up here for those controls? It's an awful long way for a few parts. Maybe it was those damn Confederates."

Just then Tuma and Roche stumbled in after rigging the tail. They were nearly out of air, exhausted, and wracked with cramps from the frigid water. "Visibility is zero," Tuma said, gnats swarming around his dripping face. "All you can do is feel with your hands. There's this kelp four or five feet long, and it's real dense. You have to just stick your face in and claw your way through. Twice Bill got stuck and I had to pull him out."

"Okay," Gary said, blowing a lungful of cigar smoke at the bugs swirling around his face, "let's see about that tail."

Reed attached a twenty-five-foot steel cable to the helicopter and took to the air. With Carroll, Gary, and Tuma standing in knee-deep bog at the lake's edge, Roche snorkeled back out to the tail. Slowly, Reed descended overhead. The air was shattered by an instant typhoon. The ground shook. Foot-high whitecaps and spray, driven by the hundred-mile-an-hour rotor wash, soaked us. We grabbed on to trees, which bent to the ground in the wind. Sighting through two small mirrors mounted on the helicopter's nose, and abetted by Gary on the radio, Reed brought the shackle down to Roche, who, fighting the wind and water, attached it to the four-inch-wide nylon straps on the tail. Reed tried to rise. The helicopter strained at full throttle just twenty-five feet overhead. It felt like the end of the world. Wind-driven water slashed my face. Slowly, Reed worked the load back and forth, trying to loosen it from the sucking weeds and muck. We cowered behind trees, but Gary, stogie hard between his teeth, stood inured to the cyclone, filming with his video camera. He, the camera, and the cigar were drenched.

Inch by inch the tail rose out of the water. Twenty-five feet of B-17 fuselage and tail, the green paint and blue-and-white star-and-bar U.S. Army Air Force symbol, outlined in fluorescent orange, as perfect as the day it was painted. From the two side windows and the ball turret on the bottom hung six .50-caliber machine guns. "Goddamn!" shouted Gary. "Now we've got the whole damn airplane!" He lived for moments like this. You never knew what you'd find when you went after an airplane. He'd been hoping for a bit of the tail, but never would he have thought there'd be so much of it, so well preserved, the paint so fresh. Time flashed. This was no *Kee Bird*, but this is what it looked like when it crashed. Jack Erickson would be pleased.

Nothing, however, is that easy. The turret suddenly slipped from the fuselage and disappeared beneath the lake's cold blackness. And Reed's big Bell, two turbines running at full power, couldn't fly with the load. All he could do was drag it to the marshy shore, drop the line and land. No matter. Gary splashed through the swamp and clambered onto the tail, grinning. He was sopping wet, covered with dirt and mosquito bites, and hadn't had a bite to eat since five that morning. But the machine guns looked brand new, belts of .50-caliber ammo still fed right into the chambers. "God, I love this shit," he yelled, like a kid on Christmas morning. "That .50-cal is brand spanking new!"

Time was short and the meter was ticking. He could admire the tail later. Gary thrashed back through the brush to the center section. He and Don Carroll passed short loops of inch-thick steel cable through each of the wing attach points on the fuselage, then connected those to two three-inch-wide nylon straps. Reed spooled up again and hovered over Gary, who straddled the fuselage the way his hero the Duke might have straddled a horse. Again, the hurricane-force winds whipped the trees. Dust, sticks, and brush hurtled by. Roche, Tuma, and I huddled against the ground. Straining against the driving wind, the helicopter swaying ten feet over his head, Gary looked maniacal, his blue jeans soaked, a cigar clenched between his teeth, his face covered with dirt. He fastened the straps to the steel cable dangling from the helicopter and bolted into the whipping brush. But try as he might, Reed couldn't seem to budge the fuselage. It didn't move an inch. After ten minutes roaring at full power he gave up.

For the next few hours we piled chunks of aluminum and whatever we could carry into piles on the cargo net, which Reed ferried to Ruby, followed by an engine and one of the wings. By 8:30 P.M., fifteen hours after starting the day, Reed radioed in; by regulation he had to stop for the day. Instead of sleeping in the bush, Gary suggested we stay in Ruby, and we piled into the helo—dirty, tired, and hungry—for the short flight back. "She's a mean old bitch," shouted Gary as we lifted off, "and this Bell doesn't have enough lift."

As we blasted down onto the muddy, gray beach, the whole town of Ruby, it seemed, swarmed to meet us. Children rode on their parents' shoulders; dusty, dented pickup trucks bumped up; and clusters of boys riding rough wooden go-karts all surrounded the pile of broken, aluminum World War II treasure worth $100,000 or more. A local family with a log cabin overlooking the river invited us to stay in their kids' playhouse, a miniature log cabin eight feet square with a rack of moose antlers over the little door. We dragged a case of MREs into the playhouse and leaned against the walls. The sun was an orange ball descending over the steel-gray Yukon and the acrid-sweet smell of smoking salmon wafted past. A kid scurried over with strips of smoked salmon and Gary broke out a bottle of V.O. and fired up another cigar.

"We'll just try to wail on that center section tomorrow," Gary said, taking a swig and passing the bottle round, "and see if we can't break up the ground around it; maybe that's what's holding it down." He paused, took a long drag on the cigar, looked around the warm, dry little house and said, "I'd say the Pirates are living pretty good—eh, Rafid?"

Rafid Tuma nodded and shot a squirt of spit mixed with Kodiak snuff into an old Coke can.

Although Gary was operating on this trip under the umbrella of his "nonprofit" Institute, he preferred to think of himself and his guys as the Air Pirates. Sometimes he even still went by that name, which he'd coined after plucking a P-47 Thunderbolt off of Oahu's Sacred Falls in 1987, while he was operating under the prosaic name Air-Marine Salvors. It all depended on the job.

"We brought it out by helicopter and crated it for shipping," said Tuma.

"And," added Gary, biting a piece of salmon, "the next day I'm getting on the plane to go home when I see the newspaper: AIR PI-RATES ROBBING HAWAII OF AVIATION HERITAGE, screamed the headline. Hey, I thought, I *like* that." Gary could talk for hours, and it was late when we crawled into our sleeping bags, the sounds of barking dogs echoing through town.

I was cold and stiff in the morning when we rolled the rest of the fuel down to the helicopter and flew back out to the B-17. It was a glorious day, the sun coming up warm, the sky as clear as the water in a swimming pool. With machetes and knives, we all cut and scraped and clawed into the wet peat around the plane. Sure enough, fifty years of roots were tangled around its spars, clutching it tightly to the ground. "And here," Gary said, hacking at the ground and roots with his machete, "I was doubting that big chopper. I was thinking, too much damn emergency equipment on board weighing him down."

Two hours later the helicopter whined to life and Reed took to the sky trailing twenty-five feet of cable. The ear-splitting, chest-pounding hurricane enveloped us. Gary attached the straps to the cable and jumped clear. Reed rose and increased power, the wind and noise like 10,000 horses galloping just overhead. Louder and louder, the Bell swayed back and forth. Suddenly, up popped the ragged eight-foot-high aluminum cylinder dripping fifty years of dust and debris. Reed headed to Ruby, the load twisting slowly below the helicopter.

"Okay," Gary said, charging over to the beached tail at the lake's edge, "we're going to rig that and book on out of here. But," he said, kneeling on the green tail, "this is going to be a bitch. We've got to find the right attach points." To Tuma and Roche, swimming in the shallow muck: "I think we may have to cut her in half, if we can do it without cutting the stem bar"—part of the main aluminum frame to which the skin was attached. "I don't want to, but we once picked up a piece like this on the ice cap and it started spinning and I tried to grab it but it threw me thirty feet and we had to tell the pilot to drop it."

A droning whine signaled Reed's return. He swept in low over the lake, paused a moment, and signaled to Gary. "Shit!" Gary said, after talking to Reed over the radio. "Something is wrong with the helicopter. We gotta go. Now!" Gary dropped his tools, leaped over the power saw, and crashed into the brush. Roche, Tuma, and I scurried after him. The helo was thundering at full power in the clearing. "Grab your packs," Gary shouted, "and leave everything else. Move fast!" We bolted into the helicopter like grunts being rescued from a firefight in Vietnam, leaving the tools, the rigging,

$8,000 worth of diving equipment. Before we could even close the doors Reed was up, racing toward Ruby high and fast in case an engine died and he had to autorotate to the ground.

The engines held and ten minutes later we landed at a gravel airstrip a mile outside of the village. The B-17 fuselage section, Reed said as we piled out of the helicopter, starting spinning wildly en route to Ruby. Just as he was banking over the Yukon to drop the load, it cut the throttle linkage to one of the engines, severing his control over it. Reed didn't panic. He set the fuselage gently on the dock and came back to get us. But for now, the four-million-dollar helicopter was shot. Reed scurried off to find a telephone and call his office, returning a few minutes later. A light Bell JetRanger helicopter was en route from Fairbanks to extricate the gear and whatever it could still get out of the B-17 site, including the tail. A commercial puddle jumper would fly Tuma and Roche and me out. Everything arranged, Gary flopped against the skids of the grounded Bell and fell asleep.

That afternoon, under a warm, late-summer Arctic sun, Charlie Hnilicka loaded the wreckage onto his Yukon River barge, to be offloaded in Fairbanks three days later. The treasure didn't look like much: one broken, burnt-out wing; one engine; a pile of twisted cowling, hydraulic lines, oxygen bottles, odd switches, crew seats, a carburetor, miscellaneous sheet metal, and the big center section of fuselage. It sure wasn't the *Kee Bird*, and it was hard to believe that it was worth so much money and effort. "Jack Erickson will be happy that we got that center section," Gary said, as a front-end loader eased the aluminum hulk onto the barge, "but I know what Jack will say: 'You stay up there until you get it done.' Well, there's always a good bar in Fairbanks and a pretty woman to pour your whiskey."

The clatter of a helicopter broke the quiet and the JetRanger from Fairbanks swooped onto the beach. "Gotta go," Gary shouted as he bounded down the beach and climbed into the waiting helicopter.

In two quick trips Gary and the JetRanger brought out the gear and one of the ball turrets, which the helicopter set down on Hnilicka's already moving barge. They had to leave the tail. In Fairbanks three days later the trucking company that had been contracted to bring the salvaged parts to Tillamook suddenly tripled its price, to $16,000. So Gary and Don Carroll rented a van and U-Haul trailer for $2,600, strapped the pieces on, drove four days and nights down the AlCan Highway, and delivered the goods to the front door of Erickson's museum. And three weeks later, Gary and two assistants flew back up, cut the tail section in half, and flew it out, too. As warbird recoveries went, it had been quick and easy. In a few years, with a lot of money, craftsmanship, and elbow grease, the world's only flying B-17E would take wing and grace Erickson's growing collection of vintage airplanes.

THIRTEEN

—

A PECULIAR PASSION

Polk City, Florida, and Tillamook, Oregon

It is the handful of wealthy collectors, like Jack Erickson, who ultimately fuel these recovery missions. Had Darryl Greenamyer managed to fly the *Kee Bird* out of Greenland, he might have buzzed the screaming fans at Reno, or he might have paraded the plane at the Experimental Aviation Association's huge annual summer "fly-in" at Oshkosh, Wisconsin, basking in the glow of his rare artifact. But he wouldn't have kept it long. He couldn't afford to. Simply flying it would cost nearly a thousand dollars an hour for fuel alone. Add constant maintenance, insurance, the requisite big crew to operate it, and a thousand square feet of hangar space, and the half-century-old four-engine bomber was like a turbocharged Hoover money-sucker. Darryl had done well over the years, but he hadn't done that well. Flying the *Kee Bird* at Reno would have been a big ego boost. More importantly it would have been a shrewd business move: He would have been showing it off, advertising it, driving its value up, ultimately hoping for a payoff in the millions of dollars.

Everyday men and women loved to see the airplanes and they eagerly shelled out a few bucks for a tour or a day's admission to an air show, but the age of someone like Walter Soplota scurrying home with a saved warbird on a rickety trailer were long over.

There were only twenty-nine B-29s and forty-five B-17s, including the nonflying ones displayed in museums, in the whole world. Only four P/F-82 Twin Mustangs and four P-61 Black Widows. And those airplanes weren't like some obscure da Vinci codex or van Gogh sunflower painting that most people had never heard of and couldn't identify with. Warbirds were historic icons that evoked deep and powerful emotions. There were literally tens of millions of Americans whose fathers or mothers or grandfathers or grandmothers or brothers or sisters had flown or made a warbird; there were millions of Americans and Europeans who associated the sound and technology of a B-17 or a B-29 with their very freedom and economic well-being. A Twin Mustang or a B-29 was rarer than gold, rarer than diamonds, rarer even than a Picasso. More people had slogged to the top of Mount Everest than all the world's owners of a B-29, B-17, and B-25 combined. And for the increasing numbers of rich people in the world, it was getting harder and harder to stand out. But own a B-17 and you were instantly catapulted into the ranks of the unique, the special. You were someone. Friends wanted a ride in your plane. Air shows hired you. Hollywood directors wanted your airplanes for their war movies. Museums courted you. Veterans adored you. Magazines like *Air Classics* and *Fly Past* and *Warbirds Worldwide* wanted to snap photos of you and your airplane. And on top of it all, you weren't just being selfish, you were protecting a historical artifact, preserving history (and getting a massive tax write-off, to boot, if you did things right). These days the cult of the warbird depended on a handful of rich private collectors. They fueled the whole industry, from the guys like Darryl and Gary, who recovered the airplanes, to the restoration shops and aviation museums springing up all over the country.

The biggest collector of them all was Kermit Weeks, and there wasn't a soul in the subculture who hadn't heard of him. His family had amassed a fortune in the oil business, a fortune that was now Kermit's. He had a museum in Miami and an even bigger museum in Polk City, Florida, just down the road from Orlando. Unlike a lot of wealthy collectors, known more for the size of their wallets than their flying skills, Weeks was a two-time U.S. National Aerobatic Champion. Gary Larkins had looked for a plane or two for him; Weeks had loaned Darryl parts for the *Kee Bird*, and he was known to have paid large sums for the treasures of a few faltering collectors.

Everyone had a Kermit Weeks story, even Walter Soplota. "I went to Weeks's place and there's this dirty, long-haired guy mowing the lawn out front," Soplota had told me. "Well, when I went to the front desk and said I wanted to see Kermit Weeks, the girl said, 'That's Kermit Weeks!' pointing to the guy mowing the lawn."

"One day I was up in Kermit's penthouse," Gary Larkins told me, "and he's got this huge pad with giant windows overlooking his flight line and this hot tub big enough for a keg party, and I was trying to talk to him when he picks up this violin and just starts fiddling as if I wasn't even there!"

Weeks invited me for a visit. Twenty miles southwest of the sprawling housing tracts and attractions of Orlando, I came upon the first billboards: RARE WARBIRDS. A few miles farther there was a DC-3 artfully posed nose-down in the grass at the edge of the highway, a mannequin clothed as a flyer dangling by parachute straps from the upended tail. Polk City was old Florida, orange groves, dangling Spanish moss, and little more than a crossroads with a gas station, a mom-and-pop pizza joint, and a drug store. And Kermit's "Fantasy of Flight." A spotless, new brown stucco complex rose from the orange groves, on the edge of a blue lake. A grass runway paralleled the lake. Fantasy of Flight was huge, and it all looked like it had been built yesterday. Just inside the door stood the Compass Rose, a restaurant built to look like a 1930s airport waiting room, featuring sandwiches named Spitfire, P-63 King Cobra, or Corsair (char-grilled chicken breast, blackened, served with herbed new potatoes).

A World War I biplane hung from a cathedral ceiling outside of Weeks's office in the back of the museum. The walls and ceiling were covered in mirrors, the biplane suspended in a reflected void that was supposed to be skylike. "Upstairs, the last office in back," said the receptionist. I climbed the staircase onto a balcony perched in the mirrored "sky" and found Weeks bent over a computer in a small office down a narrow hall. The man who stood to shake my hand surprised me. From the stories, I'd expected some wild-looking character, maybe a younger-looking Walter Soplota. But wearing a T-shirt tucked into clean, faded blue jeans, the tall, strongly built forty-seven-year-old collector looked like a model from *Outside* magazine. He had a bushy mustache and long hair pulled into a neat ponytail. He settled behind a wooden desk piled with papers and said, "What can I do for you?"

Why were people so fascinated by World War II airplanes, I asked. "There's just a lot of romance to the past," he said, quickly, "whether it's sailing ships or whatever. World War II aircraft represent a lot of feeling and emotion—the desperation, the conflict, people were busting their butts and losing their friends—and that's what they think of when they see the airplanes." What made him amass such a huge collection? "I've just always been fascinated by the things that fascinated me," he said elliptically. No doubt he'd been asked all this a thousand times before. It was a relief when the telephone rang.

"Yup," Weeks told the caller. As he curtly talked into the phone, I looked around his office. It was a working office that betrayed almost no trace of the kind of egocentrism I expected of a wealthy collector. Rolls of packing tape were piled on the green carpet. Over his computer was a big watercolor of a Spitfire landing on a grass field. Lining the wall were rows of black file cabinets piled with airplane models and a globe. Tacked across a wall by his desk were blueprints and a site map of Fantasy of Flight. The only hint of self-promotion was a small plaque on the wall, the Pitts Aerobatic Trophy, from 1979.

Weeks hung up the phone. "People call me all the time, offering to sell me stuff for a lot of money," he said. "But now I've curbed my acquisitions and I'm just waiting for the deals to come along. And anyway, I'm out of space. I've got forty-six thousand square feet here, and it's packed. I've got planes in California and planes in England and planes all over. I haven't really started Fantasy of Flight yet. Until I can get the permits to build the rest of the next phase—it'll feel like you're at a World War II airfield when I'm done—I'm not buying."

Then, leaning back in his chair, his long legs draped across the top of his desk, Weeks began to speak more personally. By his mid-twenties, when he'd come into his inheritance, "I could afford to have something really cool," he said. "Everybody worth anything in aviation said I had to have a P-51 Mustang. So I bought myself a T-6 for $28,000." The T-6 was the advanced trainer of World War II; you had to master flying one before you tried the powerful and temperamental Mustang. "I'd never flown anything like that before!" he said, hunching forward in his seat. "And within six months a P-51 came up for sale. I thought, 'What the hell!' and then it was downhill from there!" He had more money than he knew what to do with and he acquired warbirds with a frenzy. He didn't care about their values and he didn't care how much work they needed. He snatched up a P-38 Lightning for $75,000, the Mustang for $155,000.

"Now they're priceless," he said, shrugging his shoulders. "But I've always collected airplanes for what they are, not for what they're worth." By 1985 he had fifty airplanes and opened his first museum, donating the airplanes to the museum and taking a huge tax write-off—"*and* I could still fly 'em." He collected World War I biplanes, Japanese and German airplanes, rare engines, "whatever struck my fancy. Initially it was collecting indiscriminately, but now it's pretty much only to fill a hole in the collection." He had reproductions of Lindbergh's *Spirit of St. Louis* and the famous *Gee Bee* racer built. He opened Fantasy of Flight in 1995 on 300 acres in

Polk City—"a sucky place to attract tourists," he admitted—but it "was a cool place to fly my airplanes, and I needed a five-thousand-foot runway, and a lake for my vintage seaplanes. There are a few planes I'd love to have that I don't, but I won't mention them. Other than some German and Japanese stuff, there's not much left in World War II that I don't have." When Davis Tallichet, a collector who had obtained a permit to salvage the *Kee Bird* around the same time as Gary Larkins, got into financial trouble and had to sell his airplanes, Weeks ponied up millions for Tallichet's bomber collection, including the only B-26 Marauder and one of two flying B-24 Liberators left in the world. "That was the most I'd spent for anything, but it was the only opportunity for something like that and they were really original, and that was important to me. If someone else got 'em, well . . ."

Weeks was acquisitive—he now had somewhere around 150 airplanes, even he wasn't sure exactly how many, worth who knew how much ("I couldn't even speculate")—but it was the "spiritual" part of the collecting that really motivated him, he said. More than just wanting to own them, he wanted to fly them. "My personal goal in all this is to experience aviation history by flying the planes from different periods in history. When I'm flying the *Spirit of St. Louis*, I'm, like, 'What the hell was Lindbergh thinking!' I'm scared flying across water and he's flying across the damn Atlantic Ocean! When I'm flying the Mustang I'm looking for bandits, I'm thinking about what they were feeling on a mission." For safety and comfort's sake, most warbird owners add modern wiring and avionics to their airplanes, sometimes extra fuel tanks for more range. But not Weeks. When his planes are restored, Weeks wants them exactly as they were built. "I want them original. The wiring is coded according to the World War II manual. If the cables in the airplane are hand-spliced, my cables are hand-spliced. If that's the way it was, that's the way it'll stay."

He leaned forward in his seat. "The airplanes are really just a means to an end," he said. He looked serious, reflective. "A lot of people have had past-life ties with the war or airplanes." I leaned forward in my seat. "I've always had this really strong attraction to aviation. Why? Because I have a really strong sense that I flew in the first World War and that I was killed in action in World War II and reborn in 1953. Your phobias, your dislikes, your passions, they're all carried over from your past lives, and aviation is an avenue where I can get in touch with mine."

Kermit Weeks loved airplanes and flying, but so did a lot of the people I met. And getting in touch with your past life didn't seem an adequate explanation for spending millions and millions of dollars on warplanes. Why old warplanes? What did they mean to collectors and fans? Surely, millions of people who otherwise loved warbirds would think Weeks's notion of past lives was a little kooky. And yet what was it about the twenties, thirties, and forties that they felt so connected to?

Pondering those questions, I headed to Tillamook, Oregon, to see collector Jack Erickson. There was nothing New Agey about him. When I mentioned the idea of getting in touch with your past in the cockpit of, say, a P-38, he looked at me like I was crazy. At sixty-five years old, the war was still real enough to Erickson that he didn't need to live it in his fantasies. The recently retired head of a logging and helicopter empire stretching from New Guinea to Oregon, Erickson met me in the cafeteria of the Tillamook Naval Air Station Museum. Wearing canvas work pants and a thick blue-and-white flannel shirt, he looked more lumberjack than CEO. He was small and wiry, with short gray hair, pale blue eyes, and the calloused hands of a blue-collar worker. "This was a quite a base during the war. I can remember coming down here and the highway was all blacked out and everybody's headlamps were nothing but little slits," he said, stuffing a dip of Copenhagen snuff under his lower lip and leading me into the largest wooden building ever erected.

A former Navy blimp hangar seventy-five miles southwest of Portland, the vast, dim wooden hangar was over 1,000 feet long and

296 feet high. The sliding doors alone weighed thirty tons. The roof arched high overhead in an intricate web of wooden beams and crosstrees. Erickson pointed to a line of airplanes. "That F-14 fighter is on loan from the Navy. All the rest of 'em, I own." We strolled past a perfectly restored B-25 Mitchell bomber, pausing at a pristine P-38. "This was surplused in 1946 and a guy bought it in 1968 for fifteen hundred dollars and used it as an aerial photo ship, and then it and another one just sat in his barn in Roseville, California. I bought and restored both of them."

The P-38 and B-25, a PV-2 Harpoon, a C-47 cargo ("It's fun to fly, nothing happens very fast"), an A-26 ("This one flew in the Bay of Pigs"), a Corsair, a Hellcat, an SBD divebomber, a PBY Catalina, a Mustang, one after another, we strolled past twenty-one of his twenty-four airplanes (the others were under restoration at various shops around the country). He wouldn't say what they were worth. "You can do the math," he said. I did, and I figured at least thirty million, if not more, and rising fast. "The good 'ol Cat," he said, pointing to a Grumman FM-2 Wildcat. "This is one airplane that can sit for a year and you can just fire it up and everything works." His two-seat Supermarine Mark XIX Spitfire was the only one left in the world. Erickson hopped up on the wing and slid the canopy back. "It's all original, even the radios," he said. "Smell it!"

He leaped over the rope around his German Messerschmitt Bf-109, a brutish-looking airplane, and yanked on the leading edge of the wing. It slid forward. "Did you know these had leading-edge slats? It's not pretty-looking, but that old German engineering was good. Ahead of its time."

Erickson's relationship with warbirds and Tillamook went way back. Impressions from the war were his first strong memories. "We lived outside of Portland, and there were a lot of Mustangs and Lightnings always dogfighting and buzzing around," he said, leading me toward the back of the cavernous hangar. "The war was all anybody ever talked about. My cousins, my uncles, they were all in the war, and it was really all you thought about when you were growing up." As with my father and the airplane room in Newport, Erickson told me that he "had every picture of every plane ever built during the war. My whole bedroom was pasted with them."

In the museum's gift shop was a ten-foot blowup of a well-known photograph showing a World War II daredevil named Swede Ralston flying through the blimp hangar, trailing a tail of smoke. It was none other than Ralston who taught Erickson how to fly in 1953, and in 1955 Erickson bought his very first warbird, a T-6, for $500. But he sold it two years later, and for nearly twenty-five years his passion for warbirds lay dormant. "You're involved in work all the time and your interest level goes other places," he said, shrugging his shoulders. Erickson pioneered the practice of harvesting timber with helicopters, and Erickson Air Crane operated lumber concessions and sawmills in New Guinea, Malaysia, Indonesia, South America, Canada, and throughout the American Pacific Northwest.

He bought his second warbird, a Mustang, in 1981, and "I've just added a plane or so every year, and now it's been twenty-odd years. In my early days I wanted the most popular fighter in the U.S.—that was the Mustang. Then England, the Spitfire. And then Germany, the Messerschmitt. I wanted the most well known airplane in each category. Then, as time went by, value came into play. No matter how much you love these planes or no matter how much you want one, you still have to be value conscious," Erickson said, arriving at fifty square yards of aluminum rubble, covered with dust and the occasional pigeon dropping. There were wings and tails, engines still wrapped in their cowling—My Gal Sal and the B-17 from Ruby, Alaska—the fruits of Gary Larkins's labors and half a million dollars of Erickson's money. I recognized the B-17 tail with the perfect star and bar from Ruby. Erickson jumped onto the pile and tiptoed like a tightrope walker across the truss of a B-17 wing. In a way, I thought watching him, Erickson was returning to a past life just like Kermit Weeks, and just as my own fascination with warbirds was rooted in those old photos in my father's bedroom. He'd grown up during the war; he loved its airplanes and loved flying so much he'd gotten his pilot's license; and now he simply loved flying the planes of his childhood. And maybe that was it: warbirds brought people back to their youth. In that light, maybe Weeks's notion of past lives wasn't so kooky after all. Maybe it was just his way of trying to connect with a gritty, romantic youth that he, the rich kid growing up in suburban Miami, never had.

But Jack Erickson wasn't very sentimental. He was known as a shrewd businessman and, ultimately, he insisted his planes were an investment. "Whether it's a car or a house or a business, you gotta buy right," he said. And that's how he'd started sending Gary Larkins into the wild. Having money, connections, and helicopters stationed throughout the world made the exotic search for warbirds easy. "I wanted a B-17," he said, atop his pile. "So if you think someone's asking price is too high, well, what's the next best choice? There's not too much original left, and about the only way to acquire one for a good price was to go out and get one.

"But, damn, that wind really fucked things up!" he said, surveying the wreckage of My Gal Sal and the B-17 from Ruby spread across the floor. "Sal's damage was worse than I thought it was, and I might not have done it if I'd realized she was in such bad condition. It looks pretty sick—you've got to have a good imagination." He paused a few moments. "But look at that duct work," he said, jumping down and poking his head into the wing. Indeed, the inside of the wing shined. Not a bubble of corrosion or a speck of rust dimmed the shiny surfaces. He grabbed a length of rubber hose. "Look at these hoses. They're damn near sixty years old and they're as full of flex and life as if they were brand new. The thing about Sal, though," he said, pausing a moment, "she was all there. All original shit that is nowadays very hard to come by. Ball turrets, top turrets— look at this top turret," he said, squeezing past a wing and coming upon a machine-gun turret perched on the concrete floor. "It's perfect!" The ceiling over the cockpit was missing, and the nose was smashed, but there were the yokes, the seats, the instruments, the dozens of toggle switches and cables that make up a B-17. You couldn't buy it anywhere. "Look at this," he said, pointing to the center section that I'd helped Gary pry away from the ground in Ruby. ("I Survived the AlCan Highway," proclaimed a bumper sticker on a truss.) We peered in the perfect tail gunner's compartment of *My Gal Sal* and Erickson kicked a piece of landing gear. "All pristine!" he said.

In 1992, Erickson started running out of room in Medford, Oregon, where he kept his airplanes. And the old Tillamook blimp hangar was an underfunded "blimp museum" with no exhibits. "Mostly just the building itself," Erickson said. He moved in and a new aviation museum was born. These days, 90,000 visitors a year troop through to see his airplanes and visit the cafeteria and gift shop he operates.

We left the B-17 wreckage and headed back past Erickson's airplanes. Beneath every one were pans lined with paper towels collecting the incessantly dripping oil. Erickson himself had more than 5,000 hours of flight time, and every one of his planes was a flyer. "From a pilot's point of view, they're just a different flying experience. It's more challenging. You have to be more aware of what you're doing." He paused a long time. "They are high-performance airplanes and they can bite you pretty fast." He paused again. "Swede Ralston, when I bought my Mustang, he said, 'What the hell are you buying that old piece of shit for?' He was from the age group that went through the war and flew those planes every day, and he couldn't imagine why anyone would want to fly one now. But for us"—he paused again, sucking on his dip of Copenhagen, fighting for words—"for us they have so much history. But the question is, how long will World War II planes be in vogue? When my generation dies off, will the interest still be there? Will they still hold their value?"

I left Erickson and headed out into the chill Oregon rain, pon-

dering his question. I decided these planes would always be compelling and valuable icons. Unless or until there was another war as
important as World War II, its planes would never be equaled in
emotional or monetary value. Still, I suppose I'd hoped that the
wealthy collectors might brag more, or jaw about the ego-boost of
owning something so big and rare, maybe confide how they felt bigger, badder, even heroic because they owned big, bad, heroic airplanes. World War II had been the most important event of the
twentieth century, and American airplanes had played a good part
in its victory. What did it feel like to own one?

Part of the problem was that the one thing that distinguished
the collectors from other fans—their money—was the one thing
they were most hesitant to talk about. It was curious, but I was beginning to feel that in the continuum of the warbird subculture, the
guys who spent the most money on the airplanes were the least
interesting—or maybe just the most reserved—and that it was a lot
more fun to talk to the guys who fetched them than the guys who
owned them.

So on the way home from visiting Jack Erickson I dropped in on
Matt Jackson, the air racer and old friend of Darryl's who'd helped
on the *Kee Bird*. He operated an airplane shop at Van Nuys Airport
and when he came walking out of his hangar I didn't recognize him.
At the *Kee Bird* site he'd been barrel-chested and brash; now he was
just brash. He'd lost a hundred pounds, and with it went the barrel
chest. He was hopping over to Palm Springs to pick up a client in a
refurbished old four-seat, single-engine Navion, and he invited me
along. First, he showed me another plane he'd recently finished: an
A-26 Invader he'd turned into an executive transport for another
client. Its owner sure wasn't interested in historical authenticity. In
place of the bomb bay was a leather sofa. "Gorgeous, eh?" he said,
shaking his head. "Don't even ask how much that cost."

In a few moments we were bumping east through a yellow haze
over L.A. "Look," he said, "in the old days the guys who loved and

owned these planes were the old World War II drivers who were flying them as crop dusters and firefighters and air racers. But in the
early 1980s, it all started changing when these guys with money
started chasing planes. Ever since, it's escalated, and they've created
almost a false economy. They're all outsized personalities with lots
of money who shoot from the hip. 'Sperm of the moment' is what I
call it. They say, 'I want that airplane,' and Gary Larkins or Darryl
run scurrying to get 'em—and that's fine, because they're in it for
the adventure as much as the money. They're all people who just
love the airplanes. It's a disease."

FOURTEEN

—

SOONER

Narsaq, Greenland; July 1999

Compared with the desolate brown rocks, dirt, and ice of northern Greenland around Thule and the *Kee Bird*, southwest Greenland is downright pastoral. Long, sheltered fjords wind inland for miles, twisting among archipelagos of small islands. In the summer the coast is dotted with emerald-green plots of hay, hard against great rising mountains of rock and glacier. As the *Kissavik*—a chartered, sixty-five-foot former Danish Coast Guard vessel—chugged through the jade-colored water, speedboats packed with black-haired Greenlanders out for a day of seal hunting and fishing zipped past. This was still Greenland, though, and even at the end of July the temperature was forty-five degrees, the wind on the water cutting. A light drizzle fell. "What am I doing here?" roared Bob Ready, simultaneously sweating and shivering on the *Kissavik*'s foredeck. "I could be sitting at home by the pool!" He paused a moment, gazed at a waterfall cascading 300 feet down a granite cliff, gazed at the low, pewter-colored sky and mountains of blue-green ice floating by, gazed at the piles of duffel bags and video equipment on the deck, and the crowd standing at the rails, and then proclaimed, "No, I'd rather be here than anywhere else in the world!"

Ready was sixty years old, the bearish, mustachioed chief executive officer and president of a two-hundred-million-dollar industrial lighting company in Blue Ash, Ohio, and he was exhibiting all the symptoms of a new disease: vintage warbirds fever. So far, unlike Jack Erickson or Kermit Weeks, he'd only partially succumbed to his passion; he was fascinated by the airplanes and loved the idea of them, but they scared him, too. For a while he'd owned a Stearman biplane, an AT-6 trainer, a B-25 Mitchell, and a Chance Vought Corsair fighter, but then he'd sold them. His company was publicly traded and he worried about the potential public-relations liability of having such expensive toys, or of killing some innocent by-stander in a crash. But he was into planes, and not only was his company located by a small municipal airport in Blue Ash, he oper-ated a maintenance and refueling facility for corporate jets (in-cluding his own Cessna Citation) at the airport. When the town started thinking about closing it, Ready had a brainstorm. He'd recently fallen into a conversation with a World War II veteran who was lamenting that today's children didn't appreciate or even know about "the tragedy, pain, and sacrifice," as he'd put it, of World War II. What if he built a memorial dedicated to the Army Air Force at his little airport? It was a great idea! It would pay trib-ute to the nearly 50,000 deaths suffered by Eighth Air Force air-crews in World War II, even as it breathed new life into the airport that was so important to his company. And what better symbol of the war, and what better anchor to the memorial, than a genuine B-17 Flying Fortress? Indeed, he could even build it right next to his maintenance hangar, with a glass wall overlooking the memorial.

There was only one problem with Bob Ready's scheme: he couldn't find a B-17. Of the forty-five still in existence, only a hand-ful were in private hands, and no one wanted to part with his for what Ready considered a reasonable sum. So, like Jack Erickson be-fore him, Bob Ready turned to Gary Larkins.

Gary had the perfect B-17 in mind for Bob Ready. It was an ex-ceptionally rare early model B-17E named the *Sooner*, which had run out of gas trying to land in near-zero visibility at the new American base called Bluie West One at Narsarsuaq, Greenland, on

June 27, 1942. Like *My Gal Sal*, it was part of the first squadron of B-17s en route to the war in Europe. Unlike *Sal*, the *Sooner* had ditched in the water just off a small island and, while all twelve crew members had paddled to safety, the plane sank in minutes in two-hundred-odd feet of water. Gary had been lusting after the plane for years.

Wherever World War II had been fought, there were downed airplanes. But after years of searching, Gary had learned a thing or two about them. Most intact airplanes in crowded Europe were long gone. Indeed, just about any airplane near any place where people went or lived was likely to be picked over. There were rumors of a lot of planes in the former Soviet Union, but that vast country was a hornet's nest of corruption. Working there and getting permission to export anything would be a nightmare. There were lots of airplanes in the South Pacific, but the moist jungle heat and warm salt water was murder on airframes. Plus, places like the Solomons and the Marshall Islands were fast creating national-heritage acts that often made it illegal to remove World War II artifacts, which attracted precious tourists and divers. Getting locked in the metal box in the Solomons made a great tale, but Gary didn't relish being locked up in another one. Then there were the Philippines, but besides the similar problems of the tropics, Gary's forays there had ended in run-ins with real pirates and guerrillas. In many ways, the Arctic was the best place on earth for warbirds, and Greenland and its waters were the best place of all. Thousands of American warbirds had passed through and over en route to the war in Europe, and dozens had crashed. The frigid air and water preserved the airplanes, and it was so remote that no one touched them. And it was no small matter that the Danish and Greenland governments were relatively easy to work with. Spend a bit of time on the paperwork, and the planes were there for the taking. The *Sooner* wasn't a *Kee Bird*, but it was the next best thing: a perfectly intact early model B-17 dressed for war. It ought to be worth millions.

The year the *Kee Bird* had burned, the year he'd recovered *My*

Gal Sal, Gary spent three weeks, on Jack Erickson's tab, trolling for the plane. He hadn't found it, but that wasn't surprising: his side-scan sonar had been held up in customs and he searched with nothing more than an underwater video camera. But the *Sooner* ought to be easy pickings: the official U.S.-government crash report included a map drawn at the time with an arrow pointing right to where the plane had crashed. And dozens of locals from the nearby village of Narsaq said that they knew where the plane was. Indeed, they reported that over the years someone had attached a steel cable to the plane, and back in the summer of '95 Gary had found the cable right where it was rumored to be. He'd tried to hook the cable and follow it to what he hoped would be the plane, but his team had no diving equipment and the cable kept slipping back into the deep. As an added bonus, Paul Blaida, the *Sooner's* bombardier, was itching to lead them to the spot he'd last seen as a twenty-two-year-old heading off to war. With powerful side-scan sonar equipment and an operator who knew what he was doing, the *Sooner* ought to stand out like the Great Wall of China.

But there was more. Gary knew of an unnamed B-17 that had crash-landed, wheels up, on a frozen fjord on the remote coast of east Greenland, on April 9, 1944. Like the *Kee Bird*, that B-17 greased onto the snow-covered ice without damage and all nine crewmen were quickly rescued. An airplane flying over the crash two weeks later reported the ice melted. The B-17 was gone. Even more incredible, before they were rescued the crew had snapped photographs of the fjord and the airplane, and Gary had them, stunning, clear, black-and-white photographs showing a B-17 against a backdrop of immense, craggy mountains. The polished aluminum B-17 shining in the Arctic sun looked like some outlandish offering in the latest Neiman Marcus Christmas catalogue. Again, it was stock, ready for war, and ought to be, as Gary would chant, "Cherry!"

Bob Ready was hooked. He loved the idea of the *Sooner* as the centerpiece of what he was planning to call the Ultimate Sacrifice Memorial. As for that other B-17, well, the expensive part of an expedition to recover a plane was assembling the recovery equipment in Greenland; once it was all there, recovering a second plane would be nearly free. He could restore that one to flying condition and have his very own flying B-17.

In Bob Ready, Gary found a salvor's dream. In his early days, he'd largely found planes for government museums, and had been paid in trade with surplus equipment. He had to find the planes the Air Force or Navy wanted, recover them, deliver them, take as payment another plane or planes, then sell those planes—all that before he saw a penny. It was all speculative. And even working for someone like Jack Erickson had its problems. Erickson, for instance, usually paid Gary a prearranged fixed sum, out of which he had to salvage and deliver the plane—no matter how long or difficult the process turned out to be. And Erickson wasn't known as a lavish spender.

Bob Ready, on the other hand, didn't like to play games. With his company and his memorial in mind, he wanted a straight, no-nonsense deal. He had loads of money. He didn't want any *Kee Bird* debacle, didn't want Gary trolling around on a shoestring without the right equipment, didn't want to be penny-wise and pound-foolish. If you planned it right and spent the right amount of money, Bob Ready figured, it ought to go like clockwork. He put Gary on a salary: for the first time in all his years of hunting winged treasure, Gary was being paid in advance, no matter what the outcome.

But unlike Jack Erickson, Ready wanted to be involved. He dug the romantic idea of looking for and recovering the *Sooner* out on the high seas of the frozen north with a guy like Gary Larkins, whom he referred to in his Ultimate Sacrifice Memorial concept presentation as "the modern-day Indiana Jones." He was a hands-on manager and he wanted to manage the recovery of the *Sooner* just like any other corporate operation. So now here Bob Ready was, riding the fjords of Greenland, surveying all he'd wrought, wondering, just like Vern Rich and Matt Jackson and Darryl Greenamyer before him, what the hell he'd gotten himself into.

The sky darkened, a rain squall pummeled the *Kissavik*, and Paul Blaida, the *Sooner*'s eighty-year-old bombardier, turned white as chalk and threw up all over his only pair of blue jeans. The expedition was only a few hours old and Bob Ready was already flooded with anxiety. He was worried about Blaida, worried about all those people crowded onto the decks of the *Kissavik*, worried they'd even find the airplanes—especially with all the journalists and photographers and filmmakers he'd brought along. "Where do you go to just relax?" he muttered.

For Gary Larkins, it was a new kind of expedition. For two and a half decades he'd been flying or slogging to the ends of the earth with a small band of pirates to muscle out winged treasure. Usually he spent one trip finding the plane, videotaping it and assessing the recovery options. A second trip would recover it. As for the *Sooner* and the plane Ready was calling the *Later*, he had never even seen them. They ought to be there, but he couldn't be sure. But under Bob Ready the plan had mutated, grown, blossomed into the biggest expedition of his career. To find the *Sooner* meant a high-powered side-scan sonar towed behind a boat. If they could find the *Sooner*, why couldn't they just recover her right then and there? That meant a barge to put the *Sooner* on, a crane to raise her, and an unmanned submarine, known in the trade as an ROV (remote-operated vehicle), to rig her. The *Sooner* ought to weigh around 35,000 pounds, and that meant a big crane, which meant a big barge. To tow the barge and crane and carry his own crew, the boat's crew, plus the side-scan and ROV crew, meant a big boat. The bill was starting to mount, so what the hell, if Gary could get the *Sooner*, why not just go get the *Later*, too, while he was at it? That meant a barge big enough for that big crane and two 35,000 pound airplanes, each with a wingspan of 103 feet. A bigger barge meant an even bigger boat. And so, on July 13, 1999, the 185-foot *Ocean Wrestler*, towing a 375-foot oceangoing barge mounted with a 250-ton lift capacity crane and a half-million-dollar ROV sailed from

Sydney, Nova Scotia, for Narsaq, Greenland. It was chartered for forty days.

Originally, Bob Ready and a handful of friends and supporters planned to fly up to Narsaq when Gary actually located the *Sooner*. But as the plan unfolded, Ready's thinking changed. If Gary was going to find the plane—and he already knew where it was and they had all the equipment in place—why not be part of the expedition from the beginning? When Gary and the Pirates flew off on a recovery adventure, they always did so with open-ended tickets. We don't know how long it will take or when we'll be back, they told their wives. But Ready didn't like that approach. The *Ocean Wrestler* and all the equipment were costing him around $15,000 a day. He budgeted $750,000 for the twin recoveries. He wanted a timetable. Gary complied. Getting the *Ocean Wrester* from Sydney to Narsaq would take four to seven days. Finding and recovering the *Sooner* ought to take four days. The trip up the east coast to the *Later* ought to take another four days. Add four days to bring up the *Later*, and a week to get it all back to Sydney—the whole deal would be done in about a month.

Somehow, even when the most speculative plans get committed to paper, they suddenly seem real, fixed, becoming true simply because the papers say they are. The plan said Gary Larkins would find and recover the *Sooner* in four days, a plane that nobody had actually even seen in half a century. So Bob Ready bought plane tickets for Gary and his team out of Greenland and home on August 13. And, since the plans said it was going to take four days to find and recover the *Sooner*, Bob Ready and twelve friends and relatives decided to join Gary for the first four days in Greenland. They'd see the rare piece of history break the water, drink some champagne, then go home happy while Gary and the Pirates went on to fish out the *Later*.

The expedition was huge. There was Gary, his team of five, two sonar operators, two ROV operators, a documentary video team of three, two still photographers, and me; Bob Ready; his son, Scott; his first cousin, Jack, a retired Navy admiral; Paul Blaida; a couple of cronies of Bob and his son; an advertising copywriter from Toronto hoping to write a book on "aircraft archaeology"; Ron Dick, a former vice-marshal of the British Royal Air Force; and assorted others. As the cameras flashed and the videotape whirred, the *Kissavik* looked like a boat full of tourists promised a plane no one had seen in fifty-eight years.

Everyone was there but Gary Larkins. He'd flown up two days before to meet the *Ocean Wrestler* in Narsaq and get things ready. No one had heard from him since.

Steve Dabagian was incredulous. A short, gnomelike oceanographer with long blond hair and mirrored sunglasses, Dabagian was a side-scan sonar expert and president of Ocean Systems, Inc. Just two weeks before, he'd found John F. Kennedy, Jr.'s, airplane at the bottom of the ocean off Martha's Vineyard. Perched on the *Kissavik*'s stern railing, at home in the wind and rain, he said, "We'll never find that plane in four days. It'll take me a day or two just to get the system up and running."

Late that afternoon, after four hours of puttering through the fjords, we rounded a bend. The *Ocean Wrestler*, a utilitarian-looking, black-hulled former North Sea oil tugboat with a great, upswept bow and a long, low fantail, was tied to a massive steel barge as big as a football field in Narsaq harbor. Quaint-looking red, yellow, green, and blue houses dotted the rocky shore. The *Kissavik* pulled up to the *Wrestler* and Gary Larkins. "Oh, it's been fun!" said Gary, who'd just spent eighteen hours coaxing the *Wrestler* and its barge to Narsaq through seventy-five miles of ice and fog-choked fjord.

Although this was high summer, Narsaq was some four hundred miles south of the Arctic Circle, which meant the sun set by ten P.M. It was already too late in the day to start the hunt. Berths were sorted out: Gary and the Pirates and the ROV and side-scan guys were on the *Wrestler*; Ready and his entourage were staying on the *Kissavik*. Dinner served in two shifts to accommodate the forty people. And, well, there was nothing to do. Here was Bob Ready and all his friends stuck on a utilitarian workboat in Greenland. The *Wrestler* was all working steel; there wasn't even a lounge on the damn thing. As dusk settled over the gray fjord, Ready and his entourage gathered on the *Kissavik* and the Pirates hunkered down in Gary's ten-foot-square berth below the *Wrestler*'s waterline.

It hadn't taken Gary long to make the berth home. A skull-and-crossbones pirate flag hung from the wall and a life-sized cardboard cutout of the mighty Duke, John Wayne, as "Hondo," sporting chaps, spurs, and iconic Winchester, watched from a corner. Wherever Gary went he carried an important-looking trunk filled with a TV/VCR combo, and a pile of "training films," classic movies starring Gregory Peck, the Duke, and Harrison Ford. Even in the wild, as long as he had a generator handy, he'd hunker down in his tent and replay the fantasies. *The Dirty Dozen, Twelve O'Clock High, Hondo, Indiana Jones and the Temple of Doom*—he'd seen them all a hundred times, but he never grew tired of them. For Gary they weren't the unrealistic fantasies of Hollywood screenwriters, they were inspiration for real life. (Once, when I said I had never seen the classic *Thirty Seconds over Tokyo*, he said, only half-joking, "What! You haven't watched it? Every real American should watch that movie every month!") He duct-taped the TV/VCR to the faux wood bulkhead and whipped out a box of cigars and a bottle of V.O., and one by one the Pirates filed in: Rick Dougherty, a red-bearded professional bartender who'd been kicking along with Gary since high school; Rafid Tuma, George Carter, Ricky Whitmire, and Wayne Lloyd, all current or former Baltimore County, Maryland, police officers and police divers who dropped whatever they were doing whenever Gary's call of the wild sounded; and the two ROV operators, the two sonar operators, and the crane operator.

They perched shoulder to shoulder on equipment trunks and

folding lawn chairs, or just stood when there wasn't any space left. Gary sat cross-legged in his narrow bunk, a glass of V.O. and one of his treasure maps in his lap, a cigar clamped between his teeth. Cigar and cigarette smoke filled the cramped room.

Someone mentioned JFK, Jr.'s, airplane. "That was recent," Gary said, taking a long drag on his cigar. "They knew the flight path of the plane and it was only one hundred feet or so down— hey, why don't you put in *Twelve O'Clock High*," he said, taking a long drag on the cigar. "And this B-17 is a detective story. Based on the difficulty, I'd much rather have to recover JFK's plane. That was easy," he said, taking a sip of V.O.

Gary paused. The room was out of ice. A moment later Whitmire, a squadron commander of the Baltimore County SWAT team when he wasn't on leave chasing planes with Gary, scurried back with a two-foot chunk of glistening iceberg. He chopped it into drink-sized pieces with his Buck knife and clinked it into glasses all around. "Just think," Gary said, "this ice might be a million years old!"

Near midnight, talk turned to the *Sooner* again. "I think she's right near that rock, where that cable we found last year is," Gary said. "Those natives in the village said that over time it was tied around a rock and that's exactly what George and I found in '95—a cable right off the beach, only we had no diving gear that year."

"If we find the cable again, maybe we can just tie a liftbag to it," Tuma said.

"Why would everyone talk about cables and then we find a cable right where it's supposed to be?" Gary said. "It's too weird to be just coincidence.

"Hey," he said, clearing a pile of maps and photos off his bed. "Time for you boys to take the party somewhere else. I need some sleep."

The *Kee Bird*, the B-17 in Alaska—the locations of those planes were known. Gary now had the map of the *Sooner's* crash location, the crash reports, the eyewitness accounts of Paul Blaida and a host of local villagers. This wasn't the middle of the ocean. The plane had been there, people had seen it, and that made him confident. For nearly thirty years he'd been recovering warbirds—no one had brought back as many as he had—but still he never acquired the fame of Darryl Greenamyer. Not long ago he'd given a slide show and talk at the Smithsonian National Air and Space Museum, and had been wined and dined before the show by Don Engen, the museum's director. He was getting closer all the time, but he was still no Darryl, no Jacques Cousteau, no Bob Ballard. Yet no one had ever recovered one, much less two, "cherry" B-17s from the ocean depths before. He wanted the *Sooner* and the *Later*. Badly. If he could just get these two planes, his days of begging for money, of picking up Greenamyer's trash, would be over. But all the money and planning and sophisticated equipment in the world couldn't obscure one simple fact: this was still a treasure hunt. Before he could recover the *Sooner* or the *Later*, Gary had to find them.

At a little after eight the next morning, leaving the barge anchored in Narsaq harbor, the *Wrestler* and the *Kissavik* headed out. A dark-gray sky covered the winding fjord, and horizontal striations of fog cut across green, craggy headlands. Light rain dribbled on the still water. Ready, his entourage, and the four divers were aboard the *Kissavik*; they planned to look for the steel cable. On the *Wrestler*'s bridge, thirty feet above the water, Gary opened a binder filled with the *Sooner*'s crash reports and the map. He was wearing a navy-blue one-piece jump suit emblazoned with the Air Pirates logo, wings sprouting from a skull beneath a star. "The cable was thirty feet offshore of this island," he said to Capt. John Meadows and sonar operator Steve Dabagian, whom he'd nicknamed the Armenian Gypsy, "and we pulled it and messed with it. Everyone says it has been there a long time. Now, we found a little old lady who grew up in Narsaq, and she remembers the plane here, right in this trough," he said, running his finger over a narrow channel between two small islands. "But Paul Blaida thought it was here," a little far-ther south.

"Did she actually see it?" asked the Gypsy, dressed in a bright-red jump suit.

"She says she saw the plane go around and around a couple times and she thinks it landed here. But she was a little girl then. But everyone says the plane landed two hundred to two hundred fifty yards out from this little island. And Paul says there was a vil-lage, that it was a straight shot from the plane to the village. Now, the locals all say there was no village there, but Paul said they lived in caves, and sure as shit in '95 we found a bunch of caves and the remains of what might be a little church. So I say let's start by scan-ning there."

Searching the ocean bottom by side-scan sonar involved towing a four-foot-long torpedo-shaped "tow fish" over a grid of equally spaced lines a few feet above the ocean bottom. The fish sent out pings of sound at forty-five-degree angles, which were picked up by a transponder hanging ten feet under the *Wrestler*, and computers translated the sound into a gray "picture" of the ocean bottom. The tow fish cost $25,000, and if it smashed into a rock it might be ru-ined. Dabagian wanted to run up and down the search area first without the fish, mapping the bottom, allowing him to know what he was "flying" over. "I don't want any surprises," he said. To en-hance the accuracy of the search, he needed to know exactly where the tow fish was at any moment. To overcome the built-in error of satellite global positioning systems, he wanted to set up a GPS sta-tion high on a peak within sight of the search area. That GPS would triangulate between the tow fish, the *Wrestler*, and the satel-lites overhead, giving him the precise position, at any given mo-ment, of the *Wrestler* and the fish itself. When the fish identified a target, the computer in his control cabin would pinpoint it to within three feet. "That will take us most of the day," he said.

———

Shortly after four P.M., the Gypsy was ready to start the hunt. The GPS base station, powered by two car batteries, had been mounted on the crest of a hill overlooking the search area. After running up and down four search lines, Dabagian was satisfied there would be no underwater surprises. "Okay, Captain," he said on the bridge, "spin around and get on line number four. Just miss the ice, that's numero uno!" While there didn't appear to be any potential surprises under the water, what was floating on it was another matter altogether. Icebergs were everywhere, huge growlers of blue and white and green, as well as smaller blobs, all slowly drifting in the narrow channels. Mounted on the bridge was a computer monitor, linked to the Gypsy's laptop computer in the sonar control room below; the monitor displayed a grid of numbered lines 3,000 feet long and 450 feet apart. A toyish outline of a boat represented the *Wrestler*, an X at the end of a dotted line represented the tow fish. The fish could see nearly 500 feet to either side. An accurate search meant following the lines exactly, but the icebergs made that impossible. Even more ominous, the icebergs were ten, twenty, even forty feet high. And that meant they were 200 to 400 feet deep; some were literally grounded on the bottom. What would fifty years of tons of ice dragging along the ocean bottom mean to a fragile aluminum airplane?

Dabagian's colleague, Paul Goodall, dumped the silver-colored torpedo off the stern and the steel cable, wrapped around a fiber-optic core, unfurled from a winch on the fantail. If Gary's calculated estimates were correct, the *Sooner* ought to be right below.

Gary lit a cigar, inhaled deeply, and plunked his lanky frame on a rickety stool. A radiator burned at his back. In front of him in the stuffy cabin, beneath the bridge, rose a wall of electronic components. They surrounded a slowly moving two-foot-wide strip of thermal paper scribbled with grainy black and gray lines: the sonar picture of the ocean bottom. The ship's diesel engines throbbed softly, the *ping, ping, ping* of the sonar like a beating heart. A pearly-white mountain of ice passed slowly by the porthole. Gary adjusted his Air Pirates baseball cap, sucked on his cigar, and stared intently at the scribbles. Hundreds of thousands of dollars and years of searching and yearning had come down to this: in any second, those scribbles ought to coalesce into a recognizable B-17 Flying Fortress.

Dabagian's knee jiggled up and down as he stared at the thermal paper. On the desk in front of him lay a tiny model B-17, part good luck charm, part identification aid. "That tail is twenty-seven feet tall, so if it's right side up and still intact, it should throw a pretty big shadow," Gary said.

Three hours later, there wasn't a sign of the *Sooner*. The *Kissavik* pulled up alongside the *Wrestler*. The divers had searched for hours where Gary and George had found the steel cable in '95, had dived to 130 feet and had found nothing. "Maybe an iceberg picked her up," Gary said to Ready. "I was absolutely sure we were in the right place." Near nine P.M., we crawled up the 1,500-foot-wide channel between the two smallest islands. Vast, tousled growlers were everywhere, their keels reflecting blue beneath the dark water. The end of the channel, narrowing to a few hundred feet, was choked clear across with a mountain of ice. "Is there any way to read under that ice?" said Bob Ready.

"No," Gary said, "and if the plane is under there it's crushed." Ready shook his head slowly.

"You can't get discouraged after just one day," Gary said. "We've got the best technology in the world and we'll find her." Dusk was beginning to settle over the fjord. Paul Blaida slowly climbed the steep steps to the bridge. He was small, compact, with a full head of silver hair and thoughtful eyes, a retired accountant who made his home outside of Chicago. He looked at the map, looked out the windows at the rocky hills, icebergs, and still water. "We flew out of Goose Bay, Labrador," he said slowly, the landscape igniting his memory. "We went out one at a time and we were the first airplane. The pilot only had a hundred fifty hours of flight time, but we had as copilot a major, and with him we didn't fear anything.

Near BW 1 [Narsarsuaq] the radio beam was garbled and the weather was real socked in. We tried to get under the clouds and made a bunch of trips down to the ocean only to be stopped by fog. We had an alternate, BW 8 [Sondre Stromfjord], five hundred miles north, and we tried that, but it was socked in, too." The *Wrestler* drummed softly as we stared at the chilly, dark water and leaden sky and Blaida's story unfolded.

"We flew and flew, hoping the fog would lift, but finally we were at the point of no return. We dropped real low and circled around and circled around," he said softly, "until we found this island about two or three miles long and then we opened the bomb-bay doors. Every time we'd pass over the island the men would grab a bag and say, 'Bombs away!' We got a big charge out of that! Then we got ready to belly in. But one of the bags got caught on the gears that closed the door and I tried to use my knife to cut the strap, but we were flying right over the water and it was bumpy and I couldn't do it. So we all got into the radio compartment and I stood next to the bomb bay, and as it hit the water I got thrown right into the open bomb bay and what saved me was a little catwalk which I hung on to. Then we all jumped onto the wing."

"Were the props feathered?" Gary asked.

"I don't know," Blaida said. "We had two dinghies but there was only room for five in each one, so the major asked for volunteers, and two dummies raised their hands. Clothes and all, they just started swimming. The plane was sinking fast because the bomb-bay doors were open, so we started paddling and the swimmers started yelling for help. We grabbed 'em by the neck and got 'em to shore. They were already discolored. We found the bags, opened some of our stuff, and, damnit, there was whiskey!"

"How'd you pick the location?" Gary asked.

"Well, the island was flat and one side went right to the water's edge so it would be easy to climb onto, and most of the others were cliffs. Anyway, we started a fire—it was cold and foggy—and stood around wondering what to do. We didn't have a radio. Then I saw two Eskimos coming out of the fog in a kayak. They got to about fifty yards from shore and started talking to us. 'Airport! Airport!' we yelled, flapping our arms. Then they paddled away, back into the fog. An hour later the mayor arrived in a boat and brought us to another island and a church, and not long after that, Bernt Balchen—he was the commander of BW 1—came to get us."

But which small, low island was it? There were a half-dozen islands and they all looked the same. Turn me around and I couldn't tell which was which. For Blaida, a lifetime separated his two trips to this spot. "I think you should take me to the church and I should look from there," he said.

"If there wasn't so much bloody ice," the Gypsy said, "we could cover a lot more ground."

Darkness was coming fast and Gary could do no more searching. The *Wrestler* headed back to Narsaq for the night.

Two days later Gary looked weary as the *Wrestler*, rumbling gently, coasted ahead at the speed of a walk.

"Why don't we throw in a line over there?" said Bob Ready's cousin, the admiral, pointing to a spot down the fjord from where Blaida believed the plane ought to be.

"The plane isn't there," said Larkins, "and we've just started over here."

"Sure your equipment is working? Maybe we should throw a barrel or something over the side to see if that side-scan is working."

"The side-scan is working perfectly," said Larkins, "and that Armenian Gypsy could find a piece of shrapnel in the middle of the Pacific Ocean."

"The way we do it in the Navy—"

"In the Pirates we work until we find it," snapped Rafid Tuma.

"Well, no one asked you," said Scott Ready, Bob's son.

"I don't know," said Paul Blaida softly, pointing to the same low island 400 yards to the right that he kept identifying, over and over again. "That sure does look like the island to me."

"Don't worry, Paul," Gary said, "your memory is sharp. It's just a tedious process of elimination that takes time."

"All these islands look the same!" worried Bob Ready, staring across the water.

For a Gary Larkins expedition, three days was nothing, but time was running out for Bob Ready and his entourage. Tensions were running high. The hangers-on were crowding the bridge and clustering in the sonar room, desperate for the *Sooner*. They had come so far. Where was the plane? There were ten islands in the fjord spread across five or six miles. And each one looked identical. Towing the fish over a line, the *Wrestler* couldn't exceed two miles an hour. A single small grid took hours. The admiral couldn't resist taking charge. He wanted to try here, there, how about over there. As soon as the tow fish went in the water and the *Wrestler* finished a line, empty-handed, he wanted the search moved. Scott Ready had his own ideas. Conflicting information flooded in. The captain of the *Kissavik* knew a local who reported that his father had helped rescue Blaida and the crew in the summer of '42. He said they'd been taken from the first small island to Narsaq, not the now-deserted island to which Blaida kept pointing. That would change the search area by five miles. Paul Blaida was ferried in the Zodiac dinghy over to the island where he believed he'd been taken, to jog his memory. "I never went to Narsaq," he insisted, standing in the foundation of a small building. He said he'd been taken to a church. Was this a former church? Nothing indicated it was. George Carter and the divers searched the smallest island for traces of the *Sooner's* luggage. More locals weighed in and most pointed to the narrow channel they'd already searched. "The problem is," Gary said, "it may just be the village story."

But he was hardly discouraged. "Paul, when you scrambled out of the plane, did it seem real open, like that?" he said pointing down the fjord, "or was it more like a trough, like that?" he said, pointing up the fjord to a narrow opening between two islands.

Blaida gazed up and down the fjord, squinting. "I'm not sure. It was so foggy, and we were all so excited to get down all right."

"I think he did a hell of a job keeping you alive," Gary said, "but he had to have an approach in mind."

"We opened the bomb-bay doors, dumped all of our stuff and then came down; I don't think we slid more than three hundred feet," Blaida said.

"I'm not a B-17 pilot," Gary said, staring into the distance, "but I wouldn't want to be coming into that narrow bit. You'd want to ease back on the throttle slowly, to really settle on back, and you'd need a big area to do that." You could almost see the film rolling in Gary's head, picturing what it would be like to be struggling to lay the four-engine bomber down gently on an Arctic fjord, the life of your eleven crew members in your hands. "Can you imagine it?" Larkins suddenly said, doffing his Air Pirates baseball cap and squinting his thick black eyebrows. "You're twenty-two years old, you've never been out of Iowa, you're on your way to war and suddenly you're ditching your plane in Greenland and talking to a bunch of Eskimos!"

Four days passed, and hour after hour the *Wrestler* tracked back and forth over a widening succession of search grids in the maze of islands. But line after sonar line revealed nothing, save a bottom scarred by icebergs as if raked by the claws of an angry pack of giant polar bears. With every passing day, Gary, John Meadows, the *Wrestler's* captain, and the Gypsy became increasingly suspicious that the plane was simply gone, ground to bits by a half-century of tumbling icebergs. Gary spent increasing amounts of time huddled over his notebook, his lap piled with charts and crash reports, gazing at the photos of the B-17 on the east coast. "This one," he said with a twinkle in his brown eyes, "will be cherry."

On Bob Ready's last day in Greenland, he, his hangers-on, and the divers motored off in the *Kissavik* again to dive around the shoal waters of the island Paul Blaida insisted he'd paddled to, and the *Wrestler* began a search in the deeper waters midchannel. "This is the deepest water, and it's the only place we haven't looked," Gary said, as the *Wrestler* rumbled slowly ahead. Great white bergs loomed out of a thin layer of fog pierced with occasional rays of sunshine. Suddenly, at ten A.M., the radio crackled. "We've found a piece of aluminum right by the shore and we want you to come over and take a look at it," Scott Ready said.

Gary shook his head and winced. "I'm telling you," he said to Meadows on the bridge, "I'm not going to stop what I'm doing to go over there. I'm going to finish this grid first. They've got enough aces over there to tell whether it's aircraft aluminum or not."

Minutes later, the Zodiac bumped alongside the *Wrestler*. The Readys and the admiral climbed on, clutching a curved, bent, three-foot-wide sheet of aluminum. They were nearly frantic, smiling, triumphant. Gary trooped down to the fantail and bent over the piece. It was remarkably well preserved, dotted with yellow spots of seaweedy growth. Suddenly the admiral jumped on top of it, leaping up and down to flatten it. "Admiral!" Gary barked, "we don't jump on the artifacts! Could be the tip of a horizontal stabilizer," he said, "but I don't think it's from the *Sooner*. The rivets are wrong—see?" he said, pointing to a rivet. "These are pop-rivets and they hadn't even invented those when they made the *Sooner*." But the admiral and Scott Ready didn't care. They wanted the search moved where the piece was found. It was noon, they'd spent thousands of dollars to witness the recovery of the *Sooner*, they had nine hours left until darkness, and plane tickets out of Narssarssuaq the next morning. "Let's do whatever they want to do," Gary said.

———

And then, on the fifth day, a Friday, the admiral, Bob Ready, his son, his cosponsors, Paul Blaida, and twelve hangers-on piled aboard the *Kissavik* and went home. Gary was reborn. His life-size cardboard cutout of the Duke appeared on the bridge, along with his portable tape deck. The sun broke out of the omnipresent clouds and a rainbow momentarily arched over the fjord. "I feeeel good!" yelled James Brown, blasting from the *Wrestler*'s PA system and echoing off the chunks of ice, suddenly glowing like giant chunks of sea glass in the Arctic sun. "Bob Ready is a great guy," Gary said, puffing on a fresh cigar, "but none of those people should ever have been here and we should have looked for the other plane first."

Gary wanted to make a thorough search in the deep channel off Blaida's favorite island, and the Gypsy had identified a couple of possible targets. And anyway, it was Friday, and Captain Meadows refused to embark for a new destination on a Friday. Bad luck, he said. You couldn't whistle on the *Wrestler*, either; that might bring winds, which, in fact, were building offshore. So although Friday turned up nothing, once again, Gary decided to spend one more day searching. And that evening, a new report of the summer of '42 came in from Narsaq. It sounded good, both confirming aspects of Paul Blaida's story while raising the possibility, again, that the village he'd been brought to hadn't been the now-abandoned one with the foundation, as Blaida had insisted, but Narsaq itself. The mayor, Blaida remembered, took them on a twenty-minute boat ride to shore, followed by a walk up a slope to a church. The *Sooner* landed, the local said, and a few fishermen spotted some men in uniform at the end of an island. The fishermen were scared, he said, so they went and got the mayor, who took the *Sooner*'s crew directly to Narsaq. Now it was a big village, with hundreds of houses. But in 1942, the native said, Narsaq was nothing but a church and he insisted that the downed flyers had been brought there. If that was true, then the search was off by five miles.

So the next morning we set out again, newly invigorated. Moods soared and plummeted by the hour; the hunt was all-consuming. The Grateful Dead echoed across the fjord as Gary paced the bridge beside the Duke. "I think she's gonna give it up today," Gary mused. "It all fits. The problem was Paul couldn't see the tops of any of these mountains because the ceiling was five hundred feet, so he couldn't get his bearings. Find this sucker, will you!" he shouted to the Gypsy. "Hey, those big old tires, you can't hurt those babies. They've got enough rubber on 'em to block a barge."

Six hours later, nothing. "I don't know where that plane is," Gary said. "I wish she'd just breach. Maybe we should just go around every island in Greenland." Thick, low clouds were rolling in and the temperature was dropping. Squalls of snow lashed the fjord as the *Wrestler*'s fax suddenly whined and beeped. It was the hourly weather report. "Shit!" said Meadows, tearing the flimsy paper out of the machine. "Winds at thirty-three feet per second—that's sixty miles an hour. You don't want to be out in that."

"This is frustrating," Gary admitted, gazing at the charts. "Usually you've got a plane and it's just a matter of work. But here we're just driving around and you don't know if it's ten feet or ten miles away, or if it even exists."

A systematic search of the new area found not a trace of the *Sooner*, and as darkness fell, the *Wrestler* headed back to Narsaq. Tomorrow, Gary decided, we'll head to the east coast.

That evening, the Pirates and I strolled through Narsaq. At a small café in the village, Tuma admired the polished red stone dangling on a gold chain from the cashier's neck. It was *tuttupit*, Inuit for "reindeer blood," and was found in only two places in the world: near Narsaq and on Russia's Kola Peninsula. Wait, the cashier said, and ran off. A few minutes later she appeared with Mike Lund, a short, black-haired Greenlander. He didn't speak English, she said, but he had a bunch of the rock. We followed him down a narrow street, into his electric-blue, two-storey wooden house. He led us past yellow foul-weather gear hanging in the vestibule, into a small living room. Big, double-paned windows overlooked the iceberg-filled harbor. He brought out a bucket filled with chunks of the pink rock. Suddenly, Ricky Whitmire whipped out a photograph of a B-17 and handed it to Lund. He smiled, and jumped to action. On a scrap of paper he drew a remarkably accurate rendition of the two islands where Blaida had insisted he'd landed, the narrow channel choked with ice where we'd looked the first day. His drawing looked exactly like the charts we'd been staring at for days. Then he wrote the names of the islands. They were one and the same. We paid a few dollars for a couple of rocks, and rushed off to the *Wrestler*.

Once again, we headed out to the channel the next morning. Seeing a row of huge grounded bergs at the far end, Gary suspected a blind spot hiding the *Sooner*, and he pressed Meadows and the Gypsy to get in close. Which wasn't easy, because the fish required forward momentum but only "saw" sideways, requiring careful and painstakingly slow maneuvering of the *Wrestler*. Divers George Carter and Rafid Tuma plunged into the twenty-nine-degree, 150-foot-deep water to see what the fish couldn't. By now the sun was hidden, the sky was bruised-looking, and snow swirled around the boat. The weather fax was spitting out warnings of hurricane-force winds and seas of thirteen to eighteen feet. Backing up to and between growlers towering higher than the *Wrestler*, with keels and ridges glowing like white underwater saw teeth, Meadows grew increasingly tense. "I tell you, would you have mobilized all this expensive equipment based on a five-minute interview with a local? We've looked everywhere within twenty miles—it's here, it's there—I'm getting sick of it!" Suddenly, with a crack like a shotgun, one of the bergs calved, a truck-sized chunk splashing into the water, the growler slowly rolling over amid its own turbulent wake. "Personally, I don't understand jeopardizing this boat for this goddamned plane," Meadows said, refusing to go closer.

For once, Gary agreed. "I gotta say," he said, "looking for this thing is kind of like looking for Jimmy Hoffa. But hey," he said, pulling out his treasure map, "there's a broken-up old PBY Catalina right in the harbor of Julianehab. Maybe we should go pick that sucker up. . . ."

"Forget it," said Meadows, "I'm at a point where I'd rather deal with the hurricane-force winds than drive around here chasing myths anymore."

FIFTEEN

—

LATER

East Greenland; August 1999

Quitting the *Sooner* hunt, the *Wrestler* plunged into the gale. Hour after hour passed in a blur of swirling gray-green skies and lashing rain as the *Wrestler* limped around Cape Farewell and edged 240 miles up the east coast at the pitifully slow speed of three knots. Foaming seas exploded against the boat, hurtling over the thirty-foot bridge, the barge a distant apparition smashing through the waves a half-mile back. Doors banged. Water sloshed from the toilets. Food littered the floor of the mess. I hoped we wouldn't disappear beneath the waves forever. The Pirates lay for hours in their bunks, delirious with nausea. Gary remained unfazed. "You know," he said one evening on the bridge, staring into the gale toward the invisible shore twenty miles away, "there's an A-20 Havoc up there on the glacier that crashed carrying twenty cases of gold to Europe. And, come to think of it, there's a B-24 Liberator just a hundred yards off the beach. I bet we could wrassle her off with the guys and the crane. How about it, Captain?" The *Wrestler* rose, rose, rose, hesitated, then dropped in a stomach-churning free fall, rolled, heaved, shook, and rose again, an amusement ride gone awry.

"This," muttered Meadows, his hair oily and dark circles growing under his eyes from his endless hours on the bridge, "is verging on the bizarre."

On the morning of the fourth day it stopped. As if the *Wrestler* had passed through some magical gate to another world, the sea was suddenly like glass. Not a breath of wind stirred. White mesas of ice fifty feet high and half a mile wide floated by. Thousands of seals bobbed in the dark water and pods of pilot whales arched their shiny black backs, all against a coastline wall of jagged and snow-topped ridges rising 5,000 feet straight out of the sea. Meadows was grouchy as he turned inland toward Fjord X, where the crash reports placed the airplane. There were few soundings on the chart and, as far as the pilot book stated, the last known vessel to enter X was the U.S. Coast Guard icebreaker *Northwind*, which rode out a gale there in 1941. "Well, we'll have to see if we can get in the fjord," Meadows said. "Then we'll have to see if we can get the barge anchored. Then we'll have to see if we can start towing."

But upon entering the fjord, moods soared as the Rolling Stones blasted across the deck. The mountains towering above the morning fog were jagged and huge and tipped with snow, like the gateway to some J.R.R. Tolkien mythical kingdom. Sheer granite walls oozing greenish-brown ice rose 500 yards to either side of the fjord as Gary, standing on the *Wrestler*'s upswept bow, lifted a black-and-white photo to the horizon. "It's taken me ten years to get here, boys!" Gary said, his dark eyes darting from the photo to the mountain range ahead. "She should be right up ahead!"

Gary had always thought the so-called *Later* was the more promising airplane. She'd left Goose Bay, Labrador, headed to a refueling stop in Iceland, on April 9, 1944. Three hours from Iceland the weather closed in. Somehow, the oxygen tanks had leaked, and without oxygen the crew couldn't climb above the soup. "When we got to where we thought Iceland was, it was really socked in, fog all over and visibility very limited," wrote the engineer in the official crash report. They turned around and headed to Greenland. Two hours later, with fuel running low, "we came out of the overcast and the coast of Greenland came into view," reported the bombardier.

They met up with a C-46, dumped the ball turret, and then, wrote the radio operator, "the crew all braced themselves in the radio room and pilot and copilot set the ship down on a fjord." "We jumped on the wing," recalled the upper turret gunner, "and were seen by the C-46." Added the pilot: "Even before we landed our position was radioed in by Captain Dana (in the C-46) and on our approach to land he followed us in. This I am told saved us from a lot of hardships. Also in less than two hours [an airplane] came and dropped us supplies and some of the best sacks that sack men have ever cuddled in." They were rescued three days later.

Gary had the photographs they'd taken of the fjord and airplane, with the location of the crew's camp circled by one of the survivors. Not only were the mountains in the background distinctive looking, but there were no icebergs frozen in the fjord and the charts showed no glaciers flowing into it, and an average depth of eight hundred feet. The possible fate of the *Sooner*—pulverized by growlers—was unlikely here. Knowing the exact latitude and longitude of the crash, all Gary needed to do was put himself in that old photo and launch the tow fish. He'd studied the picture for hours with a magnifying glass, compared it to nautical charts, even tried in vain to get top-secret U.S. military charts of the place. Now he directed the *Wrestler* farther into the middle of the fjord, closer to the coordinates listed on the crash report, expecting with every fifty yards the mountains to line up more perfectly.

He held the photo up at arm's length again: the peak like a witch's hat, the shark's-tooth ridge, the glacial ice tumbling around, the sweeping fjord in the foreground. It ought to fit as perfectly as some heirloom key in a long-lost attic chest, except this chest was one of the remotest spots on earth, and Gary's key was a single photograph taken on a cold spring day in 1944. Somewhere in the unmeasured depths below was a 35,000-pound piece of aviation history, "as shiny as a new nickel," Gary chanted, and about forty million times more valuable.

Hours later, Gary was frustrated, Meadows incredulous. The

Wrestler had anchored the barge, a tedious process that took half the day, then steamed up and down, back and forth, had even stopped dead on the latitude and longitude listed in the official crash report, but something was wrong. The mountains at the end of the fjord didn't match up to the photo. Not exactly, anyway. "I don't know," Gary said, sucking hard on a Swisher Sweet and shaking his head slowly. He studied the photo, studied the mountains. "Nothing looks quite right. We've got some pieces to the puzzle, but it's like the puzzle has changed."

By this time, we'd been wandering the seas of Greenland for twelve days. Meadows and his crew were restless. Water and food were low. Winter was coming. Bob Ready was sitting on the edge of his seat back in Ohio, waiting for word of success while spending around $15,000 a day. And it suddenly grew awfully clear that the treasure "map" was wrong. Was it the photograph? Or was it the coordinates? "I don't like it," Gary said, staring at the mountains. "I don't like it at all. Mountains don't change in fifty years, and none of the mountains match the photographs."

"How good was mapping in 1944?" said the Gypsy. "Not good, I bet. This is a huge place and it could be anywhere. We can sidescan from now until the cows come home but unless we're in the right place we're wasting our time."

"Erosion, weather, the old camera, there could be a hundred reasons why the photos don't match perfectly," Meadows said.

"Mountains just don't change in fifty years, and none of these mountains really match," Gary said.

He stared at the photo and stared at the charts. He held the photos up to the horizon and traced his finger over the contours of the mountains shown on the chart. "I say the plane's here," he said suddenly, pointing to Fjord Y, just north of the one we were in. "That fjord's a lot straighter and wider than this one, and if I was a pilot I sure as hell wouldn't be flying into some narrow, crooked hole where I couldn't turn around."

"Well," the Gypsy said, "that's only a mile as the crow flies, and if the lat and long were off by just one degree, it could be there. And the name of the ridge between here and there," he said, pointing to the chart, "is X, so maybe that's what confused them. Maybe we should go around and look."

"Hey, no problem," exploded Meadows. "We can look in every fjord in east Greenland. But that fjord," he said, pointing to the chart, "it's uncharted. There are no fucking soundings there. No one's been there since 1829 and I don't particularly want to be the next. And if we so much as touch a rock with this eight-hundred-ton vessel, there's a hole in it." Meadows lit a cigarette and paced the bridge, shaking his head. "At the end of the day, no one's responsible for this vessel but me. This is the Arctic. There is no shipyard here. This ship is our lifeline. This is how we're getting out of here. It's the only way we're getting home. We ain't towing the barge with the Zodiac! I'd say due prudence is called for. If we're going over there, we're going easy, max three knots, and that's without the barge. That's—what?—twenty-six miles, and it'll take us a whole day to get in there just to see if your photo matches while we've got a definite report of the plane being right here."

It was a common problem for Gary. The only airplanes left survived because they were in places where normal people didn't go. So he found himself in a constant battle to cajole a succession of boat captains and aircraft pilots and officials around the world to go where prudence and common sense screamed forget it. "I wanted a P-39 that was supposed to be on a mountainside on the Philippine island of Mindoro," he'd recounted one evening, "but the helicopter pilot said, 'No way, that place is full of NPA guerrillas.' I pulled out five hundred bucks. 'Nope,' he said. 'How about seven?' I said. 'Nope,' he said. Finally, at twenty-seven hundred he said, 'Okay, but wait a minute.' He dashed in the hangar and came out dragging these four huge steel plates for us to sit on. 'It sucks to get shot at, but it really sucks to get shot in the ass,' he said."

Although Gary had gone home without a plane that time, it was his willingness to risk everything that made him successful when others gave up. At seven the next morning, Larkins, two Pirates, and the *Wrestler's* second mate, Dan MacLean, climbed into the Zodiac and puttered off for Fjord Y, a fool's errand if ever there was one in Meadows's mind. "We've been here for twenty-four hours now and we haven't put the fish in yet," he railed. "And that fish is the only way we're going to find that plane. We ain't gonna *see* it. I'd feel awfully stupid if we go over there, run out of time and never even search the spot where the crash report puts the plane."

An hour and a half later, as the Zodiac putted into Fjord Y, Gary's heart started to leap. Could it be? He fished out his photo of the fjord and held it up. A cold plug of spray smacked the old photo, and the ten-foot-long orange rubber Zodiac bucked in the chop, a fragile little boat in a vast landscape of sea and mountain and ice. Yep, this was the spot all right: The peak like a witch's hat, the shark's-tooth ridge with the glacial ice tumbling around, it matched perfectly this time. Once again, he'd climbed through the frame of an old photograph. "Holy shit!" he shouted, waving his cigar. "We've found her!"

MacLean spun the Zodiac around and headed back toward the *Wrestler.* Even in August, going against the wind and tide, the air was biting. "An extra rum ration for the boys," Gary barked into his crackling radio. "We've got her cornered now. It's like a religious revelation!" he shouted. "I'm sitting right over the plane."

"Put Dan on," barked Meadows.

"There's no doubt about it," confirmed MacLean, "this is the spot."

Meadows reluctantly headed toward Gary. Two hours later, the Zodiac's twenty horsepower outboard sputtered and coughed, and then stopped dead. It was out of gas. And the *Wrestler* was just about to round the point between the two fjords when the Fathometer reading jumped from 1,000 feet to one hundred feet in a boat length. Meadows disengaged the props. A second later, traveling at six-tenths of a knot, the *Wrestler* struck a submerged rock. A grinding crunch resonated through the ship. Meadows looked like he'd seen a ghost. The engineers went running. They searched the forepeak, shined flashlights into the bilge, and clambered over the bow.

Miraculously, no water poured in.

Gary paddled up that afternoon, cursing. "I've got a million dollars' worth of equipment and I'm rowing!" he barked. Meadows gingerly steamed back up the fjord to the anchored barge. Rafid Tuma dived with an underwater video camera, revealing a four-inch-deep dent on the *Wrestler*'s stem, but no apparent gashes or buckling of seams. "You can't imagine," said Meadows, shaking his head, "how lucky we are."

The next morning the *Wrestler*'s crew and the Gypsy rigged a sonar transponder linked to the Gypsy's laptop computer in the Zodiac, enabling the Zodiac to take depth soundings. Leaving the barge safely anchored in Fjord X, Meadows followed the Gypsy and the Zodiac at a crawl into uncharted Fjord Y, a vast pool surrounded by towering mountains. "I'm feeling pretty cocky," Gary said, clutching his photos of the plane resting on the ice. "It's all about putting yourself right in this photo. I've found five of them this way. You've got to feel it." And sure enough, working from the photos, Ricky Whitmire, Rafid Tuma, and the Pirates found the crew's 1944 campsite a few yards inshore, a hodgepodge of rusted U.S. Army ration cans and piles of .50-caliber machine-gun shells tucked among the rocks. "God! If I roll my sleeves up I can almost get hold of her," he said, peering into the water. "That plane is gonna be cherry."

But nothing was easy. Fjord Y, it turned out, was a 1,500-foot-deep, two-mile-wide V, its sides granite walls riddled with deep crevasses and boulders. Even with 3,000 feet of sonar cable, the Gypsy barely had enough to reach the bottom. Thermoclines, layers of water with sharply varying densities that reflect sound waves, played havoc with the sonar, making the fish appear as if it was about to crash into the rocks. Worse still, the fish was designed to read swaths of the ocean bottom by looking down and sideways from twenty or thirty feet above the bottom, which meant it saw only narrow bands of the steep walls at each pass, sharply raising the number of lines that had to be searched. "If that plane is nose down in one of those crevasses," the Gypsy said, "we might never see it."

Six days passed. Gary and the Pirates missed their flights home. The month was nearly up and the weather was changing: an impenetrable gray sky slid over the fjord like a hatch cover. The temperature and barometer dropped. Water was rationed and showers allowed once every four days. "I'm ready to get the hell out of here," said the chief engineer.

"I tell you, that plane just floated out to sea on a big piece of ice," Meadows said. "I don't believe it's here."

But the sonar identified four possible "targets." If they didn't exactly resemble a B-17, neither did they look like rocks, and Gary didn't want to budge. "All I know is, that airplane couldn't have gone very far; it's down there," he said. "If we find it, the forty days Bob Ready budgeted for is out the window."

"Give me a day or two and I guarantee I'll find it," said Steve Saint-Amour, the freckled, chain-smoking ROV operator.

Gary took Saint-Amour up on his challenge. It took a day to fetch the barge from the first fjord, half a day for Meadows to get two of its anchors to bite in 800 feet of water just offshore. At last the barge was positioned. The crane dropped the ROV in the water to examine the targets and, if they weren't a B-17, to visually scan the steep walls. Our hopes soared again. Possibly in minutes the ghostly shape of a Flying Fortress might appear in the glare of the ROV's video cameras. We crowded around the television monitors in the ROV control van, a forty-foot-long shipping container chained to the deck of the barge.

The ROV dropped through hundreds of feet of black water. Pale fish swam by, and zillions of little shrimplike krill, like creepy-crawly snow, swirled in the bright lights. And then—just as it hit the bottom—its lights, cameras, and sonar went dead. Like a blown fuse, its electrical system had detected a "ground fault" and shut down.

Saint-Amour and his partner worked around the clock. They changed the motor, replaced the hydraulic fluid, and tinkered endlessly. But every time the ROV went in, it died. Only weeks earlier, it found an Israeli submarine at 10,000 feet in the Mediterranean and worked flawlessly. Now it wouldn't work at all. And through it all, one of the anchors on the barge kept dragging, forcing Meadows to hold the barge in place with the bow of the *Wrestler*.

"I'm going to find that plane if it takes me until Christmas," Gary shouted, standing on the barge in his blue jumpsuit, a biting wind howling up the fjord in the dusk.

But there was nothing he could do. This time it wasn't a matter of more elbow grease or staying longer, as it was on the ice cap with *My Gal Sal*, or in the Yukon with a P-39 that he'd recovered. Just like in the last days of the *Kee Bird*, when everything started to unravel at the top of the world, all the optimism and will that Gary could muster couldn't stop the chaos of the ROV, the sonar, the tug, the barge, the weather, the deep uncharted fjord, from spiraling out of his control. Yes, he had put himself in that old photo, but he might as well have been a thousand miles away.

Early the next morning, under heavy clouds, the *Wrestler* weighed anchor. A sheen of hydraulic fluid swirled purple and blue and gold on the green water. "I feel bad for Gary," said Rafid Tuma, squirting a wad of chewing tobacco into the swirl. "For me the plane is just another object to be picked up, another adventure. But for Gary, it's different. The planes are his passion."

Surprisingly, though, Gary hardly missed a beat. A moment later he was on the bridge, poring over his maps and crash reports, and thumbing through the box of artifacts from shore. "Look, we'll just have to come back next summer," he said, examining an old, spent .45-caliber cartridge. "Those guys crashed their plane in the middle of nowhere and sat around waiting to get rescued, firing off their guns. What do you supposed they were shooting at?" He paused and the question hung in the air. "The plane's here and we're gonna get it. Hell, if it was easy, everyone would do it."

SIXTEEN

THE LAST GOOD MACHINES

Kissimmee, Florida

Kissimmee, Florida, was hardly exotic Fjord Y, but my heart quickened when I spotted Tom Reilly's place through trees thick with Spanish moss. At the end of a short dirt road stood a beige metal hangar, REILLY AVIATION in faded red block letters across its side, two B-25 Mitchell bombers visible over a rickety wooden fence. Pulling into the parking lot, I saw more: a jumble of jet fighters piled like junk cars next to an A-26 Invader.

Four months had passed since I'd left Gary and the Pirates, and I still felt unsated. Since the first flight over the *Kee Bird* six years ago, I'd spent months in Greenland and Alaska in pursuit of winged treasure, had hung out with the Confederate Air Force, and guys who spent more money on one plane than I'd probably earn in a lifetime. But I was still puzzled over the question of why these antiquated machines held such power over so many people—including me—and I hoped Reilly's little corner of the Kissimmee Municipal Airport might suggest an answer.

Tom Reilly restored warbirds. Or at least that's what he started doing. Now he called his operation the Flying Tigers Warbird Restoration Museum. "The Smithsonian is completely at the other end of the pendulum," he said, explaining the obvious, as I walked into his hangar. Most airplane hangars and aviation museums were

223

spotless, spacious, well-organized places. Reilly's hangar was a giant workshop-cum-grandmother's-attic. Crossing its threshold plunged you into the heavy, sweet smell of oil and the mustiness of old things. You had to squeeze between the planes, everything from a perfectly restored, bright-yellow Stearman biplane to a MiG-21 and an F-104 Starfighter. An old plywood Link Trainer stood in a corner; biplanes hung from the ceiling, two B-17 fuselages and B-17 wings and stabilizers were piled ten feet high, among racks and racks of grimy old sheet-metal parts. A P-38 Lightning was scattered in a zillion pieces on a wooden rack. In the back, perched on oil drums, was a wingless Corsair, nearing the end of a ground-up restoration. A P-40 Warhawk fuselage, all ribs and stringers, like a kid's balsa-wood model in the early stages of construction, was on a stand. Heavy, antiquated lathes and sheet-metal formers squatted along the walls. Around a corner a team of men crawled over a B-17 wing, a puzzle of exposed ribs, spars, and trusses. And in the midst of it all were clusters of sunburned tourists milling about, snapping photos, jawing with the guys working on the airplanes. "Just watch yourself as you wander around," tour guide Richard Bozarth, a former B-29 flight engineer, said at the end of the tour. "No one will bother you."

"Really, it's a museum of airplane construction," Reilly said to me, surveying his little empire. "You can come in here and see the inside of a wing."

Reilly himself looked like a cross between a professor and an Irish prizefighter. Fifty-eight years old, he had a freckled face, a small red mustache, thick wire-rimmed glasses, and the strong fingers of a man who'd wrenched a lot of nuts over the years. He walked with a bounce. A native of New Jersey, he'd been slipping and sliding across New York City's George Washington Bridge—his college commute—one day in the late 1960s, when he decided he'd had enough of cold and snow. He pointed the car south and didn't stop until he got to Orlando. He started buying, renovating, and selling run-down houses, earned his private pilot's license, and was teaching skydiving when the economy turned bad in the early 1970s. Looking around for something else to do, he bought thirteen North American Yales, an early fixed-landing-gear version of the AT-6 trainer. He shined them up, sold them for a modest profit, and then bought a B-25 Mitchell for $10,000. Within a year he had the Mitchell flying, and sold it for $17,000. He liked working on planes a lot more than selling real estate. In 1985 he met Bob Collings, a wealthy collector whose Collings Foundation, in Stow, Massachusetts, was growing into a large aviation museum. For Collings he restored another B-25 and a B-17, and then a B-24 Liberator. Two years and 97,000 man-hours later, the Liberator was judged Grand Champion at the Experimental Aircraft Association's annual fly-in in Oshkosh, Wisconsin. "The B-24," he said, "put me on the map." Seven more B-25s, three B-17s, and a flock of other warbirds later, his Flying Tigers Warbird Restoration Museum had evolved into an oasis of the thirties and forties in a desert of Gatorlands and Walt Disney make-believe. Observed Reilly: "You can look at Mickey Mouse only so much." Unable to keep the curious at bay, he threw open the doors of his workshop in 1988. Forty thousand visitors a year now come through, at eight dollars a head. The more people who came by, the more little mementos of their dad or their uncle or their own war years they brought. Their donated medals, helmets, uniforms, letters, bullets, radios, models, and dozens of oddities from the war filled a room. In 1997, Reilly started offering five-day hands-on classes twice a year in warbird restoration, mostly to people who didn't even own a warbird.

Still, it was the restoration projects that anchored it all, and Reilly finished an average of one airplane a year, which meant that some years he didn't finish anything at all. "You can't imagine how long it takes to make nothing," he said, meaning that a seemingly simple part could take hours and hours to fabricate. Reilly stopped in front of a long table where a four-foot-by-twelve-foot piece of sheet metal had just been cut. "Hey! Who cut this?" he barked, peering closely at the freshly cut edge.

"I did," said a new sheet-metal worker.

"There's something wrong with your cutters. See this nick?" We examined the cut. It looked perfectly straight to me, save a minute scratch every inch or so. Reilly picked up a heavy pair of shears and made a cut. The scratch appeared. "We can't live with that," he said. He tightened the shears with a screwdriver, sprayed them with a squirt of WD-40, and ran them across a sharpening wheel. When he tested them, the nick was gone. "I'm a perfectionist and a workaholic," Reilly said, striding to the Corsair. "I'm the worst type-A personality you've ever seen. I work constantly," he said, launching into the basic restoration process.

To keep his shop consistently busy and the cash flowing in, Reilly discovered he couldn't just wait around for some rich collector to bring in a warbird to be restored. Instead, Reilly scoured the countryside looking for wrecks and parts to acquire. Not to recover from the wild, the way Gary did, but simply to buy. The Corsair, for instance, came from Bishop, California, where it crashed into a mountain in 1944. Reilly pointed to photos taped on the front of the fuselage: it was a heap of twisted, broken aluminum. The B-17 he acquired from the New England Air Museum, in Windsor Locks, Connecticut, in exchange for restoring a B-25. It was largely intact, but had been lengthened and a fifth engine mounted on the nose, to make a test bed for Pratt and Whitney engines. Once Reilly got enough parts to make a shadow of the plane on the ground, he sold the yet-to-be completed project, much the way a builder sells a house when he's acquired the land, the blueprints, and dug the foundation. Then he took the plane (or parts) apart down to "Dixie Cup size." The sheet metal. The castings. The hydraulic lines. The bearings. The ribs and trusses and spars and stringers, every rivet was drilled out and every piece reduced to its smallest component. That was the easy part.

Reassembling a B-17 or a Corsair to flying condition was another matter altogether. Originally, the airplanes were built on assembly lines by thousands of workers. Tom Reilly's shop rebuilt them one-by-one, by hand. Every stringer and rib had to be examined, cleaned, stripped in an acid bath, and painted with a corrosion inhibitor. And, depending on the airplane, many had to be remade from scratch. The Corsair contained 80 percent original parts; the P-40 only 20 percent. Bolts; nuts; hydraulic lines; the complex, beautiful compound sheet-metal curves; all had to be made by hand, one piece at a time. "We have tons of applicants for jobs here," Reilly said, leading me back to a workbench, "and a lot of them are retired from the military or the big airlines. They're experienced mechanics, but they're parts changers. When something breaks they take the part out and put a new part in. But when you're restoring an old airplane, many times there are virtually no parts to be had." Reilly grabbed a two-foot-long screw-jack assembly, which operated the B-17's wing flaps. "We have to have people who can take a piece like this and can then build it from scratch, who can put metal on a mill and make it. We need craftsmen."

Reilly's shop reassembled the airplane one section at a time, tail, stabilizers, wings, and fuselage. When the sheet-metal work was complete "we're sixty to seventy percent done with the airplane." The sections were assembled, then the plane was wired, plumbed with oil, fuel, and hydraulic lines, and, finally, the restored engines mounted. "Then we put fuel in and fly her out."

The process sounded simple enough, but it took years. Over the course of the week I spent at the shop, a dozen guys made an awful small amount of progress.

Richard Van Meeteren was working on the Corsair. After five years and $1.2 million, it was starting to look like a finished airplane, although it still lacked landing gear, an engine and all its wiring, control cables, and plumbing. With its curves and inverted gull wing, the Corsair was especially graceful-looking—and complex to rebuild. Van Meeteren, thirty-seven, was working on its left wing. He was balding on top, having salvaged what was left of his hair in a short black ponytail. "This place," Van Meeteren said, "is a fantasy for me." A German, he'd come to Reilly's to learn the craft. "There is nothing like this at home. I'm a romantic. I love old things and I love old airplanes, and there's no place in Germany where you can go and learn this."

The structure of the wing was just like a balsawood airplane model: an aluminum spar ran perpendicular to a series of ribs, reinforced with delicate stringers running the length of the wing, the whole covered with sheet metal. It was a miracle of elegant engineering. Like the skeleton of a bird, none of the components was heavy or strong by itself. Brute strength played no role in its structural integrity. But riveted together as a unit, the wing could support a 2,000-horsepower fighter flipping through the sky at over 400 miles per hour. Van Meeteren was making a new rib. He had the original one—a curved teardrop-shaped piece of aluminum, the last half-inch of which, all the way around, was bent in a ninety-degree angle so the rib could be fastened to the stringers and sheet-metal skin—but it had been cracked during the Corsair's crash sixty-six years ago. The challenge was the half-inch bend. It was easy enough to cut a new piece of aluminum to the right size, but the bend, running along the curving leading edge of the wing, had to be bent to precisely the right size and shape, and it had to be achieved without weakening the metal's structure. "It's the alloys in aluminum that give it rigidity and temperate strength, but they also make it brittle," Van Meeteren said. So to recreate the piece, he outlined it on a sheet of five-eighths-inch plywood. Cut and sanded to the precise size, he had a form, around which he could slowly and carefully bend the end, tap by gentle hammer tap. Once shaped, the rib would be drilled with more than a hundred small rivet holes, heat treated to harden the aluminum, and sprayed with corrosion inhibitor. That was one rib.

A Corsair had dozens of them, a B-17 hundreds. Every rivet hole had to be drilled by hand, every rivet shot by hand. Ultimately, how long a restoration took depended on one thing: "Money," said

Gari Murphy, working around the corner from Van Meeteren. "Ninety percent of the work here is by hand. If I take a two-hundred-seventy-five-dollar piece of sheet metal, by the time it's turned into a part it's worth twenty-five hundred dollars. That's why parts are so important. Look," he said, striding over to the Corsair. He was tall and lean, with ragged teeth, a wiry mustache, and long blond hair held in a ponytail with a girl's scrunchy. He wore cowboy boots, a tie-dyed T-shirt, and thick trifocal glasses that always looked about ready to slip from his nose. He pointed to a solid chunk of metal that connected the two portions of the Corsair's wings. The part was original. "This is the pivot point on the wings. It's made of forged steel with all the grains aligned for strength. Try to find one! To have that one part remade to Chance Vought specs would cost twelve thousand dollars. That's why crumpled wrecks are so valuable."

At one of the old forming machines nearby, I started talking to Syd Jones. He was making the aluminum cover for the landing light on an AT-6, gently bending the piece of metal and lovingly beveling its edges with a hand-held rasp. For seventeen years, Syd and his wife, KT, had worked for legendary treasure hunter Mel Fisher, recovering the treasure of the seventeenth-century Spanish galleon *Atocha*. Syd and KT had done it all, starting as divers and graduating to ship captains and finally to being in charge of all the artifacts brought up from the galleon. But tired of treasure hunting and Key West, they'd driven north and discovered Reilly's little warbird oasis. Both were pilots, and the history swept them in. They bought and restored their own AT-6, a gleaming gray machine sitting in the hangar, and went to work for Reilly. "It's a unique window on time right now," Jones said, pondering the light cover's fit on the airplane wing's leading edge.

"I was going through my preflight check the other morning," said KT, a strong, tan woman with frosted blond hair who walked up and joined the conversation, "and it hit me that this same thing had been done thousands of times, the exact same procedure. It's almost a religious ritual! You're connected to the past when you do it."

"When we were doing the *Atocha* we had thousands and thousands of five-hundred-year-old artifacts but no people," Syd said. He was tall and skinny and quiet. "The people who owned the jewels and crosses and gold and cannons were lost forever, and we could never put the galleon together again. We could only make assumptions about the people and the artifacts we found. But the guys who flew these airplanes are still around. We can talk to them. They come in here all the time. But fifty years from now, will they still be around? No! Will people be doing this with F-16s? I don't think so. They're too expensive and too complex."

"With these," KT said, "you can see how everything works. They're big machines. Powerful machines and you have a respect for the men who flew them, because they weren't easy to fly."

"Look at that plane up there," said Syd, pointing to an OX-5 Bird hanging from the ceiling. It was a fabric-covered biplane with a wooden propeller, as different in appearance from the T-6 as a typewriter was from a computer. "Just ten years separates these two airplanes. Amazing, isn't it?"

After so many months on the warbird trail, it began to make sense. When you asked people like Thad Dulin or Gary Larkins or Kermit Weeks to explain their fascination with warbirds, they answered much like Tom Reilly did: "They're big, fat, and ugly. They smell bad and they drip oil, and they have a heart and soul of their own. You just don't hear round engines run anymore, and there's a romance to them," Reilly said. The answers at first seemed strange; that they'd won the war usually wasn't the first thing people highlighted. Instead it was always the sound, the oil, the smoke—the machinery—that captivated people. But why was that so romantic? Why were Corsairs and Flying Fortresses so much more romantic than a 1944 Buick or even a World War II–era Sherman tank? If the ten years separating the Bird biplane from the T-6 Syd Jones was restoring seemed like two centuries, the leap in aircraft technology and design over the next ten years was equally dramatic. Parked next to the T-6 was a de Havilland Vampire, one of the earliest jet fighters. All streamlined curves, it had no propeller, no visible engine, no dripping oil, and, when "fired up," its powerful turbine sounded like a vacuum cleaner. It flew circles around the old piston-powered warbirds, but there was nothing romantic about it. Why were Hellcats or Superfortresses so much more romantic than Vampires or F-100s or F-16s?

Hearing the airplanes from World War II, working on them, flying in them, talking to people like Syd and Thad and Gari Murphy made me understand: These warbirds were the last good machines.

From the start of the Industrial Revolution, technology inspired reverence, awe, and deep emotion. In steam power, electricity, railroads, and factories, writes David Nye in *American Technological Sublime*, "the improvement of machines in precision and reliability became a metaphor for social improvement. The steam engine, the spinning jenny . . . were inherently moral objects both because they were based on natural laws and because they improved the condition of mankind. . . . The contemplation of complex machinery had seemed an act of sublime meditation that ennobled the observer." Indeed, writes Edwin Tenner, "Americans from 1889 to 1929 were probably more optimistic about the electrical, mechanical and chemical transformation of society than any other people has ever been."

Machinery and mechanical objects captivated Americans, the pistons and gears works of beauty and awe that would only make life better. William Dean Howells described the 600-ton Corliss steam engine at the Philadelphia Exposition in 1876 as "an athlete of steel and iron with not a superfluous ounce of metal on it." Electricity, the telegraph, the automobile, the skyscraper, these were things that would bring us together and make the world better. Nye notes that there were virtually no Luddites among American workers in the nineteenth century. And airplanes were the ultimate machine. Airplanes were cool in the way that all machines were—they spit fire, roared, and were fast, like everything from steam engines to railroad engines—but they also flew, defying gravity and lifting a man into the realm of the birds and gods. Until World War I, the mere appearance of an airplane overhead brought people running outside to marvel at the machine buzzing overhead. When the first airplane flew over Chicago in 1910 as many as a million people streamed out of their homes and offices to watch it. When Charles Lindbergh landed in Paris in 1927, 150,000 people crowded the airfield, whipped into such a frenzy by his feat that souvenir hunters literally began ripping his airplane to pieces. Suddenly Europe and the United States seemed connected in a way the two continents had never been before, and a whole new world of possibility beckoned. Two hundred thousand peopled jammed Santa Monica, California, to witness the end of the first aerial circumnavigation of the world.

I'd been fascinated with airplanes since I was a kid, and working on the *Kee Bird* had made me comprehend the challenge of flight. But wandering Tom Reilly's restoration shop, peering inside wings and complex, symmetrical, radial piston engines, I began to fully understand the marvel of powered flight. Although the 1903 Wright Flyer looks whimsically simple and fragile, it was, writes Walter Boyne, "immensely sturdy, a brilliant arrangement of thin wooden spars and tightly strung wires creating a structure of enormous resilience and strength." Substitute aluminum for wood and wire, and the airplanes of World War II were not that different. Stick an engine in a car and as long as there's enough power, it goes. A kid can make a go-kart out of wood and a lawn mower. But to break the bounds of gravity, as does even the simplest airplane, requires a harmony of weight and balance and strength and power. The B-17 Flying Fortress was a big, powerful, sturdy, all-metal airplane; fully loaded for war, it weighed 65,000 pounds and it seems as different from the Wright Flyer as a supercomputer does from a slide rule. But the big wing under restoration in Reilly's shop was an elegant marvel of delicate stringers, fragile ribs, and thin sheet metal fastened together into a wing, like those on the Wright Flyer, of enormous resilience and strength. And powering it were four eighteen-cylinder radial internal-combustion engines, engineering marvels equal to any wing or fuselage. Again, it's hard to get any better than Walter Boyne's description: "The internal combustion engine is a machine of rocking, jolting, opposing forces; its nature is to knock, rattle, and come apart. Keeping the various forces—some reciprocal, some rotating, some centrifugal, some centripetal—all contained, while simultaneously powering them by the improbable means of igniting thousands of individual explosions per minute by means of a precise mix of gasoline and air, is extraordinarily difficult. Doing it flawlessly over hundreds and even thousands of hours under constantly varying conditions of pressure, temperature, and stress demands exceptionally fine engineering and precise machining."

The engines and airframes of the 1940s were different in degree, not in kind, from the Wright Brothers' marvel. The engine was the same, only bigger and more complex, as was the airframe. The whole was operated with mechanical linkages; the ailerons and flaps and rudder controlled by cables operated by the pilot's own hands. You could see the propellers turning, see and smell the oil and exhaust spitting from the engine. And as they grew more powerful, they simply grew bigger. Longer propellers. More cylinders. Bigger cylinders. It was technology that you could see, touch, hear—intuitive technology that you didn't need a college degree to understand (after all, in 1939 only 4 percent of Americans had graduated from college). That these machines came of age during the world's most destructive war, after the country's worst economic depression, only made them more powerful symbols of human achievement and possibility. The big piston engines and ever more sophisticated airframes were not only marvelous displays of technology, but inherently represented good; they were waging war on murderous scoundrels bent on taking over the world.

Although the B-29 Superfortress is one of the rarest and most coveted of all World War II–era warbirds, if you look closely at the plane, it bears hints of forthcoming technological change. Its rivets are flush—you can't see or feel them as you can on a B-17. And no gunner's fingers clutch the .50-caliber machine guns, as they do on B-17s; the B-29's machine guns were remotely and electrically controlled. These changes, among many others, gave the B-29 less drag and enabled it to carry its heavy load over long distances.

That final cargo, the atomic bomb, changed everything about our relationship to technology. Nothing human beings had ever made was as powerful or deadly. Nye notes that while the 1939 World's Fair promised regular flights to London by the 1960s, the succeeding generation already worried about nuclear armed missiles. "In the 19th century," he writes, "the technological sublime had exalted human reason and made heroic the inventor, the builder, the entrepreneur and the solo pilot. But by the end of the 20th century technology had become so complex and inhuman that they could make a mockery of the individual. A technology so terrifying ceased to . . . be an engine of moral enlightenment. . . . Who identifies with the bomb?"

The end of World War II was the end of one brand of innocence. The war completed America's transformation into a world industrial power and a society driven by technology. In the technological race of postwar years, machines changed fundamentally—and so did our relationship to them. They became more powerful, but more opaque, mechanical linkages replaced by mysterious microprocessors, the mighty crankshafts replaced by digital codes, elaborate strings of ones and zeros. Typewriters were replaced by computers, piston engines by jets, mechanical gauges in the cockpit by TV screens. "My father's Depression-era Underwood typewriter," writes Tenner, "reveals its bars, shafts, gears, and even its bell for all to see." But in the postwar years, those mechanical innards became increasingly concealed. "Messy ribbons were packaged in cartridges and cassettes, and durable cloth yielded to disposable film. As the

new models were finished in almost every color but black, typewriters were already on their way to being black boxes in the technological sense: mechanisms opaque to the user. Likewise audio and
videotape, as well as computer diskettes, have retreated into hard
plastic shells." Machines got more powerful, but also smaller and infinitely more complex. Anybody could take apart a piston engine;
few people can work on a jet, or even fathom the inner workings of
a computer chip.

Nowhere is this technological change starker and more obvious
than in the airplane. By the time the B-29 was performing its deadly
task the jet had taken wing. When the *Kee Bird* was abandoned in
1947 it was already obsolete. With a few exceptions, from 1945 on-
ward, every warplane built would be a jet. No propellers. No thumping pistons. No more mechanical contact with the ailerons or
rudder. Now, "pilots no longer even manage tools, but manage tools
that manage other tools," writes Tenner. If you were to line a bunch
of typewriters or cars or tanks from 1920 to 1960 up in a row, you'd
be hard-pressed to separate exactly the prewar and postwar models.
But line up a similar progression of warplanes and anybody could
walk right up to them and identify at a glance the pre- and postwar
models. You could likely do it by sound alone.

The Flying Fortresses and Corsairs and Hellcats loved by hundreds of thousands of people won a war. They lifted people out of
poverty and gave them hope in dark times. But even more important, they symbolized a time when machines promised nothing but
progress, and when you could see and touch and repair the insides of
those machines. People would never worship an F-16 or a B-52
Stratofortress—or even a Messerschmitt ME 262 or a Gloster Me-
teor, the German and British jets developed during the war. Not
only technically too complex for the average person to comprehend, they carried a kind of moral ambiguity. Even a kid could grasp
the difference, as I did in the 1960s. I knew what the Flying Fortress
had done—I'd seen it in all the movies. But the B-52? What was it
doing in Vietnam, and why? Watching a swept-wing Stratofortress

take off and hearing its turbines roar filled you with anxiety and plugged you into all the technological fears of the postwar era—nuclear weapons, pollution, loss of privacy, repetitive stress disorders, automatic weapons in the hands of postal workers or school kids, electromagnetic radiation—you name it, we're filled with technological anxiety. But vintage warbirds take us back to our technological youth, and to a sureness of purpose.

Back in Reilly's shop, Gari Murphy clomped up, curled his huge cowboy boots under him on a rough two-by-four workbench like a cat, and lit a Mustang cigarette—"Whatever's cheapest, man." He regathered his long hair in a red scrunchy and offered me his opinion about the source of warbirds' popularity. "This country reached its highest level in the 1940s. I read about it and discuss it with all the old guys who come into the shop. When we entered World War II, the Japanese and the Germans were the best pilots in the world. But it was a war of technology and industrial might. Now we don't make anything anymore. We're a service economy. Go to Wal-Mart: 'Where America Shops!' Ha! . . . Nothing is made here anymore. I mean, stop and think what a master machinist makes compared to a computer guy. This country has turned into a nation of techno-geeks. What do you need a computer for? Why spend fourteen hundred dollars on a piece of equipment to send someone a note electronically? Why? I don't get it! It's hard to get excited about a computer. I'd rather see a guy polishing a connecting rod."

That you could engineer better connecting rods, faster and more efficiently, with a computer may not have occurred to Murphy. But I understood his point. In the social and emotional history of technology, a connecting rod was good—it was big, simple, and mechanical, with no hidden parts or hidden bugs. You could hold it in your palm and feel its heft. A guy could love a connecting rod, could love a Wright Cyclone 3350 full of oil and eighteen pistons and connecting rods, could love a half-century-old B-17 Flying Fortress, could love its throaty cough and stinky black exhaust. Could anybody really love a memory chip? Could anybody love their laptop? Computers grow obsolete so fast people get a new one every few years. They feel no connection to its smaller components.

Shaded from the hot morning sun beneath his big B-25 Mitchell bomber, the next day, I found Larry Kelly. He and Tom Reilly were fiddling with *Panchito*, parked on the grass outside the hangar, their hands covered with oil. Reilly had restored it and Kelly, a fifty-two-year-old pharmacy and medical-supply mogul, passionately loved it. Not just because it was rare, and not just because it was worth more than half a million dollars. All polished aluminum, bristling with turrets and machine guns and sporting graceful propellers mounted on big twin radial engines, *Panchito* was big and brutish and elegant and utilitarian at the same time. But there was nothing ambiguous about it. Embodied in its spars and wings and pistons and machine guns was a time lost forever, a time when machines, and even war, seemed good. It radiated the hope and the innocence that brute power would be enough, that mad dictators and emperors would be defeated, and that progress was inexorable. Flying his B-25—just standing next to it—made Kelly feel better, more heroic, in a rather unheroic age.

"I think I was born one generation too late," Kelly said, wiping the oil off his hands on a paper towel, "and flying these old combat planes is all part of connecting to that time. But, really, the greatest thrill isn't flying them, it's meeting the old guys who flew them."

"One time we took Jack Sims, one of Doolittle's Raiders, for a flight," Reilly said. He adjusted his glasses and stared into the blue sky. "I was in the left seat and he was in the right seat. We climbed out over the Gulf of Mexico and he didn't say a word. Then I gave him the controls. He descended and descended and flew a couple of hundred feet over the waves—that's how they'd flown to Japan during the raid. Still, he didn't say anything. Suddenly the St. Petersburg tower calls up and says we're heading into heavy traffic and why are we so low. I told him we were a B-25 with one of Doolittle's

Raiders at the controls. At that point he gave us all the airspace west and south of St. Pete and cleared all the other traffic away. We were skimming over the waves and suddenly Sims said, 'Boy, does this bring back memories.' I let him take us back and he greased a landing better than any of us."

The *tap-tap-tap* of a rivet gun echoed from the hangar. Reilly's guys were skinning the section of B-17 wing they'd been working on all week. In a few years, after untold thousands of hours of hand labor, another B-17 would take wing. According to legend, the Phoenix rose from its ashes and magically flew again after five hundred years. In Kissimmee, Florida, Reilly's guys were resurrecting Phoenixes every day, part by part, rivet by rivet.

We stood underneath the big, shining plane, listening to the rivet gun at work, and smiling at the vision of an old man flying over the wave tops of the Gulf Stream.

EPILOGUE

—

RETURN OF THE *KEE BIRD*

When the *Kee Bird* skidded to a stop on that cold morning in February 1947, it came to rest on the frozen lake about thirty feet from shore. There, the lake was only a foot or so deep. When the *Kee Bird* caught fire forty-eight years later, it was in the middle of the lake. In the throes of grief, Darryl Greenamyer piled the bulldozer, the mess tent, the heater, the grader, and extra barrels of fuel under the wings. In a few weeks, he expected, the ice would melt and all traces of the *Kee Bird* would sink into the depths and disappear.

When Gary Larkins arrived nine days later, he dragged everything he could off the lake. That's what the Danes wanted. But he couldn't budge the wreck of the *Kee Bird*.

Vernon Rich, who had worked so hard on the *Kee Bird* and saved the Caribou, never got to go back in to the site in May when it burned. For him, the *Kee Bird* was an open wound that wouldn't heal. Then one day in 1998, Niels Jensen called from Denmark. The Danish fireman who had flown the Caribou cylinder out to the *Kee Bird* during those last, desperate days in August of 1994 had startling news. What remained of the *Kee Bird* lay in shallow water. The *Kee Bird*'s big center section, its four new engines and new propellers, and its tail, all were still visible and close to shore. And the parts were worth a small fortune to the right buyer.

Meanwhile, Kermit Weeks still had a couple of B-29s in pieces. The Confederate Air Force's *Fifi* always needed parts. Tucked away in museum hangars around the world were numerous incomplete B-29s, the restoration of any one of which would require new parts. And a collector named Anthony Mazzolini had discovered the last B-29 remaining at the China Lake Naval Weapons Center. It was missing a tail, was riddled with bullet holes, and needed new leading edges on the wings and four new engines and props to make it flyable. Boeing agreed to help restore it, but parts might be a problem. Mazzolini approached Gary Larkins about possibly recovering the remains of the *Kee Bird*. It's sunk in the lake, Gary said, but I'll go get it for $600,000. And the word was that Davis Tallichet, the collector who'd obtained a permit in 1993 to recover the *Kee Bird*, had a permit, again, for the *Kee Bird*'s remains.

But Vern, pining away in his fabrication shop in Scottsdale, knew better. He approached one of his wealthy clients who'd long followed the *Kee Bird* saga. "I want to recover the *Kee Bird*," Vern said. The client agreed to finance him. Vern hatched a plan: he'd fly up to the *Kee Bird* in a chartered Twin Otter to videotape and examine the site and airplane. That would be cheap and easy. If it looked feasible, he and Niels would fly a chartered C-130 transport up, dismantle the engines, props, and wings, and bring it all home in a single load.

Figuring the governments of Denmark and Greenland wouldn't be inclined to permit another American, no less a former member of Darryl Greenamyer's crew, back to the site, Niels Jensen applied for the permit.

It arrived on March 18, 1999. He and Vern had three years, until 2001, to recover the plane. "Niels called," Vern told me over the telephone. "He's got a one-hundred-percent, no-bullshit copy of the permit and he's been drinking ever since!"

Nine months later, Gary Larkins was on the phone with me.

He'd just finished talking to Bob Ready. "The *Later* is there," he said. "I've got no doubt about it and now I know exactly where it is." He was fired up; he was close to convincing Ready to send him back for a second try. "But we're going lean and mean," he said, "just me, the Pirates, and a small boat with a light ROV that can search those walls. When we find it, then we'll worry about recovering it." And the captain of the *Kissavik* had met a fisherman who swore he knew were the *Sooner* was. "He says he snagged his fishing net on it," Gary said. "Here we go again!" But for good measure, Bob Ready had persuaded Jack Erickson to sell him *My Gal Sal* and the remains of the B-17 recovered from Ruby, Alaska, to assemble as a static display for his memorial. Gary had just signed a two-year contract to restore it, and was pouring the footings for a new shed in which to do the work.

"I've always wanted a B-17," said Erickson, "but *My Gal Sal* was just too much work. And, you know," he said with a twinkle in his eye, "I think I know where there's another one!"

Meanwhile, Gary said, Tommy Hauptman was about to ferry an S-61 helicopter from Brunei to Manila. "Wanna come?" he said. "I know where there's a cherry Japanese Zero just sitting on a reef. . . ."

And Darryl Greenamyer? He sold all his airplanes except the Tigercat ("That's my daughters' inheritance"), sold his house in Rancho Santa Fe. And, while Gary Larkins sued Tom Hess and Ascher Ward for the expenses he incurred cleaning up the *Kee Bird* site, Darryl laid low on a big, lonely stretch of hilltop he'd acquired in the mountains east of San Diego. Finally, Hess and Ward and Gary settled out of court. Soon after, I received an email from Darryl: "I just bought a new Lancair to go racing at Reno. All I need now is to put it together. Tom Hauptman said it was like going back to an old girlfriend. It isn't—she's an old slut. I'll never learn."

ACKNOWLEDGMENTS

—

I owe a huge debt to Darryl Greenamyer and Gary Larkins. Even as their dreams went up in flames or their search proved fruitless, they let me look over their shoulders and never winced at my perpetual note-taking. I don't know if I could have done the same, revealing an openness that probably took as much bravery as their expeditions. Over the years each has taken dozens of phone calls from me and suffered withering barrages of questions, and never once did they express the least frustration. I admire them both and can't ever thank them enough.

Much the same can be said for their colleagues, the supporting actors and actresses who welcomed a reporter into their midst as if I were one of them. On the *Kee Bird*, Roger von Grote, Matt Jackson, Cecelio Grande, Bob Vanderveen, John Cater, Al and Cathy Hanson, and Tom Hess all deserve my thanks, as does Rick Kriege, even though he's no longer here to thank. And thanks to the *Nova* crew: Michael Rossiter, Noel Smart, Albert Bailey, and Lawrence Dodd.

Vernon Rich deserves a special mention. He welcomed me from the moment I stepped off the Caribou, and he has proved to be not just a great source but a good friend as well. His technical help, memory, journal, and friendship have been invaluable.

Air Pirates George Carter, Rick Dougherty, Wayne Lloyd,

Ricky Whitmire, and Bill Carter proved equally welcoming. They always moved over a space or pulled out a chair for me to join them, a cold beer (or two) usually with it. Rafid Tuma deserves extra-special thanks for sharing his precious stock of Kodiak. In the wild, that was a mark of true generosity. Also thanks to Steve Dabagian and Paul Goodall of Ocean Systems International, Inc.; Steve Saint-Amour of Phoenix Marine, Inc.; and the entire crew of the *Ocean Wrestler*, particularly her master, John Meadows.

I wouldn't have been able to make the journey to Greenland in the summer of 1999 without Bob Ready.

Thad Dulin and his family put me up in fine Texas style, helped me on numerous little technical details, and, even more important, got me airborne in *Sentimental Journey*. That little flight meant more to me than they realize.

Even though it was painful for her, Irene Kriege graciously explained the details of Rick's death, for which I am grateful to her.

For taking time out from their busy lives to show me their planes and share their thoughts on warbirds, I thank Jack Erickson, Kermit Weeks, and Walter Soplota.

I visited Tom Reilly's Flying Tigers Warbird Restoration Museum twice, and each time I was treated like a VIP. For that I thank everyone, especially Tom Reilly, K.T. Budde-Jones, Syd Jones, Gari Murphy, and Rick Reeves. And thanks to Thom Richards for the loops, barrel rolls, and dog fight. I owe all of you a story or two.

I am greatly in debt to Ernie Stewart, Lucky Luedke, Howard Adams, Russ Jordan, and Bobbie Joe Cavnar for sharing their memories of their last flight and rescue with me. I never tire of hearing their stories. I also owe thanks to Maynard White and Kenneth White for their wealth of knowledge about the 46th Reconnaissance Squadron and the *Kee Bird*. Ken White's *World in Peril* is required reading for anyone interested in Project Nanook.

Thanks to Niels Jensen for his detective work.

Tim Wright, Scott Highton, and Michael Moore took great photos and were always good traveling companions. I can't thank

them enough for generously letting me illustrate this book with
their work.

Without Ann Hawthorne I never would have gone to Greenland or learned about the *Kee Bird*.

I owe much to the editors who have kept me fed and inspired,
and who have believed in me. They include Joan Tapper, Jon
Gluck, David Willey, Diane Smith, Kathy Ely, who first put me on
Darryl's trail, and Jim Doherty at *Smithsonian*, who sent me back to
Greenland in 1995. This book wouldn't exist without *Air &
Space/Smithsonian*'s Linda Shiner, who sent me to Thule for the first
time, who rekindled my dormant love of flight, and whose editorial
comments made this a better book. And last, but not least, Mark
Jannot, who sent me to Greenland in August 1999 and offered his
valuable insight and criticism on my manuscript. He is the kind of
editor and friend every writer needs.

There are countless others who have helped me in the preparation of this book: Mrs. Lynn Gamma, archivist of the Air Force;
Barbara Young at the U.S. Air Force Museum; Jason Adams and
Alicia Hoge, for their hospitality in Los Angeles; and Larry Berko-
witz, for hunting down you know who. Peter Hess and David Paul
Horan provided much needed windows into admiralty law; Doug
Champlin and Robert Mester shared their tales, put me face to face
with the world's only known TBD devastator, 500 feet under the
ocean, and invited me into their courtroom; and Walter Boyne, Bob
Mikesh, and Tom Alison clarified some thoughts and patiently answered many a question. I thank you all.

A writer might spend day after day alone at his desk, but the
nourishment he gets away from it makes all the difference. The
Dawsons, Ryans, Renee Blankenau, Mike Rock, the McMahons,
Barb Power, and Pete Larkin, to name a few, nourished me with eager ears and fireside whiskeys. And Joel Achenbach's encourage-
ment and early comments on my manuscript provided helpful
guidance.

Jake and Susanne Page showed that being a freelance writer was possible and have helped at every step of the way, generously sharing editors, agents, editing, and advice. It's no hyperbole to say that without them—particularly Jake—this book would not exist. Every writer should be so lucky to have a Jake a phone call away.

Thanks to Sally Stone Halvorson for my author's photo.

My agent, Joe Regal, believed in me through a couple of false starts, helped craft a winning proposal, and stayed on top of everything the whole way through.

At Ballantine Books, Peter Borland will never know my relief when he showed more interest in his father's bomber than the next *Titanic*. His editing has been just as true and his enthusiasm everything a writer could ask for. And thanks to Mark Tavani for his assistance.

Finally, and in so many ways, this book belongs to my parents. It is a tribute to them—to their love of reading, writing, books, and me. Had they showed less patience for many an overly long early tale, there certainly would be no book now.

ABOUT THE AUTHOR

—

CARL HOFFMAN is a freelance journalist who writes for numerous magazines, including *Men's Journal*, *Air & Space*, *Smithsonian Magazine*, and *National Geographic Adventure*. He lives in Washington, D.C., with his wife and three children.